Palgrave European Film and Media Studies

Series Editors

Ib Bondebjerg
University of Copenhagen
Copenhagen, Denmark

Andrew Higson
York, United Kingdom

Caroline Pauwels
Vrije Universiteit Brussel (VUB)
Brussels, Belgium

Aim of the Series

Palgrave European Film and Media Studies is dedicated to historical and contemporary studies of film and media in a European context and to the study of the role of film and media in European societies and cultures. The series invite research done in both humanities and social sciences and invite scholars working with the role of film and other media in relation to the development of a European society, culture and identity. Books in the series can deal with both media content and media genres, with national and transnational aspects of film and media policy, with the sociology of media as institutions and with audiences and reception, and the impact of film and media on everyday life, culture and society. The series encourage books working with European integration or themes cutting across nation states in Europe and books working with Europe in a more global perspective. The series especially invite publications with a comparative, European perspective based on research outside a traditional nation state perspective. In an era of increased European integration and globalization there is a need to move away from the single nation study focus and the single discipline study of Europe.

More information about this series at
http://www.springer.com/series/14704

Henry Bacon
Editor

Finnish Cinema

A Transnational Enterprise

Editor
Henry Bacon
University of Helsinki
Finland

Palgrave European Film and Media Studies
ISBN 978-1-349-84675-7   ISBN 978-1-137-57651-4   (eBook)
DOI 10.1057/978-1-137-57651-4

Library of Congress Control Number: 2016950022

Cover illustration: PR-photo for the film Mother of Mine (Äideistä parhain) by Malla Hukkanen. With the kind permission of Hukkanen and Matila Röhr Production Oy.

Printed on acid-free paper

This Palgrave Macmillan imprint is published by Springer Nature
The registered company is Macmillan Publishers Ltd. London

ALSO BY THE AUTHORS

Bacon, H. (1992). *Tiikerikissan aika – Luchino Viscontin elämä ja eloku-vat* (The Age of the Leopard – The life and films of Luchino Visconti). Helsinki: Suomen Elokuva-Arkisto/VAPK-kustannus.

Bacon, H. (1994). *Continuity and transformation – The influence of literature and drama on cinema as a process of cultural continuity and renewal.* Helsinki: Suomalainen Tiedeakatemia.

Bacon, H. (1995). *Oopperan historia* (History of Opera). Helsinki: Kustannusosakeyhtiö Otava. (Second edition in 2001.)

Bacon, H. (1998). *Luchino Visconti – Explorations of beauty and decay.* Cambrdige/New York: Cambridge University Press.

Bacon, H. (2000). *Audiovisuaalisen kerronnan teoria* (Theory of Audiovisual Narration). Helsinki: Suomen elokuva-arkisto/Suomalaisen kirjallisuuden Seura. (2nd edition in 2003.)

Bacon, H. (2005). *Seitsemäs taide – elokuva ja muut taiteet* (Seventh art – Film in relation to other arts). Helsinki: Suomen elokuva-arkisto/ Suomalaisen Kirjallisuuden Seura.

Bacon, H., Anneli, L., & Pasi, N. (Eds.). (2007). *Suomalaisuus valkokankaalla. Kotimainen elokuva toisin katsoen* [Finnishness on screen anthology]. Helsinki: Like.

Bacon, H. (2010). *Väkivallan lumo – elokuvaväkivallan kauheus ja viihdyttävyys* (The enchantment of violence – The horror and fascination of film violence). Helsinki: Like.

Bacon, H. (2013). *Visconti – Güzelliğin ve çürümenin keşfi.* Translated in into Turkish by Nilgün Şarman. Istanbul: Payle yayinevi.

Bacon, H. (2015). *Fascination of film violence.* Houndmills: Palgrave Macmillan.

Hupaniittu, O. (2012). *Tutkijoiden ääni ja sähköiset aineistot. Selvitys muistiorganisaatioiden asiakkaitten digitoitujen aineistojen tarpeista ja saatavuudesta.* (Researchers' voice and digital material. Survey of the users' needs and accessibility of the digitized material in cultural memory organizations). Helsinki: Svenska litteratursällskapet för Finland. www.sls.fi/forskaransrost

Hupaniittu, O. (2013). *Biografiliiketoiminnan valtakausi. Toimijuus ja kilpailu suomalaisella elokuva-alalla 1900–1920-luvuilla.* (The Reign of the Biografi business – Operators and competition in Finnish Cinema from the 1900s to the 1920s). Turku: Turun yliopisto & Arkistolaitos.

Kääpä, P. (2010). *The national and beyond: The globalisation of Finnish Cinema in the films of Aki and Mika Kaurismäki* (New studies in European cinema series). Oxford: Peter Lang.

Kääpä, P. (2011). *The cinema of Mika Kaurismäki: Transvergent Cinescapes, Emergent Identities.* Bristol: Intellect.

Kääpä, P. (2014). *Ecology and contemporary nordic cinemas* (Issues and methodologies in national cinema series). New York: Continuum.

Laine, K. (1994). *Murheenkryyneistä miehiä? Suomalainen sotilasfarssi 1930-luvulta 1950-luvulle* (Finnish Military Comedy from the 1930s to the 1950s). Turku: Suomen elokuvatutkimuksen seura.

Honka-Hallila, A., Laine, K., & Pantti, M. (1995). *Markan tähden. Yli sata vuotta suomalaista elokuvahistoriaa* (More than a century of Finnish film history). Turku: Turun yliopiston täydennyskoulutuskeskus.

Laine, K., Lukkarila, M., & Seitajärvi, J. (Eds.). (2004). *Valentin Vaala.* Helsinki: Suomalaisen Kirjallisuuden Seura.

Laine, K., & Seitajärvi, J. (Eds.). (2008). *Valkoiset ruusut. Hannu Lemisen ja Helena Karan elokuvat* (The films of Hannu Leminen and Helena Kara). Helsinki: Suomalaisen Kirjallisuuden Seura.

Koukkunen, K., Laine, K., & Seitajärvi, J. (Eds.). (2013). *Elokuvat kertovat, Matti Kassila* (Films will tell, Matti Kassila). Helsinki: Suomalaisen Kirjallisuuden Seura.

Lehtisalo, A. (2011). *Kuin elävinä edessämme. Suomalaiset elämäkertaelokuvat populaarina historiakulttuurina 1937—1955* (As if alive before us. Finnish biographical films as popular historical culture 1937–1955). Doctoral dissertation. Suomen Kirjallisuuden Seuran toimituksia, 1315 Tiede, Kansallisen audiovisuaalisen arkiston julkaisuja. Helsinki: Finnish Literature Society.

Lehtisalo, A. (2011). "*Kaikki tänne nyt moi*". *Tyttöjenlehdet kohtaamisen ja vuorovaikutuksen tiloina* ('Hey, come here all together.' Girls' magazines as spaces for encounter and interaction). COMET – Tampere Research Centre for Journalism, Media and Communication, http://tampub.uta.fi/T/tanne_kaikki_nyt_moi_2011.pdf. Tampere: University of Tampere, School of Communication, Media and Theatre.

Seppälä, J. (2012). *Hollywood tulee Suomeen – Yhdysvaltalaisten elokuvien maahantuonti ja vastaanotto kaksikymmentä luvun Suomessa* (Hollywood Comes to Finland – The importation and reception of American films in Finland in the twenties). Helsinki: The University of Helsinki.

ACKNOWLEDGEMENTS

Finnish Cinema: A Transnational Enterprise is the result of a project, *A Transnational History of Finnish Cinema*, funded by the Academy of Finland. Under the leadership of Professor Henry Bacon, it was located in the department of Philosophy, History, Culture and Art Studies at the University of Helsinki. Many of the members of the project, particularly its initiators Anneli Lehtisalo and Pietari Kääpä, had focused previously not only on national but also on transnational questions related to exploring Finnish film history. They were joined by two fellow scholars, Outi Hupaniittu and Jaakko Seppälä, who during the project completed their PhDs on the history of the silent era of Finnish cinema on the basis of their earlier research. The distinguished film historian Kimmo Laine, whose period as a fellow at the University of Turku Research Collegium coincided with our transnational project, has also in effect fully participated in all phases of the project. Pietari Kääpä left the project when he assumed the position of lecturer at the University of Stirling, but nevertheless delivered the contributions that had been assigned to him. He also kept in touch with the research group by email throughout the three-year research period (1 January 2012–31 December 2014). All the chapters that appear in this volume were extensively discussed—not to say fiercely debated—among the project members (Kimmo Laine included). With her solid training as a historian and archivist, Outi Hupaniittu did the important job of compiling and unifying a joint bibliography.

The project had an Advisory Board consisting of some of the leading scholars who have focused on issues related to transnational approaches related to film history: Professor Andrew Higson (University of York),

Professor Mette Hjort (Lingnan University), Professor Tytti Soila (University of Stockholm), Research Fellow Jari Sedergren (KAVI) and Associate Professor Andrew Nestingen (University of Washington). Their support gave us confidence and a sense of direction. Professor Higson had a crucial role in securing the publication of this study.

Among other colleagues with whom we were happy to create new or deepen existing relationships were Anders Marklund (University of Lund), Erik Hedling (University of Lund), Tommy Gustafsson (Linnaeus University) and Lyuba Bugajeva (St Petersburg State University). Our Transnational Baltic Cinema Conference helped us to establish new connections between film scholars working in Scandinavia and the Baltic countries.

The project would not have been possible without the institutional support provided by the National Audiovisual Institute and the Finnish Film Foundation. At the Institute the friendly assistance of many people, starting from the Head of the Institute, Matti Lukkarila, and above all Jorma Junttila, Timo Matoniemi and Tommi Partanen, was absolutely invaluable for the realization of the project. We are similarly grateful to the helpful staff of the Central Archives for Finnish Business Records, the Swedish Film Institute, the Labour Movement Archives and Library in Sweden and the National Library of Sweden. We are similarly grateful to the helpful staff of the Central Archives for Finnish Business Records.

For the use of images we would like to thank Erkka Blomberg, Jörn Donner (Jörn Donner Productions), Matti Lukkarila (National Audiovisual Institute), Raija Pösö (Finnish Broadcasting Company), Haije Tulokas (Sputnik Oy) and Claes Olsson (Kinoproduction Oy).

Our understanding of the various challenges filmmakers meet in producing and creating films with both national and transnational appeal was significantly enhanced by interviews granted by Klaus Härö, Matti Kassila, Tero Kaukomaa, Petri Kemppinen, Maunu Kurkvaara, Jarkko T. Laine, Ilkka Matila, Marko Röhr and Markus Selin.

Collaboration with the Finnish Society of Film Studies significantly facilitated organization of the Transnational Baltic Cinema Conference, for which we received generous support from the Finnish Film Foundation and the Federation of Finnish Learned Societies. We are also grateful to Outi Hakola for her expert advice on conference organization.

The home base of the project was at the department of Philosophy, History, Cultural and Art Studies, where our work was supported by the two consecutive Directors of the Department, Hannes Saarinen and Matti Sintonen, as well as the Financial Administrators Kirsti Nymark and Tuija

Modinos. Many of the practical problems were sorted out with the kind and expert assistance of Office Secretary Säde Stenbacka and Department Secretary Tiina Erkkilä. Eija Peltonen, Financial Assistant at the Topelia Project Administration, had the all-important role of keeping the financial records straight all through the project.

We are also very grateful for the sensitive and precise language revision done by Michael Owston of Team Owston Company.

Completing this publication with the guidance of first Chris Penfold and then Lina Aboujieb, who have acted as Commissioning Editors of the Palgrave Macmillan Film and Television Studies series, as well as Editorial Assistant Harry Fanshawe, has been a great pleasure.

The chapter on Klaus Härö is based on Henry Bacon's article "Nordic practices and Nordic sensibilities in Finnish–Swedish co-productions: The case of Klaus Härö and Jarkko T. Laine." *Journal of Scandinavian Cinema*. 4, 2, 2014.

CONTENTS

CONTRIBUTORS

Henry Bacon, PhD is Professor of Film and Television Studies at the University of Helsinki, Finland. He has published nine books and a number of articles on film theory and history. Among his major interests are the interrelationships between perceiving and understanding of the environment on the one hand and perceiving and understanding audiovisual fiction on the other, transnational aspects of film culture, film in relation to other arts and film acting.

Outi Hupaniittu, PhD is Director of Archives at the Finnish Literature Society and Vice-Chair of the Finnish Society for Cinema Studies. She specializes in the economics of film and cinema history, and has also researched digitized cultural heritage and users' perspectives of archival material.

Pietari Kääpä, PhD is Lecturer in Media and Communications at the University of Stirling, UK. He has published seven books, edited four journal issues and contributed several articles to peer-reviewed collections on various areas in transnational film studies.

Kimmo Laine, PhD is Lecturer of Film Studies at the University of Oulu, Finland. He has published two books and a number of articles on film history. His ongoing research seeks ways to analyse film style in relation to contextual factors.

Anneli Lehtisalo, PhD has worked as Lecturer in Media Culture in the School of Communication, Media and Theatre at the University of Tampere, Finland. In her research she has focused on the relations between cinema and the past, cultural memory and genre, as well as questions of (trans)national cinema, film production and distribution and cross-cultural film reception.

Jaakko Seppälä, PhD is Chair of the Finnish Society for Cinema Studies and a researcher at the School of Film and Television Studies, University of Helsinki, Finland. His major research interests lie in the field of film history, in addition to which he is interested in film criticism, especially in film style and close textual analysis. In his current research project he explores the camera's role in Aki Kaurismäki's film style.

LIST OF FIGURES

LIST OF TABLES

CHAPTER 1

Introduction to the Study of Transnational Small Nation Cinema

Henry Bacon

In recent years transnational issues have emerged as one of the key issues in film studies. Much of this discussion has focused on diasporic cinemas, concerning films made for expatriate audiences dispersed around the globe, as well as on other forms of producing films outside Hollywood specifically targeted for the global market. A relatively new branch of this line of exploration is the study of the transnational nature of small nation cinemas. These produce films in languages that are not widely spoken or understood round the globe and thus their main audiences tend to be restricted to their own countries or countries with which they share the same language. The size of that audience is a crucial factor in determining how self-sufficient and continuous the production possibly can be at any given phase of film history. It also means that maintaining a thriving film culture is correspondingly dependent on transnational factors.

Technology has for the most part been developed and standards of style and quality set at the major centres of the film industry, but interesting and important developments have also taken place at minor centres and even in the periphery. While there has always been considerable pressure to gain access to the latest technology and meet cutting-edge industrial standards, small nation cinemas have above all seen it as their mission

H. Bacon (✉)
Film and Television Studies, University of Helsinki, Helsinki, Finland
e-mail: henry.bacon@helsinki.fi

© The Editor(s) (if applicable) and The Author(s) 2016
H. Bacon (ed.), *Finnish Cinema*, Palgrave European Film
and Media Studies, DOI 10.1057/978-1-137-57651-4_1

1

to create distinctly national film cultures. At times this might have taken place through appropriating stylistic means developed in the major centres of the film industry; at times it has found its inspiration from trends emerging closer to the periphery.[1] The latter has sometimes entailed going against the grain of what has been identified as the global mainstream. For Finnish cinema, Sweden has often provided both models of style and models of operation in its attempt to create a national cinematic art and industry. The production and distribution structures that had already evolved during and immediately after the First World War made these pursuits quite arduous, leading to the creation of a studio system roughly on the lines of Hollywood, but adapted to the limitations of a small nation still at a fairly early stage of industrialization. The universal demise of studio systems towards the end of the 1950s eventually necessitated the development of systems of state subsidy to protect national film industries. The present study will focus on how the Finnish film business throughout its history, even while determined to express its national culture by offering a Finnish alternative to the international mainstream and trying to keep at least a fairly significant part of this important trade in Finnish hands, has in various interrelated ways always been tied both to global trends and to other national film cultures.

FILMS AS TRANSNATIONAL ART

Until the coming of television, cinema was the most transnational of all arts. There were several innovators of the moving image, but cinema truly began in 1896 when the Lumière brothers started sending their projectionists-cum-cameramen to all corners of the globe, reaching Helsinki in June of that year. French producers, together with a number of other European entrepreneurs, remained major players in the world film market right up to the First World War. During the war the American film industry—which eventually was to be commonly referred to as Hollywood, even when talking about films that have not actually been produced there—was able to build an unprecedented financial and technical infrastructure, develop what came to be known as the classical Hollywood style and consolidate its already almost complete control of its large domestic market. Meanwhile, because of the war most of the briefly flourishing European film industries lost a significant part of their international markets and were thus not able to continue investing in production infrastructure in the way Hollywood studios were doing. As Gerben

Bakker has argued, the main reason why Hollywood succeeded in gaining a major advantage after the war was that the European film industry was not able to compete effectively in the escalation of quality.[2] Hollywood continued consistently to develop the classical style, thus setting new standards for narratively tight and emotionally involving filmic narration through effective camerawork and editing. According to Bakker's statistics, for example at the American Film Manufacturing Company, 'the number of different shots per film increased from 14 in 1911 to over 400 by 1918, while the number of set-ups increased from 7 to 230, and number of inter-titles from 5 to 177'.[3] As this development went together with increased investment in production values, the production costs multiplied.[4] It also became increasingly evident that in order to make films exportable, a certain minimum expenditure had to be invested to enhance quality.[5]

A key structural element that enabled this development was the economies of scale. The size of the US domestic market allowed for an economic stability that translated into a large output, with a great number of films being offered for foreign distributors and exhibitors more efficiently than what could be produced in those countries.[6] European film industries simply did not have the finances or the facilities to follow suit. This imbalance has structured the relationship between American and European film economies ever since: European companies are at a permanent disadvantage because of the smallness of their home markets and their negligible ability to penetrate into the American market.[7]

Recent research has suggested that before the 1970s the dominance Hollywood achieved in terms of titles screened did not necessarily translate into correspondingly big overall box-office success.[8] This opened at least a small window of opportunity for European small nation film industries. Yet exhibitors could not afford to promote only domestic output. Ian Jarvie points out:

> It is true that in some head-to-head comparisons indigenous films outgrossed Hollywood movies. It does not follow that, had foreign screens been filled with indigenous films, revenues would have held up ... The sheer quantity of Hollywood product, its reliable delivery of 'entertainment value', its professional gloss, its deployment of the tried and true, meant to the foreign exhibitor that if American films were played, week in week out, healthy annual profits would result. The option of replacing all American movies with local films was nowhere realistic because the quantities did not exist, and making them would not have been financeable anyway.[9]

The worries to which the Americanization of film culture has given rise have not been merely financial. In some ways even more significantly, Hollywood cinema has had a dominant position in the sense that for better or worse, it has been able to catch people's imagination and even define notions about what cinema really is. Gian Piero Brunetta has observed that in Italy Hollywood 'was a reality with a radiance of its own, an almost pentecostal light with the spiritual potential to bring to life desires, dreams and hopes, and to help the average man or woman, the home-owner and the *petit bourgeois*, to imagine his or her own future'.[10] Many European cultural critics in the 1920s were more critical and saw Hollywood films as harbingers of Americanization and, as such, as a threat to European civilization. The historian and cultural critic Johan Huizinga grudgingly accepted film as an art form, but thought it could only widen people's view of society through flattening of the social and cultural landscape.[11] Another Dutchman, the socialist intellectual L.J. Jordan, wrote about the struggle against '"Americanism"—against the senseless and mindless transplant of the insipid, childish mentality and the overflowing energy of a young, and newly-marketed culture onto our old, experienced and weary state of mind'.[12] Both cultural critics and filmmakers had good reason to worry. A memorandum of the Motion Picture Producers and Distributors of America (MPPDA) in 1928 stated that movies were 'demonstrably the greatest single factor in the Americanization of the world and as such may be called the most important and significant of America's exported products'.[13]

Inasmuch as cinema was not equated with Hollywood and set against 'real' arts, there was a call for European cinema that would be expressive of the values for which Europe was seen as standing. Films were expected to participate in maintaining and even constructing cultural heritage, including notions about the way of life peculiar to the nation. As Anthony Smith puts it: 'In the eyes of its devotees, the nation possesses a unique power, pathos and epic grandeur, qualities which film perhaps even more than painting or sculpture, can vividly convey.'[14] Thus, even in the small nations that had emerged as ancient European empires were shattered in the First World War, there were determined efforts to create and maintain national film production and to develop domestic knowhow and talent. Yet hardly ever were even the fairly big European national film industries able to succeed in this alone, and so they had to create international networks and incorporate global trends into their own film cultures.

The so-called Film Europe movement sought to develop 'international co-productions, the use of international production teams and cast for otherwise nationally based productions and the exploitation of international settings, themes and storylines in such films'. Naturally, this also entailed 'reciprocal distribution arrangements between renters in different nation-states, and other efforts to rationalise distribution on a pan-European basis, in order to secure long-term collective market share by establishing all Europe as their domestic market'.[15] The idea was that European film companies would create a European film market sufficiently large to rival that of the USA. This might have entailed overcoming notions about nations altogether. One of the leading figures of this movement, Erich Pommer, stated: 'It is necessary to create "European films," which will no longer be French, British, Italian, or German films; entirely "continental" films, expanding out into all Europe and amortising their enormous costs, can be produced easily.'[16] However, European film culture was in fact far too diverse for these efforts to amount to a sufficiently concentrated effort. According to Bakker's analysis:

> The idea was that European companies should increase the size of their domestic market to be able to compete internationally, by way of mergers, joint ventures, co-productions and distribution deals. The ideal was that a film producer anywhere in Europe would have access to the whole European market. ... Nevertheless, the 'Film Europe' movement failed, probably because it concerned mostly ad hoc co-productions and not mergers or a deliberate strategy.[17]

Yet another reason for the failure was the difficulty of keeping talented and successful people working in Europe. Hollywood, just like other major players in the global film market, has always been eager to recruit talent and appropriate narratives, narrative formulas, styles and techniques whenever such people or developments have turned out to be successful. As Bakker puts it: 'Artistic and technical talent ... who initially developed in European markets, would at a certain point outgrow their markets and want to maximise the rent they could capture from their popularity or their talent, which often meant going to Hollywood.' The Europeans did in turn recruit Hollywood luminaries, but 'could only afford to buy away the stars that were already past their peak of popularity in the US'.[18] Will Hays, President of the MPPDA, saw this development as a benign process of 'drawing into the American art industry the talent of other nations in order to make it more truly universal'.[19] For European film industries, this kind of transnationalism has always posed a major threat. For individual filmmakers, Hollywood has often offered budgets and equipment far beyond what has been available even in a cinematically cooperative Europe.

These developments have been fairly closely tied to politics and ideological struggles, which in various ways have at times spurred and at times restricted transnational cultural phenomena. As Susan Hayward describes it: 'Hollywood presents a major problem, precisely because of its protean capacity to enter the national space and not be seen as "other" due to the popularity of many of its offerings.'[20] Whether the American film industry had really succeeded in creating something truly universal may be debated, but the fact was that what it produced was going down well and was exceedingly profitable in Europe too. Bakker points out that the advantage the American studios had was not only a question of their having been able to create the economic basis for high-quality production that increased their market share, but also that they 'collectively established the US nationality as a brand-characteristic for feature films, because the first were American'.[21] Reinhold Wagnleitner, writing about American cultural diplomacy during the Cold War in central Europe, explains the attraction American films had in Europe at that time: 'By virtually representing the codes of modernity *and* material abundance, America signified the defeat of the old, the traditional, the small, the narrow—and the *poor*.'[22]

The appreciation of what American cinema could offer for the imaginary sphere was not restricted to consumer culture and could surpass ideological boundaries in surprising ways. However much the French Communist Party would offer Soviet films and other similarly appropriate films with the intention of increasing the class consciousness of the working class, Hollywood could offer models that appealed to even more basic needs. Fabrice Montebello has analysed what he calls 'distinct popular uses of the cinema applicable to larger groups' through 'micro-historical observations'.[23] In a survey he conducted among working-class men, it turned out that for them American cinema was what they understood cinema to be, 'in contrast to French films in general, which were believed to be too boring, artificial or wordy, and so judged absolutely useless dramatically, if not simply dismissed as "non-cinema"'.[24] For them, Humphrey Bogart served as the kind of model with whom they wished to identify, 'the womaniser who seduces all women with disconcerting ease and without being "naturally" handsome'. Bogart appeared to personify at least in the domain of seduction 'all the social qualities required within the working class social situation'.[25]

We may well ask in what sense the features that make Hollywood films so popular really are specifically American. There is nothing specifically American about heterosexual love interest or the altruistically punishing hero, but the Americans certainly did a good job of developing narrative formulas, stylistic features, genres and attractions that are conducive to creating maximal appeal to large sections of not only American but also European, if not global, audiences. Clearly, there was something to be learned from how that worked out and appropriating it to a national context at least in terms of setting, star actors and language. Popular genres were transplanted into recognizably domestic environments and attached to what were presented as national concerns and characteristics. Stylistic features were freely borrowed depending on what caught the attention of filmmakers and what kind of equipment and personnel studios were able to employ. And here, too, there would be a degree of give and take: successful European films could serve as models both for other Europeans as well as for American productions. European producers could be motivated either by a mission to make films that would above all serve as their contribution to national culture, or seek to play the game in the American way and make films that would have a popular appeal perhaps even beyond the borders of their own countries. Thus from the classical Hollywood style there emerged what may simply be referred to as the international mainstream style, which just like its model offered a fairly wide range of options, thus allowing for a variety of individual styles.

Until the end of the 1950s, the studio systems that had developed in most film-producing countries generally could offer the financial, technical and professional facilities for realizing all this. One crucial factor that made national cinemas possible at this stage was that even in small countries they had a sufficiently strong appeal among domestic audiences. There were measures that governments in different countries imposed in order to protect their national film industries—discriminatory taxes, quotas, various regulations—against which the Americans, particularly in the aftermath of the Second World War, fiercely fought in the name of free trade.[26] Europeans were as adamant as they possibly could be and insisted on their right to protect their national cultures beyond the exegesis of free trade. Such policies have been at least partly justified by nations with fairly well-established film cultures being occasionally able to come up with trends, filmmakers and individual films that have been recognized as significant events in world film culture and that could be adapted to other national contexts. Furthermore, thanks to new kinds of systems of production and distribution, even many small nation film cultures could have a transnational reach as structures of distribution better suited for their needs developed, which allowed for distant film cultures to become better known even far beyond traditional centres of film culture.

The rise of international film festivals made it possible for films to reach at least some degree of distribution by virtue of what were observed to be their distinctly national qualities. In a few key instances, trends emerging from a certain national context turned out to have major transnational influence. Of particular importance were Italian Neorealism and the French New Wave. Neorealism served as a model of how to treat local, socially important issues in a simple but compelling way, and the New Wave, together with other modernist movements in different countries, demonstrated how cinematic means could be developed further in order to explore the complexities of subjective responses to both social conditions and existential concerns. These trends were by and large domesticated, so what emerged, while participating in the upsurge of international modernism, also had a quality that at least through language, cultural contexts and settings as well as funding and production systems belonged to distinct national cinemas.

By the time of the New Wave, studio systems had lost a significant part of their big audiences and either collapsed or went through a thorough restructuring. The situation called for a radical reorganizing of funding and production, as it was recognized that a system of subsidies was needed for there to be any national cinema. This took place in an ideologically heated political and cultural situation, giving rise to the notion of art cinema, which was to offer an alternative to the narrative and technical strategies of Hollywood. The aim was to create a new kind of cinematic language as a way of resisting the dominant culture to which classical narration geared to arouse mindless emotional involvement was seen to be attached.[27] On the other hand, this was also an era of multinational film productions, giving rise to the question of how to maintain a distinct national flavour in the context of an ever more globalizing film culture. Randall Halle even suggests that '[i]n effect coproductions at that time [1970s] were primarily about raising enough of a budget to circumvent the ideological control of the subsidy system'.[28] Yet these films tended not only to lack an ideological stand, but also not to have any distinguishable national quality, giving rise to the derogative expression 'euro-pudding'.

By the time the Cold War ended, with the collapse of socialism dramatically taking place in the autumn of 1989, the European New Waves had subsided and the European Union had begun active efforts to enhance the prospects of film production and distribution in Europe. There were more than 300 million potential spectators to be won for a 'domestic' European cinema.[29] Yet how was this to be achieved? In the 1970s American cinema had started to overcome the severe difficulties it had experienced in the 1960s and further reconsolidated its position in the world markets. Major company mergers gave a new boost to blockbusters and soon Hollywood commanded a bigger share of European box-office receipts than ever. This pattern has continued until today. The risks are correspondingly greater, and Hollywood has also become more dependent on its foreign markets.

Thus, more than ever centre–periphery asymmetries are prevalent in respect of all aspects of filmmaking. One crucial aspect is the dual position-ing that those in the periphery often have to assume. In the age of block-busters, those acting in the culturally widely acknowledged and financially robust centres have to be able to reach global audiences in order to make profits—or just to break even. Those acting in the periphery have to nego-tiate between the need to be faithful to the cultural and possibly national-istic aspirations of their own social and historical context, and the necessity of taking into account the tastes of their domestic audiences, moulded by the ever more globalizing film culture and the consequent financial realities. While European producers might suffer a structural disadvantage because of the vagaries of political and economic history, Europeans audi-ences arguably enjoy a privileged position. Bakker points out the irony of the situation: 'while their countries lacked a film industry comparable to Hollywood, these consumers probably enjoyed a far larger variety of filmed entertainment than their American counterparts'.[30]

The history of Finnish cinema has followed these developments in broad outline. However, there are many distinguishing features that give a specific quality to the particular dialectic between the efforts to launch and maintain a national cinema on the one hand, and the desire to keep abreast with various international developments on the other. These derive partly from historical, political and cultural factors that have provided the frame-work for a Finnish film culture, partly from economic realities that have prescribed certain limiting conditions for the production, distribution and exhibition of films. What can be achieved in otherwise highly similar small nation film cultures can differ significantly due to relatively small differ-ences in the size of their domestic audiences. In some countries, address-ing a fairly large audience that can be expected to recognize the products of a national film industry as somehow its own has allowed for a degree of continuity of production, within which it has been possible to cultivate some professionalism and a sense of tradition.

The studio system in Finland got truly underway in the 1930s and fell less than three decades later, as Finnish films lost much of their domestic audience; there was not much of a foreign audience to lose. Most susidized Finnish New Wave films—like modernist films elsewhere—failed miserably at the box office. By the 1980s, it was obvious that there was no point in subsidizing a national cinema that the nation did not care to watch. This recognition led eventually to yet another reconfiguring of the system of subsidies by stipulating that about half the funding should come from private sources. This went together with wide international networking in terms of funding, production and distribution. In regard to content, the main feature of the new strategy was referred to by successful Finnish producers as 'the return of the genre film'. A staggering rise in average attendance figures was a clear indication that once again the Finnish film industry was doing something right. At the same time, Finnish auteurs led by Aki and Mika Kaurismäki began winning recognition abroad to an unprecedented degree, culminating in Aki Kaurismäki's *The Man without a Past* winning the Grand Prize of the Jury at the Cannes Film Festival in 2002.

NOTIONS OF NATIONS AND NATIONAL CINEMAS

How can one define the particular 'national quality' that domestic cinema is supposed to express? The construction of national identity and of a national cinema to go with it is always a dynamic process in which notions of national specificity are negotiated and defined in the context of, first of all, models and notions about other nations and national traits, and secondly by the political, ideological, social and cultural influences that various other nations exert in a given political and cultural situation. All this takes place in historical frameworks of long- and short-term political allegiances and enmities, which offer either parallels or contrasts that may for various reasons be highlighted or played down. Transnational and national should be thought of as reciprocal concepts in the same manner as texts and contexts mutually define each other. One of the most fundamental background notions is, following Benedict Anderson, the construction of a nation as an imaginary community. Great efforts have been made to prove the authenticity of such communities, but what really matters is simply that in the minds of members there 'lives the image of their communion'.[31] And, as E.J. Hobsbawm emphasizes, ideas about nationhood must also appeal to 'the assumptions, hopes, needs, longings and interests of ordinary people'.[32] This entails 'seeking for, and consequently finding, things in common, places, practices, personages, memories, signs and symbols'.[33] To varying degrees this takes place in terms of differentiation; that is, how our characteristic traits, traditions and customs differ from those of other nations. Thus, the construction of a sense of nationhood entails a transnational perspective.

Anderson emphasizes the importance over the course of the nineteenth century of the print medium in this process. In the first half of the twentieth century its functions, particularly as regards attempts to reach the population at large, were partly taken over by cinema and the broadcast media. This was particularly manifest in the cinemas of the interwar period, one of the boldest phases of nation building ever. Nationalism was fervent and cinema was shamelessly exploited in propagating it and related ideas in whatever ways the various different styles of government—democratic or authoritarian—saw fit. There was a strong tendency to depict the nation as ethnically and culturally homogeneous, and at times this would also entail cruel depictions of any form of otherness judged to be a threat to the nation, either from outside or inside. Threatening otherness could be defined in terms of other nations, ideologies, ethnicities, or just about any human trait that could be used as a basis for classification.

In the eyes of most people, this kind of nationalism was put to shame by the atrocities of the Second World War and further questioned by the increasing multiethnicity of the former colonial powers as they sought to come to terms with various ethnic groups immigrating from the distant parts of their crumbling empires. To some extent the notion of nationalism has retained the stigma of exclusivity, partly because it has been maintained by populist groups hostile to immigration and any social element that they deem not to belong to the nation. However, in the contemporary world even the smaller and over their formative period more homogeneous nations have had to face the fact of increasing ethnic, linguistic and religious diversification. Somewhat paradoxically, the fact that today even smaller nations actually are quite heterogeneous has generally been accepted among all but the most obsessively nationalistically minded. Arguably, inasmuch as national cinemas today reflect on the nation itself, they do so through exploring the nation's ethnic, cultural, religious and social dynamics, as well as the various ways in which the nation connects with other nations, cultures and various global phenomena.

Considering these developments, it becomes apparent that we are in dire need of a transnational approach to film studies, which would both challenge and complement the writing of national film histories through exploring how film cultures have always and everywhere connected with developments that have transcended national limits. This can be seen in the fields of technology, economy and production as well as aesthetics and content, not to speak of ideological trends. Earlier on, the transnational approach to film studies focused primarily on globalization and questions related to diasporic cinema. In this context, small nation film cultures have been rather marginalized—a phenomenon that itself would be worth transnational study. Two notable exceptions are Mette Hjort's *Small Nation, Global Cinema—The New Danish Cinema* (2005) and the anthology she edited with Duncan Petrie, *The Cinema of Small Nations* (2007), both of which focus on the impact that small nation film cultures have had on the global level. Now is the time to launch a new line of study, *the transnational study of small nation cinemas.*

FINNISH CINEMA AS A TRANSNATIONAL SMALL NATION CINEMA CASE STUDY

The present study will track how Finnish film culture throughout its history has sought to find a balance between maintaining a national identity and economic viability, through creating a variety of transnational networks at all levels of its activities. There are certain parameters that make Finnish cinema particularly suitable for a pioneering transnational study of small nation film cultures:

- The corpus of feature films produced in Finland is quite manageable—about 1300 titles—and the basic metadata has been comprehensively compiled in the *Finnish National Filmography.*
- As an exceptionally high percentage (possibly even as much 95%, depending on the exact definition) of this output has survived, it is possible to conduct a near exhaustive stylistic study focused on how aesthetic influences have been adapted.
- Finland's position between East and West for most of the twentieth century has made the definition of the nation particularly pertinent and related ideological tensions have often been reflected in film policies and connected debates.
- Throughout the history of Finnish cinema there have been well-documented debates about how domestic filmmaking should respond to the fact of the dominance of foreign films at the box office, as well as about why national cinema merits the support of the state.

A transnational study of Finnish cinema entails briefly charting first of all the *historical, political and cultural factors* that have formed the framework both for nationalist aspirations and the desire to develop film production within the nation state. This requires sorting out how international and national political contexts have in their different phases influenced the development of Finnish film production, the absorption of ideological and aesthetic influences, and their appeal to audiences.

All this connects firmly with the *economic and practical factors of film production*. This entails first of all exploring how profits have been made within the field of film culture, beginning from distribution and exhibition and seeking to find a balance between offering foreign and domestically produced films. Examination of film production practices and the politics of subsidization furnishes an illuminating view of the various ways in which the Finnish film industry has sought to cope with competition with foreign films. Key questions are how required levels of competence have been achieved, how this has taken place through transnational collaboration, how production companies have improved practitioners' competence to reach international standards and, finally, how individual filmmakers have developed technical competence in their pursuit of aesthetic ideals.

Answering these questions leads to exploration of the *aesthetic and thematic connections* between Finnish and foreign cinemas. Foreign film cultures and transnational trends such as modernism have always had a major influence on the development of Finnish film culture. How has the tension between the need to foster national heritage and the desire to meet the norms of international cinema been negotiated in different phases of Finnish film history? The circulation of foreign films in Finland and, to a considerably lesser degree, the wish to distribute Finnish films abroad have always had an influence on the Finnish film industry. Much of the necessary material for this is available at the National Audiovisual Institute and certain other collections, where a large amount of important work in this field has already been accomplished.

Sorting out the cross-influence between these dimensions requires rough periodization, each dimension developing partly in terms of its own historical conditions, partly through being linked with the others (see Table 1.1).

THEORETICAL AND METHODOLOGICAL APPROACH

In order to capture the crucial transnational factors that in these three sectors and in different historical phases have influenced the development of Finnish cinema, and to explore the conditioning economical and

Table 1.1   Periodization of Finnish film history

Political–Cultural	Economic–Industrial	Aesthetic–Thematic
To 1917 Era of autonomy	**To 1920** Early film culture: foreign imports and emergence of small-scale domestic production	**To 1920** Adaptation of international genres and domestic literary and theatrical tradition
1917–1939 Establishing nationhood	**1920–1930** Establishing domestic film production vs increasing prevalence of US cinema	**1920–1930** Establishing a national film culture vs responding to foreign competition
	1930–1939 Emergence of the studio system	**1930–1960** Standardizing narrative and stylistic techniques of 'classical Finnish cinema'
1939–1945 Second World War	**1939–1945** Adaptation to wartime conditions	
1945–1989 Cold War between East and West	**1945–1960** Heyday and fall of the studio system	
	1960–1990 Subsidizing quality cinema and founding of the Finnish Film Foundation	**1960–1990** Widening gap between subsidized art house cinema and popular films
From 1989 End of Cold War. Finland joins the European Union	**From 1990** 'New commercialism', increase of transnational production and recognition won at international film festivals	**From 1990** Return of genres and hybridization of cinema and television

cultural structures, modes of production and the films themselves, a range of carefully chosen approaches has been selected. First of all, in line with 'new cinema history', Outi Hupaniittu examines the factors that influenced the production, distribution and exhibition of films in the silent era and how these operations linked together in the formation of a national film culture. This entails exploring a variety of archival sources in an effort to analyse the aims and strategies that different operators in the field have set for themselves, as well as to assess their success in competition with other similar operators. How have commercial interests been negotiated and even integrated with ostensibly more noble aims such as creating a basis for a national cinema and expressing what has been thought to be national culture and characteristics? What have been the models offered by more firmly established film cultures that entrepreneurs, filmmakers and cultural commentators had at their disposal when figuring out what could be achieved—and for what purpose? What kind of prospects for exporting

Finnish films emerged from this process? And how have all these aims, strategies and prospects as well as the enabling commercial and institutional structures evolved within the framework of changing political and ideological circumstances?

Answering these questions entails interpreting and combining information and data garnered from a variety of archival sources, an activity that is hindered by certain materials not being available and even having been destroyed at a time when their value for historical study was not yet appreciated. Information about ticket sales is poor if available at all for a great part of the period studied, and thus our knowledge of how successful films were at the box office often remains insufficient. The archives of the Finnish film production companies have been preserved only fragmentarily. For example, there are board and company meeting minutes of the most long-lived company, Suomi-Filmi, for about the first 25 years (1919–early 1940s), but the correspondence has survived only partially from two years (1936 and 1938) and ledgers are available from only half a dozen years (1932–1935 and 1937–1939). All the other records of Suomi-Filmi as well as the archives of other production companies have survived even more randomly, if at all. The situation with the import, distribution and exhibition companies is not any better, as only one comprehensive archive (Adams Filmi) has been preserved. A special challenge has been the fact that the archival material in the collection of the National Audiovisual Institute (all remaining company archives except for Adams Filmi) have been out of reach during the time span of this project, and thus the usage of these sources has been based on the archival work done for previous projects.

The scarcity of company archives is a major hindrance to the study of the economic basis of film culture. For example, as there is no information on box-office receipts before 1970, the financial outcome is known for only a couple of films. To some extent it is possible to overcome these shortcomings by using other material, such as official records and published sources. For example, the archive of the Finnish Board of Film Classification contains the basic information on all publicly screened films produced and imported over the years 1911–2011. The Finnish Film Foundation for its part has gathered information about audiences since 1970. Also the records of the trade register, export licences, taxation and many other areas yield important information, as do newspapers, the trade press and film-oriented periodicals, to mention only a few. Nevertheless, it is difficult to assess with sufficient precision how well domestic films did financially as compared with foreign imports. Much useful information can be gained through analysing public debates at the time, although these may, of course, be biased by ideological positions as well as financial interests.

The complementary aspect of the study of the financial determinants that have shaped film culture is the comparative stylistic analysis of the films themselves. This entails classifying, measuring and verbally describing the stylistic characteristics of Finnish films and comparing the findings to similar data on foreign films and cinemas. Jaakko Seppälä's study reveals similarities and differences on the basis of which it is possible to assess, first of all, how distinctive Finnish silent cinema was and to what extent foreign cinemas affected its stylistic development. Indispensable for this analysis is the web-based research tool Cinemetrics, a database containing statistics of shot lengths and framings of a great many films made throughout film history. However, unquantifiable stylistic features also have to be analysed, calling for an even higher degree of acute observation and interpretation in examining the cinematic devices that at the time were considered to be most suitable for expressing Finnishness—or rather, how they allowed for such a quality to be constructed and appreciated. This study is further complicated by the vast number of foreign films of which Finnish filmmakers can be expected to have been aware and the small number of available studies on the style of other small nation cinemas. These problems can be overcome by concentrating on potentially influential individual films and widespread stylistic trends, the reception of which can be traced from film magazines and other written accounts.

The coming of sound roughly coincided with the establishment of the major Finnish film studios, leading eventually to the only period when the Finnish film industry was self-supporting. Films were considered to have an important role in expressing Finnish national qualities, and the studios even competed for prominence in this respect. Politically, the consolidation of national institutions and the identity of the newly independent nation took place in an extremely tense world context, leading the country first to military collaboration with Nazi Germany during the Second World War and then a Treaty of Friendship, Cooperation and Mutual Assistance with the Soviet Union after the war. This naturally had its influence on the international connections of the Finnish film industry. These political vicissitudes had remarkably little influence on the content of the films, but occasionally they opened export channels for individual titles. On the whole, however, not even during these 'golden years' of Finnish cinema did the Finnish film industry have the resources to promote its products abroad and export them on a large scale. Anneli Lehtisalo explores how

Finnish films were steadily exported in small numbers during the years 1930–1960, and how the film industry constantly upheld hopes of exporting its products, to which countries films were exported and when, as well as how political and cultural circumstances affected these efforts. Lehtisalo also discusses the strategies for exporting films: what kind of films were chosen for foreign distribution and how these films were marketed.

Kimmo Laine in his two chapters explores the stylistic development of Finnish cinema over two phases of the sound era. It began with the founding of two big studios and led to the emergence of Finnish film genres. Stylistically the output of the studio era was fairly uniform, with just about as much variation as the mainstream allows, even containing some more specifically—although by no means exclusively—Finnish features. The examination of these features can easily take place within the terms of established formalist film analysis. Methodologically much more complex is the stylistic analysis of the New Waves. The transition from studio production to the post-studio era, the 'long 1960s', was a complex phenomenon and a multiplicity of factors has be taken into account. On the other hand, there are factors unifying an apparent diversity, and even continuities at the breaking point. Film histories have tended to discuss art cinema and popular cinema as two distinct phenomena. Laine proposes that returning to the common ground between the two might shed new light on both popular cinema and cinematic modernism. For all the undeniable aesthetic and ideological differences, there are also common denominators between the art and popular cinemas of the era: a willingness for cinematic experiments to varying degrees, the reworking of genres, a certain tendency towards sensationalism and, more generally, a willingness in different ways to react to and process the rapid changes that took place in the modernizing society. As Pietari Kääpä points out in his examination of how certain modernist filmic devices such as the jump cut were employed by Finnish New Wave filmmakers, adapting these features was a dynamic process of creatively adapting new devices in a specific political and cultural situation, and not just a secondary imitation of international patterns.

However, neither the employment of modernist devices in popular filmmaking nor the establishment of the Finnish Film Foundation (FFF) in 1969 to provide subsidies mainly for art film production saved the Finnish film industry from reaching its lowest point of production since the establishment of more or less regular film production. By the mid-1970s the prospects of domestic cinema looked dire indeed. Kääpä continues his analysis by comparing the situation of the new generation of film producers at the time of the fall of the studio system towards the end of the 1950s, and the emergence of filmmakers in the 1980s and 1990s who draw their conclusions about the dire situation of the domestic film industry and started actively to gear film production towards more commercial, producer-led modes of operation. Major alterations in the policies of the FFF together with its international networks and participation in transnational systems of financing helped them to realize these ideas. In terms of domestic box-office receipts, their approach was an unqualified success. In this context, not only the genre films they produced, but also children's films, documentaries and even the distinctively art house films of Aki Kaurismäki could find an audience. Most remarkably, as Lehtisalo demonstrates in her second contribution, the prominence and success of Fisnnish films at international festivals have also improved quite considerably. As the conclusion of this volume reveals, in this day and age a small nation cinema can make a relatively big impact even on a global level.

NOTES

1. As Dina Iordanova, David Martin-Jones and Belén Vidal point out in the introduction to their *Cinema at the Periphery*: 'In the context of globalization and the realities of the post–cold war world, the relationship between center and periphery is no longer ne cessarily a straightforward, hierarchical one, where a center seeks to subsume its margins. It is often not even a case of margins struggling toward a center by virtue of some actively functioning centripetal force' (2010, 6–7).
2. Bakker, 2008: 192.
3. Ibid: 200.
4. Ibid: 202.
5. Ibid: 235.
6. Maltby, 2011: 27.
7. Ibid: 222, 269–270.
8. Maltby, 2011: 26; Krämer, 2011: 171–172.
9. Jarvie, 1994: 171.
10. Brunetta, 1994: 143.
11. Kroes, 1994: 29.
12. Quoted in Kroes, 1994: 32.
13. Ellwood, 2012: 119.
14. Smith, 2000: 50.
15. Higson and Maltby, 1999: 3.
16. Quoted in Thompson, 1999: 60.
17. Bakker, 2008: 253.

18. Ibid: 260.
19. Higson and Maltby, 1999: 5.
20. Hayward, 2000: 26.
21. Bakker, 2008: 265.
22. Wagnleitner, 1994: 197.
23. Montebello, 1994: 215.
24. Ibid: 227.
25. Ibid: 232.
26. Jarvie, 1994: 162.
27. Kaplan, 2010: 289; Farahmand, 2010: 266.
28. Halle, 2010: 305.
29. Ibid: 303.
30. Bakker, 2008: 340.
31. Anderson, 2002: 6.
32. Hobsbawm, 1990: 10.
33. Ibid: 90.

PART I

Beginnings: −1930

CHAPTER 2

A Young Nation Seeking to Define Itself: Finland in 1900–1930

Outi Hupaniittu

Finland gained independence in December 1917 in the aftermath of the Russian October Revolution as an administrative process without a single gunshot. However, independence had been preceded by political turmoil and was soon followed by a civil war.

Finland had been an autonomous Grand Duchy of the Russian Empire since Sweden ceded it in 1809. Although the Tsar held the highest power, the autonomous status secured the old laws, civil liberties and the Evangelical Lutheran religion. It also brought a number of reforms. Throughout the nineteenth century Finnish political institutions, economy and culture developed considerably. The notion of Finland as a nation was born during the first decades under Russian rule. At first it did not encompass the idea of independence and focused on developing a national identity, crystallized in the dictum 'Swedes we are no longer, Russians we will not become, let us therefore be Finns'.

A major aspect of the nationalist endeavour was the advancement of the Finnish language. The majority of Finns were Finnish speakers, but Swedish was the tongue of the upper class and written works. Gradually, Finnish was developed to meet the needs of the written culture of a

O. Hupaniittu (✉)
Finnish Literature Society, Helsinki, Finland
e-mail: outi.hupaniittu@finlit.fi

modern society. Finnish emerged as a truly literary language in the 1870s, giving rise to a language struggle between the Fennoman and Svecoman movements. Little by little the status of Finnish improved, and in 1900 it was declared to be equal with Swedish in all official uses. This did not end the language struggle. On the contrary, that only came to an end at the beginning of the Second World War.

The conflicts with the Russian central government came to a head towards the end of the nineteenth century. The policy of Russification— the cultural, political and societal assimilation of all peoples living within the empire—evoked widespread resistance in Finland. The first wave of Russification came to an end in the aftermath of the Russian Revolution of 1905. The suppression was suspended for a couple of years, full suffrage was granted and a new unicameral parliament established. Then after a couple of years an even stronger forced assimilation began, spurring a more determined effort towards independence.

The late nineteenth and early twentieth centuries are considered a golden age of Finnish art. Internationally renowned artists such as the composer Jean Sibelius and painters such as Albert Edelfelt, Akseli Gallen-Kallela and Helene Schjerfbeck created some of their major masterpieces. They, as well as the majority of Finnish artists, were Swedish speakers. However, those who were Finnish speaking were advancing towards professionalism. The language struggle divided most of the cultural sphere into two blocs—theatres, schools, newspapers, sport clubs and so on—but on both sides participants were taking a stand in the creation of Finnishness and resistance to Russification.

The struggle for national identity and independence coincided with the emergence of cinema. Its development followed similar patterns as in other countries: cinema was not established as an art, but as an entertainment for those either not interested in fine arts or unable to pay the relatively high admission fees of art institutions. Little by little, by the turn of 1910s, cinema began to attract middle-class viewers, although the old audiences were not abandoned. The number of cinemas grew and a division between elegant and modest venues became visible. Imported films followed international trends. In the early years most films originated in France; in the 1910s Danish and Italian melodramas were popular; and from 1916 onwards films from the USA became increasingly prominent. The large-scale film business was in the hands of Swedish speakers until the turn of the 1920s, but the modes of operation were bilingual. Most importantly, intertitles were made in both languages. The programmes consisted almost entirely of imported films, as domestic production remained insignificant. During the First World War, the little amount of filmmaking decreased, films from hostile countries were banned and Russian text became obligatory in the intertitles thus making them trilingual. Because of state-governed film inspection, established in 1911, and Russification measures, the possibilities for nationalistic manifestations on film were limited. The first actuality filmed by a Finnish company depicted the reburial of Eugen Schauman, hero of the active resistance who had assassinated Nicolai Bobrikov, the Governor-General of Finland. The film was screened without problems in the atmosphere after the 1905 revolution, but in 1912 another film depicting Magistrate Gustaf Blom, a convicted opponent of Russian rule, was banned. Likewise, the film of the nationalistic funeral of the 'First lady of the Finnish-speaking stage', Ida Aalberg, was not allowed to be screened in 1915. Moreover, the last feature made before independence, a triangle melodrama featuring a military officer, was banned in 1916, most probably due to presumed political overtones. Expressions of openly nationalistic sentiments were few and far between, as film companies concentrated on business and avoided confrontation. Quite possibly even the banned films were not intended as active resistance; more likely they were attempts at exploiting popular topics expected to find large audiences.

Immediately after independence was gained in 1917, the young nation faced a confrontation of a formidably greater order. The seeds of this had been planted over the past decades, as the struggle between social classes escalated and economic division between rich and poor deepened. In January 1918, the country plunged into a civil war. The Red Guard—mostly industrial and agrarian labourers—received some help from Russian soldiers still in Finland, whereas the White Guard—mostly landowners and members of the middle and upper classes—allied with Germany. The well-trained Jägers—members of the Finnish active resistance who had fled to be trained in Germany—together with a division of the German army returned to fight on the side of the Whites. After three and a half months the Reds were defeated and tens of thousands of them were taken to prison camps. In total almost 40,000 people (1.2% of the population) lost their lives, more than 90% of them in summary executions and prison camps after the actual fighting had ceased. The victors, the right-wing 'White Finland', ruled the nation over the interwar period and the country remained divided. The political activity of the left wing was severely restricted, but parliamentary rule was respected and many social and economic reforms were introduced.

Art had an important role in the process of legitimizing national institutions and in establishing a national culture. Although patriotic right-wing

nationalism was at the core of the official culture, even within these confines different ideas about Finnishness and Finnish art competed with one
another. The language divide remained as strong as ever and both right-
wing and left-wing cultural activists sought to develop Finnish-speaking
national institutions. Theatres were divided both according to language
and by class into bourgeois and workers' theatres. The language struggle continued also in the film world. During the 1920s there were both
Finnish- and Swedish-speaking film companies, but the most prominent of
them, Suomi-Filmi, was a stern supporter of the Finnish language. Other
producers were not able to challenge this market leader, which thus had a
decisive role in establishing notions about Finnish cinema. The number of
Finnish productions was still insignificant compared with the number of
imported films, and the USA remained the dominant source of films. The
share of German and other European productions continued to be significant, but Soviet Russian films were not imported until the late 1920s,
and even then their efforts were smothered by the Film Inspection Board.

Despite the influx of exports, at the beginning of the 1920s companies
were established solely for the purpose of filmmaking. Production became
more consistent and filmmakers wanted to take an active part in the creation of Finnishness and a national culture. Simultaneously, film sought
the status of legitimized art by adapting nationally significant literature
and engaging prominent writers, actors and directors from the world of
literature and drama. However, the process of professionalising Finnish literature and drama was still underway, making the field unwilling to admit
yet another form of art to compete with it.

The language struggle was still acute, and in 1926 the so-called trust
war was publicly debated in these terms, although it was basically a competition for market share. The Swedish language was accused of being
tainted by foreignness, whereas the pro-Finnish bloc was depicted as the
protector of a genuinely Finnish film business.

Over the silent era the language struggle was not all that evident in
the films themselves, as intertitles were bilingual. As regards literary adaptations and themes, the Finnish-speaking culture held the upper hand,
although there were companies operating in Swedish. The coming of
sound changed the situation completely. Through the entire studio era
(1930s–early 1960s) no films were made solely in Swedish, and only the
opening titles remained bilingual. The sound also restricted the possibilities for Swedish-speaking actors to work in films. Thus, by the beginning
of the 1930s, when 'the Golden Years of Finnish Cinema' were about to
start, Finnish films were Finnish speaking.

CHAPTER 3

The Emergence of Finnish Film Production and Its Linkages to Cinema Businesses During the Silent Era

Outi Hupaniittu

The first Finnish fiction film was made in 1907 and the transition to sound occurred in 1931. During the silent era there was no public funding or subsidies as there are today. Tax relief on domestic features was only introduced in 1930,[1] and production costs had to be covered entirely by self-financing. How were companies able to sustain production and what kind of difficulties did they encounter? How was Finnish cinema connected to the international film business?

Cinema requires a significant amount of capital, but also creates prospects for great incomes. High profitability has been an integral feature of the industry ever since its emergence. Gerben Bakker divides cinema into 11 activities, each of which increases the value of the product. He emphasizes that the most lucrative of them have been distribution and exhibition.[2] The many connections between producing and exhibiting films in Finland during the silent era must be explored in this vein. In terms of terminology, an important distinction has to be made between film companies and cinema companies, with the former signifying production companies and the latter those primarily operating as importers, distributors and/or exhibitors.

O. Hupaniittu (✉)
Finnish Literature Society, Helsinki, Finland
e-mail: outi.hupaniittu@finlit.fi

© The Editor(s) (if applicable) and The Author(s) 2016
H. Bacon (ed.), *Finnish Cinema*, Palgrave European Film and Media Studies, DOI 10.1057/978-1-137-57651-4_3

27

The key notions in this study are the first-mover advantage and the minimization of transaction costs. The former denotes the advantage gained by the initial operator in its field: the company that has been the first to set up the structures (for production: studio, equipment, laboratories; for other operations: exhibition, import, distribution functions; for both: finances, personnel, expertise, reputation and networks) is not easily challenged by newcomers. In order to succeed in reaching a similar position, the newcomer needs significant investment, but is likely not to have adequate income. Meanwhile, the first-mover is able to advance its own structures and thus maintain the lead.[3] For both first-movers and newcomers, minimization of transaction costs is lucrative, as it standardizes functions and enhances profitability. Companies tend to rely on persistence and constancy, as it brings stability and predictability.[4] Neither of these factors prevents business change, but they both create stability.

EARLY PRODUCTIONS WITHIN THE CINEMA COMPANIES

In 1915, Erik Estlander estimated that to cover the production costs of a feature film, 18–20 copies needed to be sold. He was one of the most adept cinema businesspeople in Finland, with a thorough knowledge of the field. He had imported films since 1908 and produced actualities since 1912. Estlander already had plans for very significant non-fiction film production, but they had not succeeded as hoped. Nevertheless, he was the most important actuality producer planning to expand into features. He confidently assessed that half of the copies could be easily sold to Sweden and Russia, but did not explain what was to be done with the rest.[5]

Despite his experience, Estlander's business proposal was completely infeasible. The 18–20 copies would have made production lucrative, and even lower sales volumes would have been sufficient to enable continuity of production, but no copies were sold. Estlander produced two features, both of which his company distributed only in Finland with a single copy. This was standard practice at the time. There were fewer than ten distributors in Finland, all of which guaranteed exclusive rental rights.[6] Thus, it would have been impossible to get more than one copy, or two at the most, into domestic circulation. Exporting was even more improbable: reliable sources date the first exports to the 1920s, and even then success was rare. In 1920 a couple of non-fiction films were sold to the USA, aimed at the Finnish immigrant audience, one of them even at a very good price. The first records of sales of feature films date from 1922.[7]

Before the end of the First World War, when Finland was an autonomous part of the Russian Empire, only 23 domestic features attained commercial distribution.[8] This was minuscule compared with Denmark, Sweden and Russia, where several companies were producing an increasing number of features each year. Also their domestic audiences were much larger, which made the initial phase of development easier and facilitated the move into international sales.[9] The population in Finland and Denmark was about the same, but Denmark's degree of urbanization was much greater. In Sweden, there were approximately twice as many inhabitants. In Russia, large-scale production and export started during the First World War. In Finland, the low volume, combined with the severe limits of domestic distribution, created barriers to the development of production.

In many ways the Finnish situation resembled that in Norway, where the domestic market was also small and fiction production did not bloom. Gunnar Iversen has noted that in Norway there were no strong individuals promoting productions like there were in Sweden and Denmark. Furthermore, municipal cinemas created yet another and even more severe hindrance from 1913 onwards,[10] around the time when in Finland the largest production volume of the pre-independence era was reached. In Finland, Erik Estlander and some of his peers wanted production to take place, but the economics did not support the plan. This suggests that large-scale production was the result of many factors, ranging from the economic preconditions to the individuals working with film. When compared to Sweden and Denmark, which held the position of first-movers and offered intense competition, it is no surprise that no Finnish films were exported. They were not able to attract foreign distributors, as the films lagged behind technically and/or artistically and the volume was too low. As Finnish production was structurally unprofitable, production numbers remained small and little professional experience was accumulated.

Considering this background, it is not surprising that 20 of the early features were produced by cinema companies that had their financial backbone in the lucrative distribution and exhibition businesses. Already around 1906–1907, when the era of permanent theatres began, most of the business lay in the few companies that imported and distributed films as well as owned cinema chains, the biggest of them spanning several cities across southern Finland.[11] After the leading companies had quickly seized power and built up the infrastructure, thus becoming the first-movers in the field, others had to settle for operating one or two cinemas. This structure was stable throughout the first dozen years as the operations grew slowly but steadily. For newcomers, it was too difficult to challenge the leaders outright, but with long-term work some of those new operators were able to enhance their status. Meanwhile, the first-movers competed with one another, and in this race producing films was one way to gain a competitive advantage despite the financial unprofitability.[12]

Most probably, the Finnish film business did not differ notably from other countries with low production numbers. It relied heavily on vertical integration, where large companies operated in as many stages of the value chain as possible, but the key difference from the major film producing countries was that production was not the basis of operations. From this difference emerge the two main models within the film industry. In countries with large-scale film production, the first-movers were the producers and their business plan was to make profits by making films. In order to secure their revenues, the producers also distributed, exhibited and/or exported their films.[13] In countries like Finland, the first-movers based their business on exhibition, and to support this they imported, distributed and on a small scale also produced films. The major production companies, like the French Gaumont and Pathé, soon established subsidiaries abroad to enhance their revenues, but it seems that the scale of the Finnish film business was too small to attract foreign companies. Thus, the export offices of the large producers sold their films to their Finnish business partners either directly or via special agencies focusing on film trade across borders. Hence, the constant need for films connected the Finnish companies to the international film business with similar structures, although the basis of profitability of the business lay elsewhere.[14]

The big Finnish companies were financially balanced. The profits from other activities brought the funding for filmmaking, while the distribution operations provided the necessary outlet for exhibition and box-office income. They had on their payroll professional staff such as projectionists and laboratory workers (mostly focusing on the translation of intertitles), who could assume responsibility for the technical side of production. For the artistic side of fiction films, well-known figures from Helsinki theatres were contracted. Despite all of this, the production numbers remained low and consisted mainly of non-fiction newsreels and travel films. There were also plenty of stumbles and blunders, which demonstrate that overcoming the technical challenges was not easy even for large companies.

Because of the way the field was structured and the preconditions of the value process, filmmaking was not profitable even for the major companies that gained revenues from their own box offices.[15] Nevertheless, it was the only way to strive to make even. Internationally, production costs were growing, especially during the 1910s, but investments created even larger profits than before, as the whole industry was in a state of rapid growth.[16] Moreover, in Finland the largest feature production numbers were reached just before the First World War, although because of financial difficulties the boom did not last long.[17] Nevertheless, production was not inconsequential, as the first-movers put efforts into it and did not only focus only on the financially more lucrative parts of their business.

NATIONALISTIC FILMMAKING IN THE AFTERMATH OF THE FIRST WORLD WAR

The civil war of 1918 and its aftermath strongly affected the ideologies behind filmmaking. In 1919, two new companies were established with the aim of producing nationalistic films. Both companies, Suomen Filmikuvaamo ('Finland's Film Manufacturer') and Finsk Filmkonst ('Finnish Film Art'), promised to bring to life the greatest achievements of Finnish literature with the help of leading actors, writers, composers and artists. Both emphasized their aim of promoting Finland abroad, as films would 'turn the floods of tourism' to Finland. Thus, the project of nationalistic film production did not focus on the domestic audience, but had broader ideas of exporting films depicting the uniqueness of Finland.[18] This was a fresh approach compared to the earlier features that had been modelled on contemporary films imported to Finland. At the turn of the 1920s, the new companies no longer wanted to emulate international trends, but to bring forth Finnishness in their productions.[19]

According to the declarations made by the film companies, everything depended on timing. The founder of Finsk Filmkonst, the renowned actor Adolf Lindfors, emphasized that if Finnish film production did not commence soon, the Germans, Swedes or Danes would come and set up production companies. As a result, not only would the outsiders gain the financial profits, but themes and texts would be filmed in 'an un-Finnish way'.[20]

Adolf Lindfors' fears were based on what he saw happening. One could even say that there was seldom as much of a transnational film cultural phenomenon in Finland as at the turn of the 1920s. The years of the First World War had shown the importance of film, since the belligerent states produced propagandist fiction and newsreels as well as attempting to establish or overtake cinema chains in allied or neutral countries. The German UFA (Universum Film AG) had come into Finland by force in 1918 and established a subsidiary.[21] There had been rumours of the Western powers planning to take similar actions, which led to speculations that Soviet

Russia would be next to follow. In the aftermath of the war, film was seen as a political medium with important economic effects. It was not yet certain whether the large nations would continue creating cross-border operations or if the peace would denote a return to mostly nation-based structures. The political aspects were even discussed in the Finnish Parliament, with the purpose of ensuring that the field of film would not end up in hands that would exploit it to promote the 'wrong kind' of politics.[22]

It was not just a question of politics and economics, but also of culture and art. Only weeks after the interview with Adolf Lindfors, the Swedish film *Song of the Scarlet Flower* (*Sången om den eldröda blomman*, 1919) received its Helsinki premiere.[23] At the time, the film was credited as being 'almost Finnish', as it was based on a Finnish novel, both the scriptwriter Gustaf Molander and the director Mauritz Stiller were born in Helsinki, and the music score was composed by the Finn Armas Järnefelt. However, for some it also served as evidence of how distorted the result would be if foreigners attempted to film Finnish texts.[24] Soon afterwards, Erik Estlander organized a publicity premiere for the propaganda feature *Under Bolshevism's Yoke* (*Bolshevismin ikeen alla*, 1919). This had been filmed in Finland by Russian emigrants and it is credited as being produced by Estlander.[25] In his interview, Lindfors also claimed that the Germans were filming the Finnish epic poem *The Tales of Ensign Stål*.[26] In 1921, further attestation of his view was received: the Danish feature *Leaves from Satan's Book* (*Blade af Satans bok*) depicted Finns in a very unfavourable fashion. The negative response received in Finland was such that the director Carl Th. Dryer replied to it, but this did nothing to soothe the wrath.[27] Thus it appeared that Finland and Finnish literature were of interest abroad, but that their renditions were not always becoming.

As it turned out, the Finnish film business was not taken over by either Bolsheviks or Westerners. The filmmaking Russian emigrants did not settle in Finland, and the German adaptation of *The Tales of Ensign Stål* never appeared. Still, the epic was filmed twice during the silent era, in 1910 and 1926, both times by Swedes. Furthermore, the establishment of a UFA subsidiary and other events demonstrated that something like that could happen. However implausible the threat, it featured in debates and was mentioned among the central motivations for the establishment of Finnish nationalistic filmmaking. The idea was to outpace the foreigners: to be faster than them in order to film Finnish masterpieces properly and also to collect profits from foreign markets.[28]

During the First World War, many European countries had restricted their imports from enemy countries. Thus, until the October Revolution all German products were illegal in Finland. After the peace such restrictions were removed, but during the 1920s some countries introduced import quotas or other measures to protect domestic production.[29] In Finland there were no such rules, although Soviet films did not usually pass the Board of Film Inspections. Nevertheless, discussion about foreign interest in the early 1920s can be seen as an instance of the same concern: Finnish production and economics had to be protected.

Nationalistic ideology was not the only revolutionary feature of the new companies, as their aim was also to focus solely on filmmaking. The two film companies established in late 1919 were each other's major competitors and in the winter of 1919–1920 they raced for the status of the leading film producer. Of the two, Finsk Filmkonst was the more likely to succeed, because the capital invested in it was ten times that gathered by Suomen Filmikuvaamo, and because among its shareholders was Suomen Biografi ('Finland's Cinema'), the most prominent cinema company in Finland. Considering these advantages, it is surprising that Finsk Filmkonst's journey ended practically before it had begun, while Suomen Filmikuvaamo eventually became the longest-lasting and second most prolific producer of all time in Finland.

Finsk Filmkonst declared that its output would consist solely of national art films. Its first project was the national epic *Kalevala*. Jean Sibelius, the internationally recognized national cultural hero, was engaged to compose an original score for the film. The company also aimed to build a state-of-the-art film studio complete with several supporting facilities, in the manner of the most advanced film cities.[30] By contrast, Suomen Filmikuvaamo began its operations much more modestly. It was established by a group of theatrical scene painters who teamed up with a well-known National Theatre actor in order to convert their scene-painting workshop into a film company. For the first few years, the company actually first and foremost made sets, for 32 productions in total in the first year alone. This did not mean that the plans for film production had been put aside. Quite the contrary: at the first board meeting a cinematographer was employed with a permanent contract and fixed salary. As the painters (who were also the owners) were only paid by the hour, it is obvious that the investment in a cinematographer was crucial. Also among the first acquisitions were a camera, a printing machine, lighting equipment and film stock.[31]

Although the main objective of Suomen Filmikuvaamo was the creation of nationalistic film art and the filming of nationally important literature, the company did not discard other sorts of filmmaking. The aim
was to commence newsreel production immediately on the arrival of the
equipment, and to explore the possibility of making advertising films for
Finnish companies. Producing comedies was also deemed to be accept-
able in order to gain experience little by little.[32] Nevertheless, Suomen
Filmikuvaamo (the name was abbreviated to Suomi-Filmi, 'Finland Film',
in 1921) survived its first years only because of scene painting and advertising films.[33] The cash flow these produced together with a generally
realistic business plan enabled the company to function, whereas its competitor, despite its greater resources, was ruined by its grand, economically
and practically unrealistic plans.

IT ALL COMES DOWN TO DISTRIBUTION

Despite its successful trade on the theatrical scene, the survival of Suomi-
Filmi was not self-evident. The main problem was that the basic structure of the Finnish cinema business did not accommodate film production
independent of distribution and exhibition. The distributors were in the
process of reforming their activities at the turn of the 1920s and lost all
interest in filmmaking. This did not diminish their significance, as they
were growing into larger and more powerful entities. Whereas during the
1910s there had been six or eight leading companies, in the 1920s this
large-scale business was in the hands of only four of them.[34] This meant
that there were not as many competing distributors as there had been in
the previous decade, and thus Suomi-Filmi had fewer options for negotiating exhibition deals. As the distributors were larger than they had been
in the 1910s, they were also more powerful within the field of the film
industry in Finland. Thus negotiations were more difficult for a production company in the early 1920s than they would have been in the 1910s
had there been companies operating in the film production field without
distribution and exhibition operations.[35]

A good example of the difficulties that film production encountered
was Suomi-Filmi's first feature, *Olli's Years of Apprenticeship* (*Ollin oppivuodet*). This was not based on high national literature, but a work of
contemporary juvenile fiction. It was eventually to become the most
successful Finnish feature to date, but at the time it was completed in
November 1920, it did not even get a distribution contract. Suomi-Filmi

had to organize a publicity premiere, renting a cinema and issuing invitations to the high and mighty of the young nation at its own cost. Even after the successful premiere and good reviews, the largest distributors were not interested. An independent cinema took the film and seats were sold out for three consecutive weeks. Only after this did the largest distributor, Suomen Biografi (the owner of the cinema rented for the publicity premiere), become interested and buy the exclusive distribution rights for three years with a one-off payment.[36]

The income that Suomi-Filmi received from *Olli's Years of Apprenticeship* was considerable, especially for the first three weeks: the cinema guaranteed the producer the sum of 40,000 marks, but if the net income were to exceed 80,000 marks, the producer would get 50% of it. The small independent cinema took a considerable risk with the contract, as the average weekly net income was around 26,000 marks and the screenings normally lasted only for one week. Had the film been a commercial failure, or even if it had achieved the average income, it would have mean significant losses for the cinema. However, the risk turned out to be worth taking. It seems that Suomi-Filmi received a little more than the guaranteed sum, as the net income was somewhere between 85,000 and 95,000 marks. Also the compensation for the exclusive rights for three years was quite reasonable, 33,500 marks. Both of these sums were much higher than would have been paid for imported films. There are no sources for prices in 1920–1921, but in 1919 a film programme (the main feature and the accompanying newsreel and short comedy) cost around 6000–7000 marks and the net income was around 12,000 marks (including only distribution to others, no box-office income from the company's own cinemas).[37] Even considering significant inflation, the price in 1921 would have been 7500–8700 marks and the net income 15,000 marks. The decline in the value of the mark affected imports and made foreign films significantly more expensive from the autumn of 1921 onwards, but there were no signs of this yet in late 1920 or early 1921.[38]

In total, Suomi-Filmi received about 80,000 marks, but still that was not enough. As the production costs were around 130,000 marks, an operating loss accrued that was as much as half of the capital of the company. Also, it is evident that both the independent cinema at which the film was screened and Suomen Biografi as the distributor made profits.[39] The case of *Olli's Years of Apprenticeship* highlights the core problem of Finnish film production in the 1920s. As the producers and exhibitors were separate companies, the box-office income had to be shared and the producer was not able to gain sufficient revenues.

Despite the financial setbacks, Finnish film production was starting to flourish, although the volume was still very low. The crucial change occurred around the time when the European film industry faced a significant downturn. During the First World War, European production did not suffer that badly. Quite the reverse: the situation was more difficult in the neutral European countries than the belligerent ones, as the war supported filmmaking and increased the consumption of entertainment. The downturn came when the international trade was gradually freed from wartime restrictions. Thus, the problems of the European film industry were not caused by falling production volume, but by modest growth when compared to the rapid expansion and development in Hollywood.[40] By the early 1920s, when it had become apparent that European film production had lost its lead for good and production volume was in rapid decline,[41] Finnish production improved, as for the first time there was continuous long-term fiction production, even though the volume remained low.

Suomi-Filmi was able to continue during its first few years with the support of its scenery construction arm and by expanding its capital by issuing shares. Furthermore, after the wipe-out of Finsk Filmkonst, it dominated the field. Feature production could not balance the books, but at least for the first time there was a company focusing on film production that was able to continue operations and make more than one fiction film without owning the distribution and exhibition functions.

During the 1910s, the major cinema companies had also been first-movers in film production, but in the early 1920s they and their successors willingly gave up production. During the years 1920–1925 Suomi-Filmi quickly managed to gain the position of a first-mover by producing 14 features. It was not the only operator in the field, but the competition was insignificant. One of the old companies, Lyyra, made three short comedies in 1920–1921, but soon afterwards the company was split up and sold. There were also newcomers, but none of them was able to make more than one film. All together, the competitors made only six films that gained commercial distribution.[42]

Despite Suomi-Filmi's status as a first-mover and its relative success, not all of its films were successful. No information about audience numbers remains, but a rough estimate suggests that popularity fluctuated significantly.[43] In general the operations were in the ascendant to such an extent that the company was little by little giving up scene painting and focusing solely on filmmaking. The last surviving signed contracts are from 1923, with a couple of offers dated to 1924 and 1925. Scenery construction is not mentioned in the annual report or board minutes after 1921, but there are no exact indications when the operations were closed down.[44]

It is evident that the advancement of Suomi-Filmi held back the efforts of those wishing to challenge it, as the newcomers made only one film before withdrawing from feature production. No other company managed to build up continuous production in the first half of the 1920s. This further advanced the success of Suomi-Filmi, as the domestic audience started to crave new Finnish films.

Despite significant progress, Finnish films remained marginal even on domestic screens and in comparison with crumbling European production numbers. Most of the titles were non-fiction, for example newsreels or advertising films for Finnish companies, but even with all these added together, Finnish production covered only a small percentage of screen time, as can be seen in Table 3.1.

For the distribution companies film screenings were business transactions, and this resulted in quite ruthless deals. Even though Suomi-Filmi received a higher income than was paid for imported films, the scale was too small. In 1920–1923 it was standard practice to distribute Finnish features with only one copy; only the most successful films were distributed with between two and four copies. In 1924 the number rose quickly and from 1925 onwards the standard was six.[45] Only the most successful films were exported, and of these only one or a few copies were sold. The precise numbers are difficult to deduce, as most often the records do not define the difference between commercial exports and film copies sent abroad in order to negotiate commercial export contracts. From the financial balances, it is obvious that exports were so few and far between that they had no impact on the Suomi-Filmi's economics.[46]

The domestic market was the backbone of distribution, but it is difficult to estimate how large an audience the films drew. In 1923, there were 123 cinemas with a total of 35,000 seats in Finland, which denotes 1 seat per 1000 inhabitants. One distributor only reached a small share of cinemas. In 1918 the largest distributor, Suomen Biografi, provided films for the company's 10 theatres and for 46 others,[47] but the scale of distribution networks in the 1920s is unknown. Also, when Suomi-Filmi's production was flourishing and there were several copies to distribute, the audience did not necessarily grow at the same pace.[48] Domestic audience numbers

Table 3.1   Number of Finnish films compared with the total number of films inspected in 1918–1930

	Finnish fiction films	Finnish non-fiction films	Total volume of Finnish films	Percentage of the total number of films inspected by the Finnish Board of Film Classification
1918	0	11	11	2
1919	1	28	29	4
1920	4	15	19	3
1921	4	10	14	4
1922	3	18	21	5
1923	3	18	21	4
1924	5	5	10	2
1925	2	48	50	9
1926	4	70	74	14
1927	7	36	43	6
1928	3	22	25	4
1929	6	22	28	4
1930	2	26	28	n/a
Total number	**44**	329	373	n/a

Sources: Ba:3–7 Catalogues of inspected films 1918–1929, Archive of the Board of Film Classification, NA; Filmografia Fennica 1904–1930; Cinema Owners' Calendar 1936–1937; Seppälä 2012: 33–7. Compare with Appendix, Fig. A.1

All the sources used are ambiguous and thus the numbers are estimations. Of the fictional films, only those that received commercial distribution are included. The non-fiction films include all those that were aimed at general distribution and thus approved for screening by the Board of Film Classification.

were steadily increasing, but the situation was still light years away from the distribution plans of Erik Estlander.

EXPANSION LEADS TO RIVALRY

The progress of Suomi-Filmi was not straightforward; quite the contrary, there were serious problems. Despite the increase in filmmaking, the company was not financially successful. The financial results were barely profitable, and as such insufficient to enable dividends to be paid. Only in 1922 was there an 8.2% dividend, which meant that the largest shareholders received 2500 marks, the equivalent of the monthly salary of the company's CEO, but 500 marks less than the cinematographer earned. The total amount shared in dividends was 19,250 marks, whereas the company paid 16,000 marks in salaries each month.[49]

The key question was distribution, in which the major cinema companies held the upper hand. As Suomi-Filmi had no cinemas or other means of distribution, it had to negotiate and agree to the terms of the cinema companies in order to get screenings, and thus it had to share the income. By 1923, the distribution problems seem to have caused a serious crisis as they were slowing down Suomi-Filmi's expansion.

Suomi-Filmi took a three-pronged approach to try to remedy this problematic situation. One short-term remedy was to launch a film tour to take feature films to areas where there were no permanent cinemas. Secondly, Suomi-Filmi changed its distributor in the hope of greater revenue. Until this time the entire feature production had been distributed by Suomen Biografi, but from 1923 onwards some films went to Adamsin Filmitoimisto ('Adams Film Office'), another of the big four controlling the cinema business.[50] In addition to these short-term remedies, Suomi-Filmi worked on a longer-term solution by purchasing a land lot with the intention of constructing a large residential building, which would include a new studio, a laboratory and office premises as well as the largest cinema in Helsinki.[51]

The result was not what was expected. Suomi-Filmi's attempts to force the exhibitors into competition only caused the situation to go from bad to worse. The film tour led to bitter arguments with Suomen Biografi, which was distributing some of the same features.[52] As Suomi-Filmi continued its cooperation with Suomen Biografi despite the obvious problems, it is clear that the producer was dependent on the exhibitor. Meanwhile, the construction plans did not advance and new features required distribution. However, both the success and the problems Suomi-Filmi faced drew the attention of other entrepreneurs to film production and stirred up the cinema business.

By 1925 Suomi-Filmi was, in addition to its construction plans, negotiating a merger with Adamsin Filmitoimisto, while Suomen Biografi was planning to expand into the provision of film studios and laboratory services for independent producers.[53] Gustaf Molin, also one of the big four, went even further. He was in the background creating facilities for serious competition in filmmaking. He had allied with the head cinematographer of Suomi-Filmi, Kurt Jäger, who resigned in early 1925 and established Taide-Filmi ('Art Film').[54] Despite the name, it did not produce fiction but focused on laboratory services and non-fiction films. Its proclaimed aim was to enhance the quality of Finnish filmmaking in order to expand production.[55] Although Molin was not among the owners or leaders, his participation is evident. In 1925–1926 Taide-Filmi produced almost 60 newsreels, and more than 40 of them were made for Molin. Nevertheless, the producer was not bound to the distributor, as at least 12 films went to other distributors.[56] Despite the fact that Taide-Filmi never made fiction films, it was a serious competitor to Suomi-Filmi. It multiplied Finnish non-fiction production almost overnight and also made Suomi-Filmi increase its newsreel production (see Table 3.1). Moreover, the chosen starting point did not denote that there were no plans for features. Just as Suomi-Filmi had survived its initial years by set painting, Kurt Jäger started his own company producing newsreels and undertaking laboratory services, and the link with Gustaf Molin meant that the company had a good chance of survival in the field of filmmaking.

All of a sudden, three of the four leading distributors wanted to participate in filmmaking. The only one not interested was the Finnish subsidiary of the German UFA, which was not surprising, considering that its main activity was to import the plethora of films produced by its parent company. On top of this, UFA was facing financial difficulties back home and by 1925 its foreign subsidiaries were under threat of closure.[57] Nevertheless, others were happy to sustain Suomi-Filmi's distribution problems, as their interest in film production was rekindling. Most probably this was because of the recent realization that even the cinema business was not as lucrative as had been hoped at the turn of the 1920s and that the dividends were far from what had been expected. For example, in 1920 Suomen Biografi was able to pay a 17% dividend to its A shares and 8.5% to its B shares, but in 1925 there were no dividends.[58] Thus, after some years the separation of production and distribution had been shown not to be as practical a way of working as had been thought. The problems originated from different sources, but the difficulties were significant enough for both sides to seek profitability through also engaging in the other's field.

By 1926 the owners of Suomen Biografi and UFA were contemplating selling the companies, thus stirring up competition between those willing to continue. A bidding war ensued, which resulted in major business deals. Suomi-Filmi bought the largest distribution company, Suomen Biografi, and Gustaf Molin captured the UFA subsidiary with its very lucrative import deals from UFA's new American partners. This shifted the balance and made him the biggest importer and distributor.[59]

These developments resulted in bitter rivalry nicknamed the 'trust war', in which nationalistic notions were of great importance. Suomi-Filmi declared itself to be *the* national cinema company, supporting Finnish filmmaking and the Finnish economy, whereas it claimed that Gustaf Molin represented everything foreign. Molin was a Swedish citizen and through his import rights had connections to the German and US film markets.[60] In the media campaign by the 'nationalists', the foreignness of their competitor was emphasized out of all proportion. The struggle over the domination of exhibition and distribution was pictured as a struggle for self-determination: was the field of Finnish film and cinema to be overtaken by outsiders or would the nationalists be able to prevent it?

In fact, sales in 1926 had made the Finnish film business more domestic than it had been since 1918, as there was no longer a German subsidiary steering its share of the business in accordance with commands coming from Berlin. Although Molin was a Swedish citizen, his mother was Finnish, he had lived in Finland since 1921 and he been one of the leading cinema businesspeople ever since. His cinematic ventures were entirely Finnish, as the companies operated within national borders and under the national jurisdiction and there were no shareholders or directors living outside Finland.[61] He imported films, but in that there was nothing more foreign than in the equivalent operations of Suomi-Filmi or Adams, the two other major operators and the figureheads of the 'pro-Finn' side. Perhaps because of this, the struggle did not last long. The heated debate died out in a year or two, even though the structures remained and neither side had managed to overcome the other.

While rivalry was raging in the public sphere, everyday operations went on as usual. Suomi-Filmi, with the assistance of its new import, distribution and exhibition departments, was considerably more powerful than before. This did not result in instant big profits, as the acquisition of Suomen Biografi was financed by loans that strained the company for years. Still, although no dividends could be distributed, its financial status became much better than it had even been before: the outcome for 1926 was already greater than that for the years 1920–1925 put together.[62] Over the next few years, exhibition provided an important part of the financing of the company's expansion plans. However, during the silent era, Suomi-Filmi was not yet a lucrative investment for shareholders and its expansion plans were unsuccessful, leading the company into severe losses by 1930. Until then the results revealed only marginal profitability.[63] It is evident that without the aid of its own exhibition activity, Suomi-Filmi would have gone bankrupt by the turn of the 1930s. On the other hand, without the financial backbone contributed by exhibitions, it is not likely that the company would have made such risky expansion plans.

This again emphasizes the importance of distribution and exhibition for the film business as a whole. They were not just the most lucrative parts of the value chain, but also remained the basis of the whole Finnish film business. Just as in the previous decade, the business model was based on exhibition operations, even as the 1920s had introduced film production companies that sought to focus solely on filmmaking. On the Finnish scale film production was flourishing, but in the big picture Finland was still an extension of the international film business, focusing on exhibiting films produced elsewhere.

The difference in finances is indicative of an important distinction between the motivation for producing and exhibiting. The aim of running cinemas was to make profits,[64] whereas filmmaking could be considered to be successful if the company broke even. At this stage it was not possible to make productions truly profitable, and thus the fact that filmmaking continued indicates that the motivations lay elsewhere. Still, production was not altruistic, as there was the prospect of future gains. Moreover, the salaries that Suomi-Filmi was able to pay key personnel were good, which means that it was not a financially poor choice to be a director of a film company. For example, the salary of the CEO of Suomi-Filmi, Erkki Karu, was doubled to 5000 marks in February 1923. The director of the National Theatre received the same amount starting from the following autumn, but the director of the Swedish Theatre in Helsinki reached that amount only in 1926. At the turn of the 1930s, when Suomi-Filmi was in severe financial difficulties, the salaries and especially the extra allowances and fringe benefits paid to the directors were very extravagant, and garnered severe criticism from those hoping to save the company from bankruptcy.[65]

On top of that, a distinction was emerging from the growing success of Suomi-Filmi's films. This was most notable for Karu, who largely personified the company throughout the 1920s. Before its establishment he had been a countryside scene painter and a director of a rural amateur workers' theatre. When the films started to gain success, he was heralded in the company's publicity as 'the creator of Finnish film art', a title that is still often bestowed on him.

It seems that the shareholders—many of whom were also key company personnel—were willing for the time being to settle for little if any financial gain, as the field was in steady growth, opening up the prospects of larger audiences, greater export opportunities and therefore also future profits.

COMPETITION IN FILMMAKING

The commencement of the trust war also signalled a prominent advance in filmmaking, as other producers appeared able to challenge Suomi-Filmi in fiction production. Over the years 1926–1930, the leading production company made 11 features, while the others completed in total the same number of films—a significant change when compared to previous years. Some of the new competition at least partly originated from the interest distribution companies had in Suomi-Filmi's activities. Adams produced one feature, but Gustaf Molin was backing more notable plans. Already in the spring of 1926, his ally Kurt Jäger—together with Teuvo Puro, one of the founders of Suomi-Filmi and a well-known theatre and film director—established yet another production company.[66] Komedia-Filmi ('Comedy Film') made both newsreels and features. Still, just as with Taide-Filmi, its main function was the laboratory. This time Molin's participation was much more evident. In the trust war, Komedia-Filmi was closely allied with Molin, who also both distributed features that the company made, and was the biggest client of the laboratory.[67] Before Komedia-Filmi had its first anniversary, the cinema magnate was also its largest shareholder.[68]

The features produced by Adams (*The Waves of Sea and Love; Meren ja lemmen aallot*, 1926) did not succeed particularly well, while Komedia-Filmi's first film was the most screened Finnish film of 1926. Nevertheless, the popularity of *Before the Face of the Sea* (*Meren kasvojen edessä*), directed by Teuvo Puro, was far behind when compared with Suomi-Filmi's greatest successes, indicating that after years of market domination by Suomi-Filmi other enterprises were able to compete. Despite the good start, the next and last feature by Komedia-Filmi, *On the Highway of Life* (*Elämän maantiellä*, 1927), was a commercial failure.[69] This denotes that distribution by the largest distribution company and a large accompanying publicity campaign were not enough to make a film successful. One reason for the downfall might have been that Suomi-Filmi managed to lure Teuvo Puro back, and thus the second film had a more inexperienced director. Also, the supposedly 'international style and topic' did not seem to have impressed the Finnish audience. Contemporary criticism and commentaries on the film are thoroughly colored by the trust war, as the pro-Finn side saw the film epitomizing everything negative that the other side was allegedly aiming to bring to Finland, and to the promoters of a more international Finnish culture the film was a great success. Thus, the commentators—regardless of their side in the battle—seem to have formed their opinion of the film before seeing it. This is visible even in the smaller press outside the capital, as every newspaper had a stance when it came to the language battle (Finnish vs Swedish) or nationalistic notions (Finnishness vs internationalism).

Soon Komedia-Filmi also closed down its unprofitable non-fiction production and concentrated on manufacturing intertitles.[70] Despite the backing of Gustaf Molin and a steady cash flow from the laboratory, filmmaking had yet again become too expensive. This did not daunt other entrepreneurs and in a short period three production companies were established—Aquila-Suomi, 1927; Kotka-Filmi, 1928; and Fennica, 1929—all of which made more than one feature. None of them seems to have had supportive lines of operations and their operations were very limited—and, although there are no records to attest to it, evidently unprofitable.[71]

The late 1920s were very interesting years in terms of feature production, with new directors and fresh notions of filmmaking surfacing. However, as noted before, the number of premieres or size of audience did not automatically bring big profits to the production company, as the income depended on distribution contracts. Nevertheless, a box-office success was needed in order for the production company to continue operations. For example, the films *With the Blade of the Sword* (*Miekan terällä*, 1928) and *A Song about the Heroism of Labour* (*Työn sankarilaulu*, 1929) by Kotka-Filmi achieved a large number of showings. Kalle Kaarna, the owner and director of Kotka-Filmi, was able to make one more film, *The Feast at the Seashore* (*Juhla meren rannalla*, 1929), but it did not reach a similar-sized audience. It was somewhat successful, but nevertheless the company ceased making films. This emphasizes the difference in stability between the first-mover Suomi-Filmi and the newcomers.[72] As Suomi-Filmi's operations were manifold and there were several productions to share the risk, the poor or mediocre ratings for one film were not as devastating as they were for a small company. It seems that one box-office failure was enough to end filmmaking in a small production company, most probably because it made acquiring financing for the next film too difficult. Nevertheless, setbacks did not automatically cause liquidation—for example, Kotka-Filmi never filed for bankruptcy, it only closed down its operations.

All in all, in the latter half of the 1920s Suomi-Filmi faced serious competition, but other production companies were never able to equal the strong status of the market leader, as production was dispersed over several small companies. As previously mentioned, Suomi-Filmi produced 11 features in 1926–1930. All together production by the newcomers rose to the same number, but the division and the lack of channels for distribution and exhibition resulted in operating losses, which slowed the development of film production outside of the first-mover. It did not matter that some of the films were box-office successes or critically acclaimed, or that they brought fresh ideas into Finnish filmmaking, as the structures of the industry did not support their profitability.

While Suomi-Filmi faced the challenge issued by the newcomers, the whole field was heading towards crisis. The economic depression and the transition to sound made the business even less profitable. Because of poor investments, unfulfilled plans and the difficulties brought by the conversion into sound film, Finnish cinema was about to return to the low production figures of the beginning of the 1920s. The situation was exacerbated by the large Hollywood production companies renewing their overseas tactics, which entailed establishing subsidiaries (MGM, 1929; Paramount, 1930; Fox, 1931; Warner, 1932) that took over the task of exporting their films to Finland. This severely hampered the prospects of the Finnish companies. In 1932 the four US subsidiaries held a share of 60% of imported films, although after this peak their share shrank.[73] This seem to have been an international trend, as similar development had occurred for example in Germany a couple of years beforehand.[74]

During the darkest moments in 1932 there were serious discussions at Suomi-Filmi about the future and whether there was any sense in continuing filmmaking, as the difficulties of sound technology seemed too great to overcome and only cinemas seemed to be profitable.[75] However, production was not closed down, and just around the corner were the most prosperous years of Finnish cinema during which profits could be made even by film production. Yet again, the crisis highlighted the many connections within the field of cinema that supported and enabled one another.

DOMESTIC SILENT FEATURES AS PART OF THE FINNISH FILM BUSINESS

During the silent era, feature film production in Finland was anything but trouble free. The financial constraints made long-term feature production virtually impossible except in conjunction with related fields of business. Suomi-Filmi dominated production, but even for this company profitability was unattainable—no dividends were distributed even when exhibition and distribution supported its finances.

Suomi-Filmi's lead was broad, but even it was not unaffected by competition. When Taide-Filmi started large-scale non-fiction production, Suomi-Filmi expanded similarly. Thus companies with varying business tactics kept an eye on one another and at times also did their best to copy operating models. The international scene was certainly not disregarded, but when it came to business tactics, it is evident that following the methods of large-scale producers abroad was unfeasible for Finnish film producers. Moreover, as exports remained nearly non-existent, competition was within Finnish borders and thus it was most important to be able to respond to the domestic challenges.

During the 1920s, the quality of Finnish filmmaking was constantly referred to in advertising. Each film was described as a great masterpiece, and the growing audiences testify to the advancements in its operations. At the same time, there were plenty of articles implying that the finest accolade for a Finnish film would have been its international success. The positive reception of a couple of films that were exported was meticulously reported as proof of the quality of Finnish filmmaking, yet still it was obvious that the Finnish masterpieces did not reach international standards. The quality of production was rising, but only on a Finnish scale.

Domestic production constituted only a small percentage of all the films shown. All through the silent years, the film business was financially based on the operations of exhibition and distribution. Although production numbers grew towards the end of the 1920s, the situation in which domestic film production would have formed the financial basis of operations was yet to materialize. Economically production relied on structures set up for screening imported films, despite the publicity celebrating the great achievements of Finnish filmmakers. Thus, during the silent era, the international film business was the backbone of operations in Finland.

Notes

1. Pantti 2000: 33–5.
2. Bakker 2008: 1, 179–218, passim.
3. Chandler 2004: 34–5.
4. Lamberg, Ojala, Eloranta, 1997: 26–38.
5. Augson: 'Kysymys kotimaisesta filmiyhtiöstä,' *Biograafilehti*, 3/1915, 3–4; see also Hupaniittu 2013: 190–4, 229–30.
6. Hupaniittu 2013: 127–43, 238–43.
7. Annual reports 1920 and 1922; Export and exhibition contract with Uuno Rikkonen, 9/9/1920, SuFiA, NAI.
8. In addition to these, three more were filmed during the Russian era. The film material of two of them was destroyed while in post-production and one was banned and confiscated before release. Filmographies also list one more film, but it was merely a filmed section of a cabaret show. Finnish National Filmography 1.

9. Of the importance of the domestic markets see for example Bakker 2008: 222–3.
10. Iversen 1998: 97–103.
11. Hupaniittu 2013: 143–8.
12. Ibid.: 486, 90–112, 188–212.
13. Bakker 2008: 179–82.
14. About the structures of Finnish cinema business, see Hupaniittu 2013: 112–13, 127–49.
15. Ibid.: 205–30.
16. Bakker 2008: 198–205.
17. Hupaniittu 2013: 218–21, 258–61.
18. 'Suomalainen filmiyhtiö perustettu,' Helsingin Sanomat, 3/10/1919; 'O.Y. Suomen Filmikuvaamo,' Uusi Suomi, 11/1/1920.
19. The change in the ideology of filmmaking has been noted by practically all researchers focusing on these years. See for example Laine 2007: 55; Salmi 2002: 329–31.
20. 'Suomalainen filmiyhtiö perustettu,' Helsingin Sanomat, 3/10/1919; 'Suuri filmausyritys hankkeissa,' Uusi Suomi, 3/10/1919.
21. About the German efforts in Finland, see Hupaniittu 2013: 280–397.
22. Hupaniittu 2013: 349–75. See also Representative Hannes Pulkkinen, Plenary 24/10/1922, Minutes I, Parliament Proceedings 1922.
23. 'Kino-Palatsi [advertisment],' Uusi Suomi, 12/10/1919.
24. See for example 'Suomalainen filmiyhtiö perustettu,' Helsingin Sanomat, 3/10/1919; 'Suomalainen filmiteollisuus,' Helsingin Sanomat, 17/12/1922.
25. The extent of Estlander's involvement in production is unknown. Although the theme was extremely topical, the film never achieved proper theatrical distribution even in Finland, and all export plans failed.
26. See for example 'Suomalainen filmiyhtiö perustettu,' Helsingin Sanomat, 3/10/1919.
27. Oski Talvio: 'Sananen tanskalaisesta filmistä jolla on aiheena meidän vapaustaistelumme,' Filmiaitta, 2/1922, 35; Carl Th Dryer: 'Lehtiä paholaisen kirjasta -filmin johdosta,' Filmiaitta, 5/1922, 92: Oski Talvio: 'Lehtiä paholaisen kirjasta,' Filmiaitta, 9/1922, 149.
28. 'Suomalainen filmiyhtiö perustettu,' Helsingin Sanomat, 3/10/1919; 'O.Y. Suomen Filmikuvaamo,' Uusi Suomi, 11/1/1920.
29. Bakker 2008: 223; Hupaniittu 2013: 243–58.
30. Company meeting 20/1/1920, KR 42.323, Finsk Filmkonst, Trade Register, NA; 'Kotimaisen filmitaiteen luominen,' Uusi Suomi, 17/1/1920.
31. Constitution meeting 20/12/1919; Annual report 1920; Board meeting 27/12/1919, 8/1 and 21/1/1920, SuFiA, NAI.

32. 'O.Y. Suomen Filmikuvaamo,' *Uusi Suomi*, 11/1/1920; Annual report 1921, SuFiA, NAI.
33. Annual reports 1920, 1921, SuFiA, NAI.
34. The leading cinema companies and operators of the 1920s were Suomen Biografi, Gustaf Molin, Abel Adams and UFA's subsidiary. Hupaniittu 2013: 414–33, 486.
35. Gerben Bakker has written about the same effect, where first-movers can hinder the operations of newcomers, by comparing the distribution tactics of the large US producers with those of the European film market in the 1920s. Bakker 2008: 248–50.
36. Hupaniittu 2013: 422–4.
37. Program book 1916–1921, SuFiA, NAI; 'Filmien hankinta vaikeaa,' *Uusi Suomi*, 14/9/1921.
38. Hupaniittu 2013, 325–6, 395.
39. Ibid.: 424–5.
40. Bakker 2008: 187–92.
41. Ibid.: 227–30.
42. Finnish National Filmography 1; the categorizing of companies into first-movers and others according to Hupaniittu 2013; 486, 90–112, 188–212. See also Appendix, Fig. A.1.
43. There is no information about admission numbers, but a rough index based on the number of screenings suggests that half received a high number of screenings and half a low number. However, the screening index encompasses all screenings until 1970 in the biggest cities. Still, silent films did not receive that many screenings after the introduction of sound, which suggests that estimates are more plausible than the numbers for the 1930s or later decades when estimating contemporary success. When screening indices are compared with the tax records, which only survived until early 1922, they rank the films in the same order and highlight the difference between remarkable success and a mediocre outcome, but also suggest that those films that received fewer screenings might have sold more seats per screening than those that received more screenings. Finnish National Filmography 1: Screening indexes; compare with Gab:14–6 Amusement tax ledgers 1920–1921, HPDOA, NAF.
44. Scenery painting contracts 8/11, 26/11 and 14/12/1923; scenery painting offers 3/1/1924, 17/11/1925 and s.d., SuFiA, NAI.
45. The films distributed with more than a single copy before 1924 were *Anna Liisa* (1922, 2 copies), *The Logroller's Bride* (*Koskenlaskijan morsian*, 1923, 3 copies) and *The Village Shoemakers* (*Nummisuutarit*, 1923, 4 copies). The numbers of copies are based on the estimations made for the Finnish National Filmography 1.
46. The annual reports 1921–1924, SuFiA, NAI.

47. Suomen Biografi to Film Committee 22/12/1918, Ea:1 Incoming Correspondece, BFCA, NAF.

48. When the screening index numbers are compared with the number of copies, it seems that the more copies there were, the fewer screenings each of them received. Still, the number of screenings was continually on the increase and the index only talks about the situation in the largest cities. However, this was the time when the number of cinemas in the countryside was growing rapidly. Thus, the new audience potential was outside the major cities, which suggests that the overall growth in admissions was larger than the index indicates. Finnish National Filmography 1: Screening indexes.

49. Annual meeting 27/1/1922; salary lists 1922–1923, SuFiA, NAI.

50. Distribution contracts with Suomen Biografi 20/1 and 25/4/1921, 20/3 and 17/11/1922, 22/9/1923, 9/9 and 29/10/1924, 24/3/1925; unsigned contract drafts with Suomen Biografi s.d. 1923, s.d. September 1923, 10/10/1923, s.d. autumn 1924, s.d. August 1925; distribution contracts with Abel Adams 24/10 and 12/12/1923, 15/2 and 15/4/1924, 31/10/1925; Board meeting 4/2/1923; 21/5/and 13/6/1924, 13/1 and 1/2/1925; Annual reports 1923 and 1925, SuFiA, NAI.

51. Board meeting 2/6 and 4/6/1923, 10/3 and 10/4/1924, SuFiA, NAI.

52. Contract with Suomen Biografi 24/3/1925, SuFiA, NAI.

53. Annual report 1925; Contract draft s.d. spring 1925, SuFiA, NAI; 'Uusi suuri bioteatteri Helsinkiin,' S.n. & s.d. Mar 1923, Unidentified scrapbook 1923–1930, NAI.

54. Declarations 538/3/4/1925 and 800/13/5/1925, KR 52.679, Taide-Filmi, Trade Register, NAF.

55. 'Uusi kotimainen filmiyhtiö,' *Filmiaitta*, 20/1925, 365.

56. Ba:5 Catalogue of inspected films 1923–1926, BFCA, NAF.

57. Hupaniittu 2013: 434–5; Thompson 1985: 110–7; Saunders 1994: 68–9.

58. Hupaniittu 2013: 490, see also 433–6.

59. Hupaniittu 2013: 439–40; Hupaniittu 2015c.

60. Ibid.: 439–40, see also Hupaniittu 2011: 212–14; Hupaniittu 2015c; Seppälä 2012: 265–79.

61. Hupaniittu 2013: 412–28, 494; Hupaniittu 2015c.

62. The financial outcome for 1926 was a profit of 70,000 marks. In terms of previous years, the outcome for 1920 had been a loss of almost 80,000 marks, and for the next years a total of 138,000 marks profit. The Company Meeting 12/2/1921, 27/2/1922, 22/5/1925, 12/3/1926, 29/3/1927; Board Meeting 18/2/1923, 4/2/1924, SuFiA, NAI.

63. Company Meeting 29/2/1928, 26/2/1929, 1/3/1930, SuFiA, NAI.

64. About the attitudes of the cinema companies towards profitability, see Hupaniittu 2013: 434–9.
65. The salary list, February 1923; Report by Lennart Åström, appendix to Annual meeting 3/4/1933, SuFiA, NAI; Board meeting 27/4/1923, National Theatre Archive, National Theatre; Ab:10 Salary book 1926–1927, Swedish Theatre Archive, Society of Swedish Literature in Finland.
66. Declaration 900/3/6/1926, KR 55.701, Komedia Filmi, Trade Register, NA.
67. Annual report 1926, Company Meeting 11/4/1927, Komedia Filmi Archive, NAI. Managing the business via separate companies was nothing remarkable. For example, Suomen Biografi was actually four companies, and Gustaf Molin operated as many as ten companies. Hupaniittu 2011: 220; Hupaniittu 2015c.
68. Nominally, Molin was not among the shareholders until 1929, but already two years earlier the majority of shares belonged to his 'Man Friday', Arne Söderberg, which was standard practice in Molin's business ventures. Company Meeting 11/4/1927 and 14/3/1929, Komedia Filmi Archive, NA; compare with Hupaniittu 2013: 400–14.
69. Hupaniittu 2015a.
70. Annual report 1928, Company Meeting 14/3/1929; see also Annual report 1927, Company Meeting 15/3/1928, Komedia Filmi Archive, NAI.
71. Hupaniittu 2015a.
72. Hupaniittu 2015a.
73. Ga:4 Ledger of film inspections 1930–1934, BFCA, NAF.
74. Kreimeier 1996: 152.
75. Company Meeting 31/5/1932, see also 3/4/1933, SuFiA, NAI.

CHAPTER 4

Finnish Film Style in the Silent Era

Jaakko Seppälä

This chapter traces the changes that have taken place in the style of Finnish silent fiction films and their connections to national and international cultural flows. Film style is best understood as the systematic and significant use of the techniques of the medium,[1] as David Bordwell defines it. I analyse Finnish films in their transnational context by means of classifying, measuring and verbally describing their stylistic characteristics and comparing the findings to foreign cinemas. This will reveal similarities and differences, which enable me to assess how unique Finnish silent cinema was and to what extent foreign cinemas affected its stylistic development. The vast number of films of which Finnish filmmakers can be expected to have been aware and the small number of available studies on the style of small nation cinemas are complicating factors. They can be overcome by concentrating on potentially influential individual films, which can be traced from contextual sources like film magazines, and widespread stylistic trends. The two styles to which Finnish films are compared are the tableau style and the classical style. The former is the style that was globally used prior to the 1910s when the classical style was developed in Hollywood, from where it began its spread. The overall goal in this chapter is to assess to what extent Finnish silent cinema developed from

J. Seppälä (✉)
Film and Television Studies, University of Helsinki, Helsinki, Finland
e-mail: jaakkoseppala@gmail.com

© The Editor(s) (if applicable) and The Author(s) 2016   51
H. Bacon (ed.), *Finnish Cinema*, Palgrave European Film
and Media Studies, DOI 10.1057/978-1-137-57651-4_4

the tableau style towards the classical style. What follows is not intended to be a comprehensive history of the style of Finnish silent film, but one that provides insight into its development and transnational nature.

SUPPLEMENTING IMAGES WITH WORDS

Intertitles are texts that do not belong to the diegesis of a film; this is where they differ from inserts like letters that belong to the story world. The first Finnish fiction film to contain intertitles was the short slapstick comedy *The Calf's Tail* (*Vasikan häntä*, 1908), which was the second fiction film made in the country.[2] On the basis of its synopsis, *The Calf's Tail* differed from its predecessor, *The Moonshiners* (*Salaviinanpolttajat*, 1907), in that it contained spatiotemporal transitions. Expository intertitles that are enunciated outside the diegesis were needed to make the transitions understandable. Because Finnish-language intertitles were a new phenomenon and therefore a linguistic attraction, they were mentioned in film advertisements. This indicates that written language can function as an index of national identity in the context of a silent fiction film.

At the time of *The Calf's Tail*'s production, expository intertitles were more common than other forms of intertitles on both sides of the Atlantic. In the American fiction film the shift in the early 1910s towards a more psychologically based narrative and the classical style affected the types and uses of intertitles. By the late 1910s, dialogue intertitles had outnumbered expository intertitles.[3] Dialogue intertitles belong to the diegesis, as they are a way of conveying the spoken words or unspoken thoughts of characters to audience members. As they are motivated by the actions of characters, their increasing use made cinematic narration less self-conscious. Within the classical style the story emerges above all from the action and dialogue of the characters, whereas in pre-classical films, like *The Calf's Tail*, the story is firmly fixed to the narrator's point of view. After the premises of the classical Hollywood style had been laid down, the role of expository intertitles changed. In the classical cinema they are used not so much to summarize action as to introduce characters, give an indication of the situation and tell how much time has passed between scenes.[4]

The first Finnish fiction film to make extensive use of intertitles was probably *Sylvi* (1913), shot in 1911, which was advertised as an hour-long art film.[5] The film has not survived, but many fragments that were possibly used in it remain. Whether the film contained dialogue intertitles is unlikely. *Sylvi* is based on a play of the same name written by Minna

Canth, from which dialogue could have been taken. However, the film was made in the style of Le Film d'Art productions and Danish art films,[6] especially *The Abyss* (*Afgrunden*, 1910), which displays letters but no dialogue intertitles. As fiction film production had only just begun in Finland and filmmakers were still inexperienced, *Sylvi* is likely to have been stylistically conservative rather than innovative. Its expository intertitles were probably so-called giveaway titles that appeared before the shots to which they referred. In *Olli's Years of Apprenticeship* (*Ollin oppivuodet*, 1920), a later film directed by Teuvo Puro, even dialogue intertitles are giveaway titles, which at times makes it difficult for the audience to know who is uttering a given line of dialogue. The giveaway title is a pre-classical convention, as its use further enhances the feeling that the given story is being told by a narrator. This seems to have been the last instance in which such intertitles were widely used in a Finnish fiction film.

The developments in the use of intertitles in Finnish fiction films can be studied with sufficient accuracy from 1920 on, since the majority of the films made in the decade survive. When filmmakers turned increasingly towards literature and theatre, as a result of which films became longer and more nuanced, the number of intertitles probably increased. Table 4.1 shows the number of intertitles per 500 shots in Finnish fiction films made in the 1920s. The column titled 'intertitles' shows the total number of intertitles in the film. This is followed by three other categories: 'expository intertitles', 'dialogue intertitles' and 'other intertitles'. Letters and telegrams, unless presented as inserts (texts that belong to the diegesis), have been categorized as dialogue intertitles, because they can be thought of as relayed dialogue. The last category, 'other intertitles', consists of title cards, credits and other such texts.

The numbers in Table 4.1 indicate that the use of intertitles in Finnish fiction films decreased towards the end of the 1920s, suggesting that Finnish filmmakers followed the international trend. Whereas *Olli's Years of Apprenticeship*, which premiered in 1920, has 113 intertitles per 500 shots, *The Supreme Victory* (*Korkein voitto*), which premiered in 1929, has only 75, which is almost one-third less. These numbers show that Finnish filmmakers did not strive for intertitle-less films, like some American and German filmmakers they admired. In the mid-1910s many in the USA believed that a film with no intertitles was the ideal.[7] Intertitles, it was argued, interrupted the narrative flow and indicated filmmakers' failure to convey meaning by visual means.[8] The ideal was most famously realized in Weimar Germany in the chamber films *Shattered* (*Scherben*, 1921) and *The*

Table 4.1   Intertitles in Finnish fiction films per 500 shots

Film	Year	Intertitles	Expository intertitles	Dialogue intertitles	Other
Olli's Year's of Apprenticeship	1920	113	47	64	2
The Kiljunen Boys at School	1921	166	45	89	22
Anna-Liisa	1922	138	25	109	5
The Logroller's Bride	1923	108	25	83	1
The Village Shoemakers	1923	116	16	95	5
When Father Has Toothache	1923	69	6	62	2
Evil Spells	1927	82	27	53	2
The Oaf	1927	87	3	79	5
The Young Pilot	1928	72	6	59	6
The Long Drivers	1928	97	5	88	4
Our Boys	1929	74	14	52	8
The Supreme Victory	1929	75	5	60	10

Olli's Year's of Apprenticeship (broadcast on Yle Teema, 12/12/2009), *The Kiljunen Boys at School* (DVD, archival working copy), *Anna-Liisa* (DVD, archival working copy), *The Logroller's Bride* (Yle TV1, 11/1/2012), *The Village Shoemakers* (Yle TV1, 30/4/2012), *When Father has Toothache* (DVD, archival working copy), *Evil Spells* (Yle Teema, 5/12/2010), *The Oaf* (DVD, archival working copy), *The Young Pilot* (Yle TV2, 20/8/2011), *The Log Drivers* (DVD, archival working copy), *Our Boys* (DVD, archival working copy), *The Supreme Victory* (Yle Teema, 6/1/2009)

Last Laugh (*Der letzte Mann*, 1924). Hollywood filmmakers of the 1920s found intertitles a precious tool for conveying plot information, clarifying spatiotemporal relations, intensifying intended emotional responses and presenting psychological states.[9] In addition, they realized that cleverly written intertitles contributed to the qualities of the film. The 'Loos-style' intertitles, named after Anita Loos who was recognized as their inventor, 'represent a narrating voice which goes beyond the neutral stating of facts'.[10] Such intertitles are rare in Finnish films and most of the surviving examples can be found in the films that were made in the late 1920s; that is, some ten years after their invention. One illuminating example is in *The Young Pilot* (*Nuori luotsi*, 1927). Here a village drunkard is introduced with the following expository intertitle: 'Pilot Akseli Rasi, whose love boat had once hit the rocks, was now drinking and wandering, so that he himself was sometimes in need of a pilot.' The narration makes a humorous comment on the state of the character, adding an extra level of meaning to the film. *When Father Has a Toothache* (*Kun isällä on hammassärky*) and *A Tech Student Film* (*Polyteekkarifilmi*), made in 1923 and 1924 respectively, contain intertitles written in the comic mode. I see them as predecessors of the 'Loos-style' titles in the Finnish context.

At the turn of the 1920s the number of dialogue intertitles in Finnish fiction films had exceeded the number of explanatory intertitles, and towards the end of the decade the dialogue intertitle became ever more dominant, as one can see from Table 4.1. The changing ratio of expository and dialogue intertitles corresponds to that of Hollywood films, but in Finland the change happened a few years later. Hollywood films probably accelerated the change, as the number of annually imported American films overtook that of all other films put together in 1923.[11] The result was that Hollywood films soon came to be seen as the universal standard against which other films seemed to be special cases for good or ill. Some Finnish fiction films differ from the Hollywood model in that they feature an exceptionally high number of expository intertitles in relation to dialogue intertitles. These include *Olli's Years of Apprenticeship*, *The Logroller's Bride* (*Koskenlaskijan morsian*, 1923) and *Evil Spells* (*Noidan kirot*, 1927). At the other end of the spectrum are *Anna-Liisa* (1922), *The Village Shoemakers* (*Nummisuutarit*, 1923), *The Oaf* (*Vaihdokas*, 1927), *The Young Pilot* and *The Long Drivers* (*Tukkijoella*, 1928).

Puro's *Olli's Years of Apprenticeship* contains 47 expository intertitles per 500 shots, and *Evil Spells* 27 expository intertitles per 500 shots (in both cases the actual number is 50). During the seven years that passed between the premieres, the expository intertitle became sparser, as indicated by the ratios. However, in both cases the number of both types of intertitles used is exceptionally high. Puro decreased the use of expository intertitles towards the end of the 1920s, but in these films he relied on them heavily. Things become more complicated when one examines Puro's *The Oaf*. This film contains as few as 3 expository intertitles per 500 shots (the actual number is 4), even though the film premiered the same year as *Evil Spells*. This discrepancy is something that the notion of personal style, taken at face value, does not explain.

Both *Olli's Years of Apprenticeship* and *Evil Spells* are adaptations of novels, but *The Oaf* is based on Selma Anttila's play. It was Puro's willingness to create a faithful adaptation of the play that led him to rely heavily on dialogue intertitles. Anni Swan's novel *Olli's Years of Apprenticeship* and Väinö Kataja's novel *Evil Spells* do not contain nearly as much dialogue as plays do. When it comes to these two films, Puro's willingness to be faithful to the original works was the cause for the use of a high number of expository intertitles. In that way he was able to give these films a literary feel. In short, Puro wanted the intertitles of his films to reflect the nature of the works on which the films were based.[12] As a similar pattern can be found in the films of Erkki Karu, rather than a trait of personal style, this should be thought of as a more general stylistic feature prevalent at that time in Finland. In Karu's films the highest number of expository intertitles can be found in *The Logroller's Bride*, an adaptation of a novel, whereas *The Village Shoemakers* and *The Young Pilot*, adaptations of plays, contain only a few explanatory intertitles.[13] Such faithfulness to the authors who had created the original works, which was also demanded by critics,[14] needs to be seen as one characteristic of the Finnish group style of the 1920s. The move towards a heavier reliance on dialogue intertitles was not as clear-cut in Finland as Thompson claims it was in Hollywood.

Following the examples set by their Swedish counterparts and the advice of local critics, at the turn of the 1920s Finnish filmmakers turned to canonized literary works.[15] However, whereas Swedish filmmakers adapted Scandinavian literature, Finns relied solely on Finnish fiction. The collective national spirit was high in the newly independent country and this led filmmakers to create films in which national themes and nationally loaded images were vivid. In his study of Karu's *The Village Shoemakers*, Ari Honka-Hallila argues that 'of the 146 dialogue intertitles in Karu's film 133 were taken from the play as such or as slightly altered, the silent film thus honouring [Aleksis] Kivi's language'.[16] In some cases the adapted lines of dialogue were slightly altered to suit the narration of the film better, in some cases for more ambivalent reasons. The convention of including some of the original dialogue in the film adaptations' intertitles for the audience to recognize and enjoy was presumably adapted from Swedish films of the golden era. As Eirik Frisvold Hanssen and Sofia Rossholm argue, the 'use of direct quotations implies a notion of "double authorship" underlining [the literary author's] authorial presence',[17] which is what Finnish filmmakers sought to achieve. In both countries artistic quality was synonymous with literary quality.[18]

Finnish fiction films of the 1920s are intertitle heavy. In the USA in the transitional period, the tendency was already to use expository intertitles only when necessary for the proper understanding of the film.[19] Finnish filmmakers did not shy away from expository intertitles in the early 1920s, no matter how superfluous they were. In *The Logroller's Bride*, for example, intertitles like 'Hanna couldn't sleep either' and 'Iisakki felt he loved his child more than ever before' do little to advance the story or to establish clear spatiotemporal relations. They convey information, but that same information is also conveyed via the mise-en-scène. Towards the end of the decade such use of intertitles decreased significantly, which is a further indication of the move towards the conventions that had been recently established in Hollywood at the time. In most Finnish fictional films expository intertitles serve as narration even when they are redundant, but some of them are confusing, if not misleading. In *The Logroller's Bride*, expository intertitles are used to introduce the main characters and the actors playing them. This is a classical convention that helps one to keep the characters in mind and raises expectations about their roles in the story. One of these intertitles says 'Grandma Anna—Kirsti Suonio', even though the character is not of the slightest relevance to the story. The only reason for introducing the supporting character is the actress playing the role. Suonio was a respected actress of the Finnish National Theatre during the years 1891–1930. Conventions such as introducing distinguished actors in supporting roles with intertitles were a far cry from the idea of silent cinema as a universal language, since they did little to serve cinema audiences who were unfamiliar with the names on the Finnish national stage. It is probable that such intertitles were edited out of copies shown to foreign audiences. These intertitles, like direct quotations from the canonized literature, indicate that filmmakers used written Finnish as an index of national identity.

THE PERSISTENCE OF LARGE SHOT SCALES

Most fiction films looked stylistically the same around 1908 no matter where they were made.[20] The actors were arranged in a row standing far away from the camera and, unless the film was shot outdoors, there was a canvas background drape with painted-on décor, while the camera remained static for the complete duration of the shot. The fragments of *Sylvi*, which were shot in 1911, suggest a reliance on this tradition of tableau staging. The scene where the titular character, a young woman who ends up poisoning her much older husband Axel for the love of another man, learns about her husband's bottle of strychnine is exemplary of the film's use of such a cinematographic style. The scene takes place in a room with the two characters (Fig. 4.1). As they are portrayed in a long shot,[21] their facial expressions and refined gestures are hard to see. The scene also lacked depth, which Bordwell identifies as one key characteristic of

Fig. 4.1   *Sylvi* (1913) was a midpoint between the flat and deep styles of tableau staging

the tableau films made in 1913 and later.[22] Yet painted backdrops, which belong to the older tradition of tableau staging, are not used either: the filmmakers relied on constructed coulisses. Even though there is much space around the characters, it goes largely unused, unlike in many tableau films that use constructed coulisses. As all the action takes place in the middle ground, the scene looks flat. Due to these characteristics, *Sylvi* is best understood as a transitional film, a midpoint between the flat and deep styles of tableau staging.

Most of the surviving shots in *Sylvi* are long shots. These shots, in which the actors are visible from head to toe with some space around them, were typical in the early 1910s, as most European and Russian cinematographers preferred distant front lines[23] and placed their cameras so that even the actors closest to the camera were shown in their entirety. *Sylvi* belongs to this tradition, as even the smallest shot scale in it is the full shot in which characters are seen from head to toe.[24] Due to the reliance on large shot scales, many narratively significant details, such as the bottle of strychnine that Sylvi discovers, are difficult to see. This diminishes their dramatic impact. The courtroom scene in which Sylvi is sentenced for killing her husband makes good use of the full shot, as it does a better job than the long shot in depicting head movements and facial expressions. Aili Rosvall, the actress playing the protagonist, stands still in the courtroom, struggling to look bravely ahead. Rosvall makes tiny movements, as if trying to lift her head from time to time. While the sentence is read, she gradually lets her head drop towards the ground. Had the sequence been shot in long shot, these expressions would not be this vivid and the scene would lose much of its emotional content. This shows that the director of cinematography, Frans Engström, understood how the drama could be supported through shot scales.

In the ball sequence Sylvi behaves flirtatiously in the company of a young man she loves. In the foreground an adjoining room can be seen where the drama takes place, whereas the background contains an opening that allows a view of a hall where various couples are dancing. According to Barry Salt, such use of deep staging is fairly common in European films of the time, but rather rare in American films.[25] Directors working in the USA moved the action to adjoining places with cuts and changes in camera position. *Sylvi*'s links to the theatre, such as the dynamic set, somewhat horizontal staging and the use of static long shots, were presumably intentional. As such, the film was characterized by what can be called cinematic theatricality. As Ben Brewster says, such film style was often favoured because it was easily assimilated into discussion using the familiar and prestigious terms of the legitimate theatre.[26] This is a further indication that *Sylvi* was representative of the European tradition of filmmaking.

While the tableau style was reminiscent of theatre, it offered some unique cinematographic possibilities. Bordwell sees the way of blocking and revealing as the aesthetic strength of the style.[27] On the basis of the surviving fragments, this technique was not used in *Sylvi*. In Bordwell's view, tableau filmmaking resembles theatre, but also significantly differs from it:

Theater staging, working within a wide and shallow rectangle, tends to be spacious and lateral, spreading the figures out to accommodate many sightlines. By contrast, thanks to the laws of optics, the film camera captures a pyramid chunk of space, with the tip of the pyramid at the lens and the playing space radiating out from there.... Since the camera views a unique configuration of bodies in space, you can not only pack the shot with many figures and objects. You can move each one as slightly as you like, blocking or exposing whatever area is necessary, all in the confidence that, in contrast to the live-theatre situation, every viewer can easily notice the changes.[28]

In *Sylvi*'s ball sequence the actors in the adjoining room move from time to time to block and reveal dancers in the background. These are undoubtedly instances of blocking and revealing, but they do not add anything to the drama of the film, as nothing narratively important happens in the background. The fragments of *Sylvi* do not contain flow of depth patterns that would highlight first one narratively significant action and then another. This is where *Sylvi* differs from the well-known films of Victor Sjöström, Yevgeni Bauer and other European masters. Here one needs to remember that the film was shot in 1911; that is, two years before the year of wonders, 1913, when many masterpieces were made[29] and *Sylvi* premiered. Cinematographically, it is closer to Le Film d'Art productions like *The Assassination of the Duke of Guise* (*L'Assasinat du Duc de Guise*, 1908) and early Danish art films like *The Abyss*.

Finnish films of the 1920s are cinematographically different from the fragments of *Sylvi*. These later films, and especially those made in the late 1920s, make systematic use of all shot scales except extreme close-ups. Finnish filmmakers had begun to rely on editing and were moving further away from the tableau style. In this they followed international trends. In 1919 in most films, no matter where they were made, scenes were broken down into several shots.[30] Editing-based Hollywood films had become a major force in the film world and they had begun to influence the development of Finnish cinema, both directly and indirectly. Table 4.2 shows the number of different shot scales in Finnish films of the 1920s per 500 shots.

In the 1920s the most common framing used by Finnish filmmakers was the full shot. Some film scholars, most notably Barry Salt, do not use the category of long shot as I have defined it (human body and some surroundings). Instead, they include both full shots and long shots in the category of the long shot. According to that definition, the category of long shot would comprise as much as 38% of all shots in Finnish fiction films of the 1920s. The shot scale data that Salt has collected in his database[31] indicates that the long shot, as defined by Salt, was the most common shot scale in Hollywood films as well. Nevertheless, only 23% of all shots in Hollywood films of the 1920s are long shots. This is a significant difference to the Finnish films of the 1920s, in which that number is 15% higher. Salt's data also indicates that the long medium shot was almost as common in Hollywood as the long shot. Long medium shots and medium shots came close after that. As Table 4.2 indicates, this was not the case in Finland, where filmmakers found it a great deal more important than those working in Hollywood to portray the whole body of an actor in the frame. Here one needs to remember that many Finnish film directors of the decade were professionals in the theatre and interested in

Table 4.2   Shot scales in Finnish fictional films per 500 shots

Film	Year	ELS	LS	FS	LMS	MS	MCU	CU	ECU
Olli's Years of Apprenticeship	1920	35	89	102	97	33	23	2	0
Anna-Liisa	1922	41	58	166	59	32	6	1	0
The Logroller's Bride	1923	68	75	83	74	45	40	2	0
The Village Shoemakers	1923	125	47	62	47	55	36	8	1
When Father Has Toothache	1923	3	9	198	85	88	35	9	3
Evil Spells	1927	41	51	66	78	77	62	42	1
The Oaf	1927	20	49	87	74	81	70	31	0
The Young Pilot	1928	94	62	85	42	83	23	34	1
The Long Drivers	1928	32	71	65	62	68	62	42	1
Our Boys	1929	122	81	41	30	33	39	80	1
The Supreme Victory	1929	56	60	80	75	34	44	52	14

ELS extreme long shot (human body small in the frame), *LS* long shot (human body and surroundings), *FS* full shot (whole human body), *LMS* long medium shot (human body from the knees up), *MS* medium shot (human body from the waist up), *MCU* medium close-up (human body from the chest up), *CU* close-up (head and shoulders), *ECU* extreme close-up (a detail of a human body or a tiny object)

Olli's Year's of Apprenticeship (broadcast on YLE Teema, 12/12/2009), *Anna-Liisa* (DVD, archival working copy), *The Logroller's Bride* (YLE TV1, 11/1/2012), *The Village Shoemakers* (YLE TV1, 30/4/2012), *When Father has Toothache* (DVD, archival working copy), *Evil Spells* (YLE Teema, 5/12/2010), *The Oaf* (DVD, archival working copy), *The Young Pilot* (YLE TV2, 20/8/2011), *The Log Drivers* (DVD, archival working copy), *Our Boys* (DVD, archival working copy), *The Supreme Victory* (YLE Teema, 6/1/2009)

the amalgamation of the art forms. The heavy reliance on large shot scales suggests that filmmakers were still influenced by the tableau style, even if they had begun to embrace new conventions.

On the basis of the data Salt provides in his database, German filmmakers preferred long shots as well: 38% of all shots in German films of the 1920s are long shots, as defined by Salt. The database contains information on only five Swedish silent films. Four of these were made in the latter half of the 1910s, which makes direct comparison problematical. On the basis of this small sample, as many as 44% of all shots in Swedish films of the era were long shots in Salt's terms. Here is the crucial observation: whereas 22% of all shots in the German films, 21% of all shots in the Hollywood films and 31% of all shots in the Swedish films are long medium shots where actors are portrayed from the waist up, only 16% of all shots in the Finnish films belong to this category. This makes it clear that in its use of shot scales Finnish silent cinema differs fundamentally from the other three cinemas, and presumably from many other cinemas as well. This is apparent also in the use of the largest shot scales. As many as 14% of all shots in Finnish films under scrutiny here are extreme long shots, whereas in German films this number is only 4%, in Hollywood 5% and in Swedish cinema 2%. Extreme long shots and long shots, as defined by Salt, cover as much as 52% of all shots in the analysed Finnish fiction films of the 1920s. In more than every other shot, one sees actors portrayed from head to toe with space around them or landscapes. In Swedish cinema the same number is 46%, in German cinema it is 42% and in Hollywood cinema it is only 28%, on the basis of Salt's database. The heavy use of large shot scales needs to be seen as one major characteristic of the Finnish group style of the 1920s. Such shots are especially common in films that are set close to nature, as they contain numerous landscape shots (Fig. 4.2). The figures I have presented indicate that Finnish filmmakers often positioned the spectator as if he/she were a member of the audience in a theatre. Both actors and their surroundings were visible most of the time. 'The classical cinema, on the other hand, assumes that the narration places a spectator within or on the edge of the narrative space',[32] Thompson argues.

All this indicates that the tableau tradition of filmmaking, which had been appreciated for its theatricality, and the admired Swedish cinema still influenced the ways in which Finnish filmmakers framed actors. On the basis of the figures Salt provides in his database, as many as 30% of all shots in Hollywood films of the 1920s are medium close-ups, close-ups

Fig. 4.2   Large shot scales that depict characters in Finnish nature are common in *Anna-Liisa* (1922)

and extreme close-ups. In German films this figure is 22% and in Finnish cinema it is as low as 18%. Significantly, 11% of all shots in Swedish films of the golden era, on the basis of Salt's database, belong to these three categories. This further supports the argument that Finnish filmmakers were still greatly influenced by these films. When one focuses on Finnish films made in the years 1927–1929, things look very different. The proportion of medium close-ups, close-ups and extreme close-ups in these films constitutes as much as 24% of all shots, whereas the same balance of shots was only 8% in films that were made in 1923 or earlier. This indicates that Finnish cinema became more editing based as the decade wore on and that filmmakers found small shot scales ever more useful. This also means that Finnish films of the 1920s, and especially those made late in the decade, are cinematographically closer to the classical style of filmmaking than the tableau style.

This move towards classical cinematography is most evident in the use of close-ups. European filmmakers of the 1910s tended to use the cut-in as a last resource.[33] Finnish films of the early 1920s are stylistically close to this tradition of filmmaking, as close-ups were used sparsely. It was not just that the number of close-ups increased in the latter half of the 1920s, the ways in which they were employed changed as well. Teuvo Puro, the director of *Sylvi*, was still reluctant to use close-ups when he directed *Olli's Years of Apprenticeship*. Yet as time passed, the cinematographic style of his films underwent a significant change. In the climax of Puro's later film, *Evil Spells*, the protagonist, Simo Utuniemi, is chasing a ruthless criminal, who is known as Chunky Sakari, in deep winter in Lapland. Both characters move on skis in heavy snow, but whereas Simo is actually skiing, Sakari, who tries to escape Simo, uses a reindeer to pull him. Here Puro employs numerous close-ups of Simo's skis (Fig. 4.3) to emphasize his speed, strength and relentlessness. Unlike in tableau films and films stylistically close to them, close-ups are not used as a last resource. Puro had found the device a good means of both creating tension and representing the nature of Simo's character.

In the 1920s, Finnish cinematography developed in the direction of clarity and expressivity, which reflects the filmmakers' knowledge of the techniques of the classical style. The notion of 'expressivity' that I use here is borrowed from Kristin Thompson, who employs it to mean 'those functions of cinematic devices that go beyond presenting basic narrative information and add some quality to the scene that would not be strictly necessary to our comprehension of it'.[34] This is precisely how the

Fig. 4.3   *Evil Spells* (1927) relies on close-ups that emphasize character traits

close-ups function in the chase sequence in *Evil Spells*. In the late 1920s the expressive use of the close-up was not just one stylistic option among others, but the norm.

MATTERS OF DISSECTION AND CONTINUITY

Tableau filmmakers emphasized mise-en-scène over editing. The fragments of *Sylvi* do not feature any small shot scales. Close-ups were used only sporadically even in foreign films that were distributed in Finland in 1911 when *Sylvi* was in production, mainly in those made in the USA. As Kristin Thompson says, the 'reluctance to put several shots into a single film suggests a recognition of the potentially disruptive qualities of the cut'.[35] Unless filmmakers mastered the basics of continuity editing, spectators had a hard time understanding the spatiotemporal relations depicted. Teuvo Puro, Frans Engström and Teppo Raikas all had little experience of filmmaking when *Sylvi* was made. The filmmakers, two of whom were actors from the national stage, deliberately relied on devices they found theatrical and therefore fitting for their art film. Noël Carroll maintains that variable framing gives filmmakers a level of control over their audience's attention that has no parallel in theatre.[36] On the contrary, the waist-level camera height and long takes on which Engström relied create what Ben Brewster has aptly called 'a view from the stalls'.[37] Cuts to closer views are a form of pointing and they form the basis of the analytical editing on which filmmakers of the classical style rely. 'By constantly reframing the scene', Carroll maintains, 'the filmmakers assure, by exploiting our natural perceptual tendencies, that we will be attending just where we need to be attending in order to follow what is going on'.[38] Competent tableau filmmakers achieved the same by relying on tactics of cinematic staging.

The development of editing in Finnish fictional films of the 1920s can be analysed by looking at the average shot lengths (ASL). The ASL is the length of a film divided by the number of shots in it. The figure indicates how often filmmakers cut and for how long the shots last, which tends to correlate with the tempo in which the story is told. Table 4.3 shows the ASLs of the Finnish silent fiction films accompanied by median shot lengths (MSL) and standard deviations in seconds (StDev).[39]

Table 4.3 Cutting rates in Finnish fiction films

Film	Year	ASL	MSL	StDev
Olli's Years of Apprenticeship	1920	7.6	6.6	4.9
Anna-Liisa	1922	9.4	7.5	6.8
Love Almighty	1922	10.3	8	7.5
The Logroller's Bride	1923	7.7	6.2	6.3
The Village Shoemakers	1923	7.0	5.6	6.1
The Bothnians	1925	6.4	5.6	4.6
Before the Face of the Sea	1926	5.5	4.6	3.9
On the Highway of Life	1927	6.8	4.9	6.4
Fugitives from Murmansk	1927	8.0	6.1	6.4
Evil Spells	1927	5.0	4.0	3.3
The Young Pilot	1928	9.3	8.0	6.2
The Long Drivers	1928	6.8	5.4	5.4
The Supreme Victory	1929	8.6	6.5	6.8
The Gypsy Charmer	1929	5.8	4.6	5.2
The Wide Road	1931	5.6	4.2	5.6

ASL average shot length, *MSL* median shot length, *StDev* standard deviations in seconds

Olli's Year's of Apprenticeship (broadcast on YLE Teema, 12/12/2009), *Anna-Liisa* (DVD, National Audiovisual Institute), *Love Almighty* (Yle Teema, 6/1/2013), *The Logroller's Bride* (35 mm), *The Village Shoemakers* (35 mm), *The Bothnians* (DVD, National Audiovisual Institute), *Before the Face of the Sea* (35 mm), *On the Highway of Life* (Yle Teema, 3/12/2011), *Fugitives from Murmansk* (35 mm), *Evil Spells* (YLE Teema, 5/12/2010), *The Young Pilot* (35 mm), *The Log Drivers* (35 mm), *The Supreme Victory* (YLE Teema, 6/1/2009), *The Gypsy Charmer* (DVD, National Audiovisual Institute), *The Wide Road* (DVD, National Audiovisual Institute)

The numbers indicate that the ASLs of Finnish silent fiction films became shorter towards the late 1920s. The mean Finnish ASL of the 1920–1925 period is 8.1 seconds and that of the 1926–1931 period is 6.8 seconds. The ASLs varied from 6.4 to 10.3 seconds in the first period and from 5.0 to 9.3 in the latter, which correlates with the slight increase in editing tempo. This development parallels that in other European countries. According to Salt, during the 1924–1929 period the mean ASL in Europe had decreased to 6.6 seconds, which was about 2.0 seconds slower on average than in Hollywood, where throughout the 1920s the most popular ASL was 5.0 seconds.[40] American filmmakers were fast cutters, which partly explains the popularity of their films. The editing tempo was less hurried in Finland in the late 1920s, but only slightly so when compared to other European nations. In this sense Finnish films were not especially slow.

The mean ASL of Finnish cinema would have dropped more notably if it were not for filmmakers who preferred long takes and large shot scales. This becomes obvious when one focuses on the films of Teuvo Puro and Erkki Karu. The ASL in *Olli's Years of Apprenticeship*, a film that Puro directed in 1920, is 7.6 seconds. This is a relatively long ASL compared to Hollywood films, but fairly typical for European films of the time.[41] Six years later Puro directed *Before the Face of the Sea* (*Meren kasvojen edessä*), in which he began to use numerous close-ups and shot reverse shots, resulting in an ASL of 5.5 seconds. The ASL of *Evil Spells*, which premiered in 1927, is only 5.0 seconds. In seven years the MSL of Puro's films decreased from 6.6 seconds to 4.0 seconds, while the StDev dropped from 4.9 seconds to 3.3 seconds. These figures indicate that the editing of Puro's films became faster and more editing based as the decade wore on. The ALSs of *Before the Face of the Sea* and *Evil Spells* are close to those of the Hollywood films of the 1920s, further suggesting that Puro moved away from the editing conventions of the tableau style, which he had embraced in *Sylvi*, and adapted to those of the classical style.

Two Erkki Karu films premiered in 1923, *The Logroller's Bride* and *The Village Shoemakers*. The ASL of the first is 7.7 seconds and that of the latter is 7.0 seconds. The editing tempo of these films is close to that of Puro's *Olli's Years of Apprenticeship*. Surprisingly, the ASL of *The Young Pilot*, which Karu directed in 1927, the year when Puro's *Evil Spells* premiered, is as high as 9.3 seconds. This ASL is 4.3 seconds higher than that of *Evil Spells*, which indicates how different the styles of these filmmakers had become. The MSL of Karu's films slowed from 6.2 and 5.6 seconds to 8.0 seconds while the

StDev remained about the same, just over 6.0 seconds. This means that Karu's shots grew noticeably longer while his editing remained somewhat uneven. Here one needs to keep in mind that the number of large shot scales, which in Karu's film style are remnants of tableau filmmaking, is exceptionally high in *The Young Pilot* and *Our Boys* (*Meidän poikamme*, 1929). Puro, on the contrary, preferred tight framings, which allowed for narratively important elements to be spotted quickly. Karu did not only hold on to larger shot scales, but actually slowed down the tempo of his films, which indicates that he was either unwilling or incapable of letting go of the remnants of the tableau style.

Close textual analysis of the surviving films reveals that Karu, too, relied on analytical editing, but his style of editing was different from classical editing. In relation to *The Village Shoemakers*, Ari Honka-Hallila argues: 'The editing style of Karu's film could be defined as *the insert style*, because the majority of the shot combinations are based on dividing a shot into two or more segments and another shot is placed in between ... or an intertitle.'[42] In such editing the establishing shot dominates the scene because the filmmaker keeps on cutting back and forth between the long shot and closer views. In the classical style sequences tend to open with an establishing shot from which filmmakers gradually move to closer shots, but rarely back. Another major difference to the classical editing style is that in the insert-style shots are taken from the front and reverse angles are employed as a last resource. To use the words of Gilberto Perez, such editing 'keeps the same frontal perspective in the closer view, the perspective of a spectator at the theatre who has the whole stage before his eyes and wields opera glasses for the significant detail'.[43] D.W. Griffith, whose films were appreciated as masterpieces in Finland in the early 1920s,[44] used this editing style to such an extent that Salt calls it '[t]he basic Griffith style of scene dissection'.[45] Salt adds that this style of editing 'continued to be practiced by many film-makers into the early nineteen-twenties, both in America, and particularly in Europe'. Later in the decade the combination of the insert style and long takes became known as the old country style. It had its supporters among Finnish filmmakers even in the late 1920s.

An illustrative example of the insert style can be found in Karu's *The Logroller's Bride*. In the sequence in question, Kero-Pieti, a travelling preacher, is talking to the members of the rural community he is visiting. The laterally staged sequence opens with an extreme long shot that portrays the living room of a house full of villagers who sit around Kero-Pieti waiting for Iisakki Nuottaniemi, the master of the house, to arrive (Fig. 4.4). The wall in the background with a door is clearly visible. Accompanied by his neighbour, Iisakki Nuottaniemi enters. They walk to the centre and sit down, where Nuottaniemi's daughter Hanna serves Kero-Pieti coffee. As she offers the cup of coffee, Karu cuts to a medium shot of Hanna and Kero-Pieti (Fig. 4.5). This shot, which is taken from roughly the same camera position as the extreme long shot that preceded it, is an insert. The framing is now tighter, but the perspective has not changed significantly and the wall is still visible in the background. The spatiotemporal relation of this shot to the previous one is easy to understand, because the background does not change and the action continues somewhat seamlessly. From this medium shot Karu cuts to a dialogue intertitle: 'My young daughter, does God live in your heart?' What then follows is the same medium shot that was already shown to the audience, simply spliced in two by the intertitle. Then another dialogue intertitle follows, from which Karu cuts back to the medium shot. When Kero-Pieti has had his say, Karu cuts back to the extreme long shot that opened the sequence, as if returning to the status quo (Fig. 4.6).

Fig. 4.4   A scene in *The Logroller's Bride* (1923) opens with an extreme long shot

Fig. 4.5 From the extreme long shot the film cuts to a medium shot without changing the camera's perspective

Fig. 4.6 At the end of the scene the film cuts back to the opening view, as if returning to the status quo

Clearly, as Honka-Hallila claims, 'Karu tends to cut medium close-ups and medium shots to function as kinds of inserts within larger shots.'[46] In the sequence in question the intertitles are inserts within the long medium shot, which is an insert within the extreme long shot. In short, the sequence contains inserts within an insert. Considering that such scenes can be found in all films Karu made in the 1920s, Honka-Hallila's argument can be taken further: Karu's editing style as a whole can be described as the insert style.[47] In all the sequences in question, 'the alterations in the camera's point of view and image size are motivated by making characters visible, by subjectivity ... and by enouncing a speaker'.[48] Closer views and slightly different camera positions are used as a form of pointing that clarifies the action. In essence, the insert style of editing is a kind of analytical editing, but differs from the classical analytical editing.

The insert style of editing is more restrictive than the classical style of editing, because the former prevents filmmakers from controlling cinematic space with point-of-view shots and reverse angles, as all shots need to be taken from about the same perspective. The style also complicates the controlling of time, as it prevents filmmakers from shortening screen time with elliptical editing. In the insert style ellipses would create very noticeable jump cuts. The sequences that have been edited in this style take place in real time. The style had its advantages too. It helped inexperienced filmmakers to achieve a continuous flow of space and time that was easy for the audience to follow. When filmmakers relied on this editing style they never broke the 180-degree rule. Furthermore, it added to the cinematic theatricality of their films, which was seen as positive. A further reason for the style's pre-eminence was practical. On the basis of surviving films and photographs, it appears that film sets often had only one wall, which was the convention in many European countries. 'The camera cannot move to the other side' when sets exist only behind the actors 'since there would then be no set visible',[49] Kristin Thompson points out in relation to German films. So even if filmmakers wanted to use reverse angles, they could not do so. Therefore '[t]he cameraman simply moved the camera closer to the action, generally from roughly the same vantage-point'.[50] This was a way to keep actors and sets visible without ruining the illusion of continuous space.

When determined filmmakers like Puro, who lacked both the means and the experience of their contemporaries in major filmmaking nations, tried their hand at the classical style of editing, they achieved what Thompson calls 'a loose version of continuity editing'.[51] According to Salt, 'when it came to the matter of eye-line matching in reverse-angle cutting between shots, the chances were that the average European director would get this "wrong" nearly half of the time, since he was not aware of the existence of any convention in the matter'.[52] Although it is no match in clarity to the Hollywood standard of editing, loose continuity editing is not confusing if the sequence in question is simple. *Evil Spells* features an ambitious sequence in which three logrollers approach a lone woman, Elsa, with the intention of raping her. It opens with a series of shots of Elsa rowing near the shore. As she rows into an extreme long shot, which functions as an establishing shot, there is an empty-looking boat in the far background. In the subsequent shot a logroller wakes up in the boat and looks approximately towards the camera. This shot is then followed by a shot of Elsa looking, presumably, back at him, but the eye-lines do not match. Puro continues to use parallel editing in order to show two other logrollers, first waking up and then trying with their friend to catch Elsa, who does her best to escape. As her boat gets stuck on the shore, she tries to release it. Here Puro repeatedly breaks the 180-degree rule (Figs. 4.7 and 4.8). One has to agree with Salt, who argues that 'there is no way that any profound meaning can be read into failures of eye-line matching, as some have tried

Fig. 4.7 *Evil Spells* (1927) follows the premises of the classical style of editing, but violates the 180-degree rule

Fig. 4.8   Even though the film violates the 180-degree rule, the editing patterns enhance the dramatic tension

to do in recent years'.[53] The same goes for breaking the 180-degree rule. Even so, Puro manages to enhance the tension with these means and the sequence is not difficult to follow. The example indicates that in the late 1920s there were Finnish filmmakers who understood how the classical style of editing worked and wanted to let go of the old country style.

CREATING BELIEVABLE DIEGETIC WORLDS

'The diegetic world of the film', Charlie Keil argues, 'should insist on its self-sufficiency, reinforcing believability by dispelling all marks of fictionality and pulling the viewer along in the process'.[54] This is the fundamental principle in the classical style. In tableau films, at least when seen from a contemporary perspective, the décor is often self-evidently artificial and does not recall a lived space that belongs to a larger world. In the fragments of *Sylvi*, to use the words of Gilberto Perez, 'space recalls the stage not only in its integrity but in its quality of enclosure, in our sense of a demarcated area ... within which each scene is contained'.[55] The box-style sets in which the back wall is perpendicular or only at a slight angle serve to strengthen this impression. For example, the home of Axel and Sylvi is a closed space. Their door opens to a corridor where nothing in particular can be seen and the only window in the apartment is covered with curtains that block all outside light. The walls of the living room are simple coulisses that are made to look more realistic with details like curtains, a door and a painting. In front of the back wall there are two laterally placed tables and some chairs, which the actors use. As the film was shot on the rooftop of an apartment building,[56] the sets are evenly lit by bright sunlight without a realistic motivation. As the examples pinpoint, the diegetic world is marked by fictionality.

As the sets in *Sylvi* are simple theatre coulisses, neither the door nor the window is real and as such they cannot give a proper view outside, because there is no outside. And yet, these, like the telephone that the titular character uses, are the elements of the mise-en-scène that suggest the apartment is a part of a bigger world. As V.F. Perkins has put it, 'the world is everything (in space and in time) surrounding and embedding our immediate perceptions. There is always out-of-sight just as there is always an off-screen'.[57] An important function of the elements mentioned is to reinforce this illusion, to make the diegetic world more believable. When compared to films made in the classical style, these elements do that only marginally. It is hard to get the impression that 'we are looking at the characters, and their "life" permits us, at least potentially, to go and "occupy" any space whatever',[58] which Jacques Aumont sees as the distinctive feature of the classical style. Almost the contrary is true, because everything in *Sylvi* happens in only a few locations, as if they were sufficient to contain the whole fiction.

Such marks of fictionality are much fewer in number in films made in the classical style, where all elements of the mise-en-scène are given a stronger realistic motivation. Hollywood filmmakers embraced verisimilitude to the extent that by the late 1910s their sets had become so complex that architects were needed to design them.[59] In these films doors open onto realistically motivated spaces and light streams through windows or gleams from a fireplace, unlike in many European films made in the tableau style. As astonishing as such American sets were, Finnish critics of the early 1920s often found them superficial.[60] Instead of valuing grandeur and realistic motivation as such, they sought ethnographic believability; that is, realistic depiction of national cultures and local customs, which in Hollywood was ultimately not that important.[61] In other words, whether sunlight shone in from a window was ultimately less important in Finland than whether or not the window was constructed of the right kind of timber.[62] In the representation of national cultures and local customs, Finnish critics found Swedish films exemplary. The peasant films in particular were valued for their ethnography, to the extent that critics argued that Finnish filmmakers needed to follow the Swedish example in the creation of a truly national cinema.[63] The model for the Finnish national cinema was international.

The influence of Swedish peasant films on the style of Finnish films of the 1920s can be seen in the mise-en-scène, especially in the meticulous care with which ethnographic details like customs, costumes and items are dealt with in many films. In films set in the past, the style of sets and costumes seems to be based, as in heritage cinema, on study of the interior design and couture of the era, much like in Swedish films. Antti Alanen argues that it was Mauritz Stiller's *The Song of the Scarlet Flower* (*Sången om den eldröda blomman*, 1919), a critical and commercial success in Finland, which 'taught Finns that well-known national themes could be turned into electrifying popular cinema'.[64] According to Alanen, the film 'gave Finnish cinema some basic situations for decades to come: the village dance by the river, the couple dreaming in the midsummer night, love-making in the haystack, and the climatic shooting of the rapids'.[65] It is true that a nationally charged mise-en-scène is largely missing from *Sylvi* while it is exploited in films of the 1920s. However, many of the elements to which Alanen refers were already present in Johannes Linnankoski's novel of the same name, which Stiller adapted for the screen. Furthermore, adaptations of canonized Finnish literature were made and planned in even greater numbers during the 1910s. I argue that *The Song of the Scarlet Flower* and other Swedish masterpieces were influential, but that, rather than providing the sole impetus, they strengthened the faith of Finnish production companies in the exploitation of Finnish customs, costumes and items, and probably showed how they could be narratively motivated.

One of the first Finnish films made following the Swedish model was *Anna-Liisa*, which Teuvo Puro directed in 1922. Carl Fager, who also worked on *Sylvi*, created the sets for this nineteenth-century period piece. In the opening sequence, Anna-Liisa is working in a room in her parents' house. She stands in the foreground next to a warping reel in the midst of a box-style set. There is a brightly lit window on the left, but no sunlight comes through it, even though the weather is clearly sunny. There is a realistic motivation for this. Considering that Anna-Liisa stands in bright light that falls partly from the foreground, there must be a window

in front of her in the off-screen space (Fig. 4.9). Because the sun shines
in from this window it cannot, of course, shine in from the window on
the left as well. However, there are bright lamps on the ceiling too, since
the character does not cast a long shadow. These lights are not realistically motivated. Altogether the lighting plot creates a slight chiaroscuro
effect: the background wall where a full cupboard can be seen is only
dimly lit. This lighting plot is reminiscent of canonized Finnish paintings
of the nineteenth century that depict rural homes, a good example of
which is Adolf von Becker's *Sunday Morning in an Ostrobothnian House*
(*Sunnuntaiaamu pohjalaistuvassa*). In this there is a brightly lit window
on the wall on the right, but, looking at shadows and lit areas, the main
light source must be another window in the off-screen space somewhere
on the right in the foreground. It seems that the filmmakers attempted to
achieve a similar effect. The table in the background to the left of Anna-
Liisa is staged in a lengthwise direction, unlike the table in the apartment
in *Sylvi*, and together with the chiaroscuro it heightens the depth of the
room. Soon after Johannes comes to meet Anna-Liisa, the room is shown
from a different angle, which breaks the illusion of the box-style set; the
camera shows the corner and the wall on the right, which have not been
visible in earlier shots. Fager gave *Anna-Liisa*'s décor a lived-in look and
made it seem part of a larger world. The mise-en-scène is closer to the

Fig. 4.9 *Anna-Liisa's* (1922) mise-en-scène is recognizably Finnish and conveys
a sense of a lived-in space

classical style than that of *Sylvi*, even if the lighting from above is more akin to theatre than the real world.

Anna-Liisa contains a sequence of logrolling that is not present in Minna Canth's play *Anna Liisa* and has little narrative import, as it merely provides a backdrop for a flashback. Mikko is introduced standing on logs close to the shore with a pike pole in his hands. His outfit consists of dark-coloured trousers, a white shirt, a black waistcoat and a hat with a brim. This is a traditional costume that Finns of the day associated with lumberjacks. Lumberjacks in *The Logrollers (Tukinuittajat)*, which Pekka Halonen painted in 1925, wear similar clothes. Logrolling, Mikko's costume and the pike pole are examples of Finnish customs, costumes and items that the film *Anna-Liisa* exploits. At the time *The Song of the Scarlet Flower* was already famous for its logrolling sequences and probably inspired Puro to make these additions. However, this does not mean that *The Song of the Scarlet Flower* provided the sole impetus for the cinematic exploitation of Finnish customs, costumes and items, because such elements are already present in Canth's play; good examples are Anna-Liisa's wrapping reel and her long, thick plait. These, unlike logrolling, were almost certainly seen in most stage productions and in the first film adaptation of the play, which was shot in 1911 but never completed.⁶⁶ Yet Alanen is not entirely wrong. Sequences of logrolling are not known to have precedents in earlier Finnish fiction films. The impetus to turn logrolling into electrifying popular cinema probably derived from *The Song of the Scarlet Flower*, which Stiller had adapted from a Finnish novel. This is an intriguing example of transnational influences moving from Finland to Sweden and then back in a different form. After *Anna-Liisa*, logrolling sequences were seen in *The Logroller's Bride*, *Evil Spells* and *The Long Drivers*.

The Logroller's Bride, which Erkki Karu directed in 1923, is stylistically different from *Anna-Liisa* in that most of its interiors are flat, demarcated spaces. The sequence where Hanna Nuottaniemi is working in a kitchen with grandma Anna when Hanna's father and her suitor have come to meet them is illustrative of this. Here, as in *Anna-Liisa*, the audience is able to recognize Finnish customs, costumes and items, but, in contrast, Fager's staging is horizontal. The only wall that is visible is the one at the back of the room, with a window in front of which the characters are laterally staged (Fig. 4.10). The flatness of this décor does little to echo the style of Finnish interior paintings; in fact, it is more reminiscent of the portable sets utilized by travelling theatre companies, the heavy fireplace excluded. The three carpets that lead to the window at the back create whatever sense of depth there is in the sequence. As prominent as the window is, it does

Fig. 4.10 In *The Logroller's Bride* (1923), the staging is horizontal and lacks depth, as a result of which it does not echo the style of Finnish interior paintings

not offer a view of the outside. A year earlier when *Anna-Liisa* was made, Fager had created a window behind which tree leaves can be seen. Here, the light falls from several sources from high behind the camera without creating any dark areas. As the characters stand close to the wall, their shadows can hardly be seen, which enhances the flatness of this sequence. The lighting keeps everything visible, but it is not given a realistic motivation. As such, it is hard to believe that the diegetic world continues behind the framing. In both films the world is recognizably Finnish, but in *The Logroller's Bride* the mise-en-scène does far less than that in *Anna-Liisa* to convey a sense of a lived-in space that belongs to a larger world. In the former, the décor is stylistically more reminiscent of the tableau style, where everything happens as if on a stage, than of the classical style. Yet as different as the films are stylistically, they both represent cinematic theatricality and in so doing give an indication of just how broad the concept is. Another lesson to be learned from this comparison is that there was a great deal of variety in Finnish set design in the early 1920s, even in the productions of Suomi-Filmi where Fager was responsible for the sets.

Towards the late 1920s Finnish film sets became deeper and more elaborate. This tendency peaked in Carl von Haartman's *The Supreme Victory*, the detailed décor of which is heavily influenced by Erich von

Stroheim's naturalism.[67] For the film Fager created a replica in Suomi-Filmi's studio of Hotel Kämp's luxurious restaurant. The sequence where the moving camera—which is reminiscent of the dolly shots along the hotel corridors in F.W. Murnau's *The Last Laugh*—finds the protagonist Baron Henrik von Hagen enjoying a drink is illustrative of von Haartman's approach. The moving camera intensifies the size and depth of the mise-en-scène and in so doing reminds the audience that the diegetic world is larger than anyone can see. Von Haartman's approach to cinematic staging is the opposite of the tableau style, where everything happens as if on a stage. In this sequence the mise-en-scène also differs from those already analysed in that it does not contain customs, costumes and items that are instantly recognizable as Finnish. On the contrary, the appearance of the restaurant and its customers is better described as European. Before the moving camera finds the Baron, it turns to 'greet' a gentleman who is enjoying a coffee with a cigar while reading *La Vie Parisienne*, which was a French erotic magazine of the time. This and other cosmopolitan elements in *The Supreme Victory* are contrasted with recognizably Finnish nature and nationally significant locations like Suomenlinna, the maritime fortress located off the coast of Helsinki. By combining such disparate elements in the mise-en-scène of his film, von Haartman promotes the argument that Finland is part of Europe and that Helsinki is as cosmopolitan as London or Berlin.

NOTES

1. Bordwell 1997: 4.
2. Salmi 2002: 75–76.
3. Thompson 2002: 188.
4. Thompson 2002: 185.
5. Salmi 2002: 58.
6. Salmi 2002: 96 & 108.
7. Thompson 2002: 186.
8. Bowser 1994: 140.
9. Brouwers 2010: 105.
10. Thompson 2002: 186.
11. Seppälä 2012: 41.
12. Teuvo Puro's *Anna-Liisa* is an exception to the rule, however. *Anna-Liisa* is based on a play written by Minna Canth, but it contains as many as 25 explanatory intertitles per 500 shots, many more than *The Oaf*. Two things explain the disparity. *Anna-Liisa*, first of all, is five years older than *The Oaf*. It was made at a time when expository intertitles were common in all Finnish films. The other factor is that *Anna-Liisa* contains 109 dialogue

intertitles per 500 shots. The number is higher than in any other Finnish film of the era. In other words, *Anna-Liisa*, being a Puro film based on a play, is dialogue heavy, just like *The Oaf.*

13. When it comes to Erkki Karu's films, the exception is *Our Boys*, which is based on an original screenplay. It contains a high number of expository intertitles that were needed to motivate the use of newsreel footage.

14. Seppälä 2012: 155.

15. Seppälä 2012: 150–159.

16. Honka-Hallila, 1995: 182.

17. Frisvold Hanssen and Rossholm 2012: 150.

18. Furhammar 2010: 87; Pantti 2000: 34–35.

19. Keil 2001: 61.

20. Bordwell 1997: 1.

21. Considering the amount of empty space around the characters, the shot can even be seen as an extreme long shot.

22. Bordwell 1997: 1.

23. Bordwell 1997: 184.

24. In one of the long shots in *Sylvi* actors move towards the camera until they are momentarily portrayed from their chests up.

25. Salt 2006: 248.

26. Brewster 2006: 49.

27. Bordwell 2005: 62–64.

28. Bordwell 2005: 60.

29. Bordwell 1997: 191.

30. Bordwell 1997: 1.

31. Barry Salt's database.

32. Thompson 2002: 158.

33. Bordwell 2005: 67.

34. Thompson 2004: 254.

35. Thompson 2002: 162.

36. Carroll, 2008: 125.

37. Brewster 2006: 48.

38. Carroll, 2008: 124.

39. Whereas the ASL stands for the mean shot length of the film, the MSL is that length for which half the shots in the film have longer lengths and the other half have shorter lengths. The median gives us the likely shot length, as it does not let deviant cases distort the data. StDev measures the extent of the spread of the data about the mean value. It can be used to tell whether the editing is even or not. The higher the number is, the more uneven the editing is, and vice versa.

40. Salt 1992: 174.

41. Salt 1992: 172–174.

42. Honka-Hallila, 1995: 156.

43. Perez 2000: 62.
44. Seppälä 2012: 110.
45. Salt 1992: 171.
46. Honka-Hallila, 1995: 156.
47. This is not to say that all sequences in Erkki Karu's films are edited in the same way, merely that this is the style of editing that he preferred.
48. Honka-Hallila, 1995: 156.
49. Thompson 2005: 74.
50. Thompson 2005: 74.
51. Thompson 2005: 72.
52. Salt 1992: 170.
53. Salt 1992, 171.
54. Keil 2001: 144.
55. Perez 2000, 115.
56. Salmi 2002: 119.
57. Perkins 2005: 22.
58. Aumont 2006: 350.
59. Staiger 2002: 147–148.
60. Seppälä 2012: 141.
61. Vasey 1997: 3.
62. Oski Talvio: "Sananen tanskalaisesta filmistä jolla on aiheena meidän vapaustaistelumme," *Filmiaitta*, 2/1922, 35.
63. Seppälä 2012: 140–141 & 154.
64. Alanen 1999: 78.
65. Alanen 1999: 78.
66. Salmi 2002: 113.
67. Seppälä 2012: 350–351.

The Studio Era: 1930–1960

CHAPTER 5

War and Peace: Finland Among Contending Nations

Anneli Lehtisalo

Towards the end of the 1930s, the Depression was over and the film business boomed, as people again had the money to go to the cinema. The number of cinemas increased as well as the number of film premieres. Hollywood films dominated the screens, but cinemas offered a wide variety of films from different countries such as Germany, the UK, France, Sweden—and Finland. Two major companies in Finland, Suomi-Filmi and Suomen Filmiteollisuus, established a studio-like production system with a growing number of film professionals. From 1936 onwards both studios started to produce several films in parallel, which quickly increased the number of domestic premieres per year. In addition, minor film companies such as Jäger-Filmi Oy (1938–1969) and Eloseppo Oy (1938–1942) and the filmmaker Teuvo Tulio (1911–2001) actively made films, although less regularly. All in all, these emerging Finnish film companies laid a foundation for the studio era of Finnish cinema, which lasted until the early 1960s, when the studio-based production system gave way to a new production system steered by state film policy.

The cultural atmosphere between the world wars has been characterized as the culture of the victors of the civil war, that of white Finland, which

A. Lehtisalo (✉)
e-mail: anneli.lehtisalo@kotiportti.fi

© The Editor(s) (if applicable) and The Author(s) 2016
H. Bacon (ed.), *Finnish Cinema*, Palgrave European Film
and Media Studies, DOI 10.1057/978-1-137-57651-4_5

rested on conservative values such as patriotism, bourgeois family values and religiousness. While the official culture was informed by conservatism, there were other tendencies as well. Cultural life in Finland was still sharply divided along the lines of the civil war: there were both right-wing and left-wing cultural institutions, such as theatres, newspapers and sports associations. Some artists adopted new modernist influences from Europe, thus invigorating fine arts, poetry and design. Swedish-speaking authors were particularly interested in modernist forms and ways of expression. In addition, mass-mediated popular culture began to gain ground in Finland. Along with cinema, gramophones and records of light *Schlager* music were in high demand. People also entertained themselves with Anglo-American popular literature, such as novels by Zane Grey or British detective stories.

The gradually stabilizing political situation and democratic institutions formed the basis for this more diversified cultural atmosphere. At the beginning of the decade, anti-democratic and fascist movements threatened the stability of Finnish society. Extreme-right pressure even led to the criminalization of Communist activities, lasting until the end of the Second World War. However, the popularity of extreme political movements decreased, and in 1937 the Social Democrats together with the Agrarian League formed a government, thus further strengthening the moderate political tendencies in Finland.

Towards the end of the 1930s, tensions in international politics grew. This made Finland's situation between East and West very vulnerable. The country did not succeed in finding the international allies to guarantee its national security. When the Soviet Union started to exert pressure on Finland in order to secure its own international interests, Finnish leaders refused to negotiate with it, and Finland was left isolated. In November 1939 the attack by the Soviet Union led to the so-called Winter War, which lasted approximately 100 days. Finland lost the war, but succeeded in avoiding an occupation. The reparations of peace were severe, though, and Finland had to cede large areas of the country in Karelia and the north to the Soviet Union and to rent it the Hanko peninsula, which would be used as a Soviet naval base. Discontent with the situation together with the continuing instability in northern Europe led Finland into an alliance with Germany, the old ally of White Finland during the civil war. When Operation Barbarossa began in the summer of 1941, Finland invaded the Soviet Union together with Germany and Romania. The so-called Continuation War began, and Finland fought along with Germany until the autumn of 1944, when it made a separate truce with the Soviet Union.

During the Second World War the Finnish film industry thrived despite material shortages and lack of staff. Because many other forms of entertainment could be difficult to arrange, for example dancing was forbidden, cinema increased in popularity. The number of cinemas as well as audience numbers grew throughout each of the war years. The war impeded the import of foreign films, and the screening of Soviet and British films was forbidden. There were also pressures to boycott American films, but the boycott was not comprehensive across the nation, as the film industry was divided into pro-American and pro-German factions. As a result there were fewer foreign films in circulation, and domestic films were even more popular than before the war. Finnish historical romances and romantic comedies attracted audiences of unparalleled size. Cinema was seen not only as good relaxation in the midst of the horrors of the war, but as important positive propaganda—a way to keep up the spirits of the nation.

After its defeat in the war Finland had to alter its domestic and foreign policies. Patriotic right-wing organizations were banned, and previously forbidden, underground Communist organizations could participate openly in social activities. In foreign policy Finland had to establish working relations with its former enemy, the Soviet Union. Finland did not transform into a people's democracy unlike many other countries neighbouring the Soviet Union, but throughout the Cold War it had to maintain a balanced relationship between East and West. The so called Paasikivi–Kekkonen line—a policy named after two influential presidents—meant that Finland had friendly relations with the Soviet Union and it had to adhere to a certain realpolitik; that is, always taking into account the interests of the Soviet Union. Accordingly, Finland signed the Treaty of Friendship, Cooperation and Mutual Assistance with the Soviet Union. This recognized Finland's neutrality, but it was also the basis for close economic and cultural cooperation. In fact, the treaty, together with the required reparations Finland was forced to pay to the Soviet Union in the form of industrial goods such as ships and other metal industry products, enhanced the industrialization of Finnish society. Generally, however, reconstructing and industrializing Finland was oriented towards the West. The Helsinki Olympic Games in the summer of 1952 were a showcase for Finland, as they demonstrated that it was a Western democracy open to other countries. Its status as a Western nation was significantly advanced in 1955 when Finland joined both the United Nations and the Nordic Council.

The Cold War affected Finnish cultural life as well, although to a lesser extent than it did politics. Officially there were active cultural relations with the Soviet Union as well as with other Eastern bloc countries. People also participated in various friendship associations, which enhanced cultural diplomacy in line with the Friendship Treaty. Despite this, popular culture in particular was influenced by Anglo-American entertainment. Popular music, films, fashion—and gradually altering lifestyles—were increasingly imported and reflected Western trends.

This flow of products and influences formed a challenge for the domestic film industry. It had suffered from economic depression and price control after the war, and now it had to compete with foreign films, which seemed to appeal more to younger generations. Additionally, there were other forms of entertainment and recreation that lured people away from the cinema, such as dances, music or travelling. At the beginning of the 1950s, the major film studios chose different strategies to cope with the situation. Suomi-Filmi reduced its own production and concentrated on other forms of business, such as distribution and exhibition. In contrast, Suomen Filmiteollisuus, whose business was based more on production, intensified its production. The company's quickly made, folksy musical comedies soon provoked an outcry, as a new generation of film journalists and cultural intellectuals demanded that Finnish film culture should be more seriously and artistically oriented.

Nevertheless, this strategy worked during the first half of the decade. Suomen Filmiteollisuus even had new competitors. The old distribution and exhibition company Adams merged with the production company Fenno-Filmi, forming the third major film company in Finland, Fennada-Filmi Oy. There were also filmmakers active outside Suomi-Filmi, Suomen Filmiteollisuus and Fennada-Filmi: Teuvo Tulio for one continued his career and Veikko Itkonen (1919–1990) started his own studio. By the end of the decade it was obvious, however, that a crisis was at hand. An economic depression hampered business in Finland generally, overproduction could not sustain the studios and viewing habits were about to change, as the Finnish broadcasting company Yleisradio started regular television broadcasts in 1958. By the beginning of the 1960s, the state of Finnish cinema was a major national concern. As a result of discussions a state film prize was introduced, which launched an era of state-subsidized domestic cinema production and marked the end of the studio era.

CHAPTER 6

Conceptions of National Film Style During the Studio Era

Kimmo Laine

This chapter continues from where Chapter 4 on film style in the silent era ended. The coming of recorded sound roughly coincided both with the Great Recession of the late 1920s and the early 1930s and with the reshaping of the Finnish film production system in the early part of the 1930s. Remarkable changes took place at the time in filmmaking and aesthetics, in film import and distribution, as well as in exhibition practices, whether or not they were all directly caused by recorded sound. Thus, this chapter begins by mapping the consequences of the coming of sound, especially as they concern film style and notions of national cinema in a small language area.

After that, the notion of national style—and the variety of styles contained within it—is discussed from several different, partly overlapping angles, in terms of the house styles of the major production companies, the rhetoric concerning national cinema and a national film style, and different modes of film practice: classicism, theatricalism, pictorialism and avant-garde.

K. Laine (✉)
Film Studies, University of Oulu, Oulu, Finland
e-mail: kimmo.laine@oulu.fi

© The Editor(s) (if applicable) and The Author(s) 2016   87
H. Bacon (ed.), *Finnish Cinema*, Palgrave European Film
and Media Studies, DOI 10.1057/978-1-137-57651-4_6

FILM SOUND

The relative dominance of Suomi-Filmi in domestic film production ended in the early 1930s. Investments in a theatre chain—which later proved profitable—and unsuccessful plans to build an 18-storey 'skyscraper' cinema complex in the middle of Helsinki, as well as the ever more frequent conflicts between the managing director Erkki Karu and the board of the company, coincided with a general recession and the inevitable investments in sound technology, bringing the company near to bankruptcy by 1933.[1] Suomi-Filmi survived the crisis after replacing most of its management, including Karu, who immediately started a new company, Suomen Filmiteollisuus. In terms of feature film output the new company soon rivalled the old one, thus creating a fresh situation with two strong companies leading the field of feature film production instead of just one.

In Finland, the economic boom of the post–First World War era had already ended before the 1929 crash. Despite the fact that the recession was over sooner than in many other Western countries and that by 1934 the economy prospered again, the film trade was severely affected: not until 1937 did film attendance again reach the figures of 1928.[2] In other words, the recession had an indisputable effect on the film industry, especially since it fully coincided with the coming of sound technology.

Reactions towards recorded sound were belated and, at first, quite dubious. Trade journals did not take up the subject until 1928, and when they did the focus was on the alleged negative effect that sound might have: cinema would lose its internationality and exportability, and thereafter its profitability.[3] However, depending to a considerable extent on exported films, the film exhibition business soon had to adapt to the changes, and the first sound-on-disc screening of *The Singing Fool* (1928) took place in Helsinki in the autumn of 1929. By 1932—roughly at the same time as in Germany—the majority of cinemas in cities had converted to sound.

Film historians have disagreed on the profundity of the changes that recorded sound brought to film culture. Whether sound is considered a smooth adjustment of the practices of the 'already constituted system of the classical Hollywood style'[4] or a radical rupture, especially in terms of aesthetic experience,[5] the small nation perspective appears to support Alan Williams' notion that, however little sound recording in and of itself changed Hollywood, 'it nonetheless helped change the rest of the world cinema in a quite fundamental way'.[6] The fundamentality of this change was further confirmed by the fact that the period of the late 1920s and early 1930s witnessed a general expansion of sonic culture.[7] The Finnish Broadcasting Company started radio programming in 1926, and an unforeseen gramophone boom also took place in the late 1920s. Such phenomena provided sound film with remarkable intermedial backing and accustomed audiences to hearing recorded and technologically mediated sound.

In Finnish cinema, the changes brought about by recorded sound took place at various different levels, and they often involved a considerable amount of uncertainty about the future. First, at the level of exhibition, the problems encountered did not end with the laborious and costly process of replacing sound-on-disc projectors by sound-on-film ones. A more fundamental question concerned translation. As the bulk of the programme consisted of imported films, and as the majority of the audience had little knowledge of foreign languages, different solutions were tested. For economic reasons, multiple-language versions,[8] as well as dubbing films into Finnish, were out of the question for such a small language area—and besides, part of the audience spoke Swedish, not Finnish. Instead, early solutions tested in Finland included keeping the soundtrack untouched but summarizing the film and translating part of the dialogue in the programme leaflet; inserting silent film–type intertitles amidst the dialogue, with the obvious disadvantage of interrupting the soundtrack[9]; and adding scenes with Finnish actors into imported films (for example, James Cruze's *The Great Gabbo*, 1929).

The final resolution to the problem was subtitling, as in other Nordic countries and certain other small language areas. Subtitling in itself turned out to be anything but easy: after solving the basic technical problems—whether to print or superimpose the subtitles, or project them separately—two Finnish companies, Suomi-Filmi and Jäger-Filmi, litigated over the printing patent for over a decade. Finally, not the least of the problems was that reading subtitles demanded practice, and although literacy was very high, many people were not accustomed to reading at speed. In this sense, subtitling probably paved the way for the success of domestic sound films, which could be enjoyed without reading.[10]

Second, the well-known problems in recording sound concerned filmmakers in Finland as much as anywhere else. Noise from the cameras had to be reduced by blimps; problems in synchronizing image and sound had to be resolved; the first microphones were not very sensitive, which encouraged filmmakers to favour exceedingly—and often disturbingly—articulate and overdramatic vocal acting; it was not until 1941 that Suomen Filmiteollisuus acquired microphones that were able to record relatively quiet and intimate talk.[11] Mixing different sounds also caused difficulties at the beginning: only in 1935 did Suomi-Filmi acquire the first actual sound-editing equipment; until then dialogue scenes and music had either alternated, or been 'mixed' by cutting the soundtrack in two between sound and music, with little possibility of controlling the quality or even the volume of either.

Despite such technical difficulties, Finnish filmmakers were active in constructing sound equipment, and for a few years all sound films were recorded with domestic sound technology. Furthermore, even though recorded sound is usually considered as a hindrance to transnational cooperation, for a short while in the early 1930s converting to sound actually increased the Finns' transnational filmmaking activities. For example, Yrjö Nyberg and his Lahyn-Filmi company were responsible for sound recording *Love and Home Reserve* (*Kärlek och landstorm*, 1931) and a handful of other Swedish films, and the first sound feature made in Estonia, *Children of the Sun* (*Päikese lapsed*, 1932), was co-produced and sound recorded by Suomi-Filmi. One of the remarkable consequences of the latter collaboration was that Theodor Luts, the director and cinematographer of the Estonian classic *Young Eagles* (*Noored kotkad*, 1927), immigrated to Finland, where he had a notable career as a cinematographer, director and producer.

Third, even if one concurs with David Bordwell's notion of the smooth transition from silent to sound narration in Hollywood, a small nation perspective might look remarkably different: it took several years before the standard practices of sound filmmaking became established, let alone became the norm. An illustrative example is provided by the way telephone conversations were shot. *Have I Entered a Harem?* (*Olenko mina tullut haaremiin*, 1932), shot with a silent camera and then post-dubbed, features several telephone conversations that are constructed quite differently from the practices established later. The conversations start with the caller saying his or her lines; then a cut to the recipient, whom we first see listening to the lines we have just heard and only after that answering; another cut to the caller, who, again, listens quietly to the lines with which we are already familiar, and so on. In other words, the filmmakers seem to find it necessary to provide the whole conversation from the perspective of both the caller and the recipient, even at the risk of repetition and temporal disruption. During the following years such a scene would be edited more economically, cutting between the speakers while maintaining the temporal continuity of the dialogue or, alternatively, splitting the screen between the characters.

The fourth source of uncertainty concerned the overall destiny of small nation cinemas at the coming of sound. The reservations regarding sound related to a great extent to the fact that Hollywood had during the 1920s invaded Finnish cinemas, much like other European cinemas. With the advent of sound, it was feared that the enormous popularity of Hollywood films would transform English into a universal language, just as the MGM head Louis Mayer had predicted.[12] This was not to happen, at that time at any rate, since together with the sharpening political situation, film sound seemed to contribute to the inward-looking European markets. An illustrative example is provided by two editorials from Finnish film journals written a decade apart. While in 1928 a report from a theatre owner's international conference emphasized that 'cinema brings nations together, teaches us about the nature, customs, life and cultural habits of different countries better and more accessibly than any itinerary or study',[13] an editorial from ten years later stated that sound film had resulted in a state of total nationalism: every film producing country now strived for indigenous subjects, and the driving forces behind all filmmaking were now national and political.[14]

Despite these uncertainties, sound technology proved to provide a positive boost to domestic film production in the end. The first feature films with recorded sound—*Dressed like Adam and a Bit like Eve Too* (*Aatamin puvussa ja vähän Eevankin*), *Say It in Finnish* (*Sano se suomeksi*), *The Wide Road* (*Laveata tietä*) and *The Light Infantryman's Bride* (*Jääkärin morsian*)—all premiered in 1931, and displayed sound clearly as an attraction to varying degrees. Whether they were '100% sound films' like *Say It in Finnish* or hybrid films combining recorded music, sound effects and excerpts of dialogue with intertitles, like the others, the novelty of sound was the basis for marketing each film (Fig. 6.1). The centrality of technology is evident, for example, in a 1931 advert announcing sound with 'no scratching needle, but straight from the film'.[15]

In a few years, as recorded sound became normalized and as the technical problems involved in recording and reproducing sound diminished, what had started as a questionable and possibly passing fad grew into one of the central strengths of domestic film production. Launching his new production company Suomen Filmiteollisuus in 1934, Erkki Karu no longer apologized for the poor quality of the sound. On the contrary, he did not feel shy at speaking for the audience: 'Since sound film invaded the markets, domestic and native-tongued film production has taken off again in many countries. The audience both here and elsewhere prefers to hear film performances in their own language.'[16]

Fig. 6.1 *The Wide Road* (1931) was released both as a silent version and as a sound film with recorded music and sound effects

Karu's enthusiasm, however, was not shared by all. Not only did liberal and leftist intellectuals mourn the loss of the assumed 'universal language' of silent cinema, but also, and more specifically, Swedish-speaking critics might be concerned about the status of the Swedish language in Finnish cinema. Generally, the 1930s was a culminating period of language struggle and 'Finnification', with serious attempts to diminish the influence of the Swedish minority in Finland. Indeed, even though film producers mostly avoided excluding any notable segments of the audience—if only for obvious economic reasons—the 'own language' to which Karu referred quite evidently indicated Finnish, not Swedish. The relation between Swedish-speaking critics and Suomen Filmiteollisuus remained distant even after Karu's death in 1935, when T.J. Särkkä took over the company. Over the years, Suomen Filmiteollisuus produced a number of films with negative or caricaturistic representations of Swedish-speaking characters—for example, *Scorned* (*Halveksittu*, 1939), *It Happened in Ostrobothnia* (*Lakeuksien lukko*, 1951) and *The Beautiful Adventure* (*Ihana seikkailu*, 1962). The ultimate proof of the unisonous nature of Suomen Filmiteollisuus' conception of the native tongue seemed to appear in 1936, when the company announced that it would no longer supply its films with Swedish subtitles.[17]

HOUSE STYLES

The new organization of film production into two—and by the 1950s three—equally strong companies affected not only the modes of commerce, but also the films themselves. Even though the 'studio system' in Finland was modest in scale, it produced mechanisms of standardization and differentiation not unlike those in Hollywood.[18] In terms of film expression, the most important of these was the way the studios developed distinctive studio 'looks' or house styles, in order to differentiate their films from those of their competitors.[19]

The dialectic of standardization and differentiation is, in fact, already evident in the names of the two major companies in the 1930s. When launching his new firm in 1934, Erkki Karu deliberately chose a name, Suomen Filmiteollisuus (Finnish Film Industry), that resembled that of his old company, Suomi-Filmi (Finland Film), but also alluded to the powerful Swedish production company Svensk Filmindustri (Swedish Film Industry)—and of course, at the same time recalled the industrial-economic aspect of cinema, along with the cultural and the nationalistic. Yet another association was with the Domestic Work Association (Kotimaisen Työn Liitto), an organization propagating domestic industry and products and headed by Särkkä; Suomen Filmiteollisuus adopted the octagonal trademark of this association. As a culmination of his playing with similarities and differences, Karu registered the abbreviation SF for his new company, knowing full well that Suomi-Filmi had informally used the same initials for years.

The third major production company of the studio era had its roots in two previous companies: the import and distribution firm Adams-Filmi and the production company Fenno-Filmi, which merged into Fennada-Filmi in 1950. In line with the two major competitors, both 'Fenno' (=Finnish) and 'Fennada' also connoted Finnishness.

While the distinction between house styles was never clear-cut, there were differences in emphasis between the studios in terms of both genre and style. At Suomen Filmiteollisuus, Karu and Särkkä carried on with the overtly national and rural—or ethno-symbolic, as Pietari Kääpä[20] calls it—tradition, associated with some of the prestige films by the 'old' Suomi-Filmi in the 1920s when Karu was in charge. As settings Suomen Filmiteollisuus favoured countryside and farmland or small towns, and the typical characters were farmers, craftsmen or vagabonds. Even when the films take place in a city, as in the series of films about the upper middle-class family Suominen living in Helsinki—six films between 1941 and 1959, starting with *The Suominen Family* (*Suomisen perhe*)—the atmosphere is that of a small town, emphasizing family ties, friendship and community.

The anti-urban, anti-modern and anti-international tendencies that were more or less latent in the studio's 1930s and 1940s films broke into the open in the 'rillumarei' films of the 1950s. Starting with *At the Rovaniemi Fair* (*Rovaniemen markkinoilla*, 1950), this was a cycle of Suomen Filmiteollisuus films about gold washers and vagabonds, who feel at home up north, out in the open and away from modern city life with its norms and restrictions (Fig. 6.2). This 1950s cycle was parallel to the strongly anti-urban and anti-elitist political populist movement that arose during the post-war era among small farmers and gained popularity in the late 1950s. While the ruralism of the 1930s and 1940s films had been close to the harmonizing central European *Heimat* tradition,[21] rillumarei films were more militant in nature, attacking the cultural elite directly. The most extreme manifestation of such hostility was a film called *Hei, Trala-lala-lalaa* (*Hei, rillumarei!*, 1954), in which the protagonist Severi Suhonen, a down-to-earth, accordion-playing gold washer, takes a train— a third-class train carriage with its folksy atmosphere is a central topos in

Fig. 6.2   *At the Rovaniemi Fair* (1950): Vagabonds in a third-class train car on their way to the north

these films—to Helsinki in order to get acquainted with high culture. The result is, obviously, disastrous, as visits to a classical concert, modernist theatre (an apparently absurdist play called *We Are All Insane*) and an art auction reinforce Severi's belief in the contrived and hypocritical nature of both high art and its audience.

The populist militancy is already apparent in the title of the film: the nonsensical phrase 'rillumarei' originated from the chorus of a song heard in *At the Rovaniemi Fair*, but after that it became a derogatory nickname given by critics to this cycle of films. Thus, in many ways 'rillumarei' is comparable to a cycle of Swedish folk comedies of the 1930s, christened 'pilsner' films by scornful critics.[22] By readopting the phrase 'rillumarei' in the title of its film, Suomen Filmiteollisuus apparently drew the sting from the critics and used it as an open declaration of war against the cultural elite and against the ideals of value and taste inherent in the critical discourse.

Issues of national culture and identity were very much at the core of all film-related discussions from the 1930s to the 1950s, but the interpretation of national cinema differed from studio to studio. In contrast to Suomen Filmiteollisuus, Suomi-Filmi, under new production manager Risto Orko, preferred urban themes and high-society settings, often with a deliberately international flavour. While the rural and small-town films of Suomen Filmiteollisuus were usually male oriented, Suomi-Filmi's speciality was women's films of different kinds, both drama and especially comedy. Despite the fact that the film industry never actually used the term women's film, as Anu Koivunen points out in her extensive study of this production trend, remarkably many cycles of films from the late 1930s to the late 1940s—maternal melodramas, fallen woman films, romances and screwball-spirited modern comedies—addressed predominantly female audiences and featured female protagonists and female-oriented themes.[23]

While most of the directors at Suomi-Filmi worked on women's films now and then, Valentin Vaala, who started as an independent filmmaker in the 1920s and was employed by Orko in 1935, specialized in them. His comedies were among the first major successes of the post-recession era, and the company was quick to foresee the potential success of the screwball-oriented comedy trend that was flourishing not only in Hollywood, but also in Italy and many other European countries. A dedicated admirer of Ernst Lubitsch and Frank Capra, Vaala scripted and directed a cycle of modern comedies with urban and usually high-society settings, independent and strong-minded female protagonists and swift dialogue. Several of these comedies were based on novels or plays by popular female authors like Hilja Valtonen—*Surrogate Wife*

(*Vaimoke*, 1936), *Miss Hothead* (*Neiti Tuittupää*, 1943); see Fig. 6.3—or Hella Wuolijoki—*Hulda of Juurakko* (*Juurakon Hulda*, 1937). However, more often than its main competitor at the time, Suomi-Filmi was willing to invest in original scripts too, as is evident from the fact that in 1940 the company announced a competition for potential screenwriters.[24] The winning script of the competition, which emphasized comedies and adventure stories, was *The Dead Man Falls in Love* (*Kuollut mies rakastuu*), an adventure comedy that was filmed by Ilmari Unho in 1942. It featured a mysterious, Simon Templar/The Saint–like righter of wrongs on the borderline between law and crime and was filled with international spies and *femmes fatales*, thus marking the beginning of yet another international-oriented cycle of films by Suomi-Filmi.

Even though the studios specialized in different genres, there was also overlapping in the kinds of films they produced. As Rick Altman has noted with regard to Hollywood studios,[25] cycles often emerged when one studio had a success with a certain kind of film, and other studios soon followed suit. Such was the case with, for example, the social problem films of the post–Second World War years, when almost all production companies—including several small ones that emerged in the aftermath of the war—invested in depictions of crime, venereal diseases, problems of the homecoming soldiers and fallen women. The result was a cycle of films that resonated with what has recently been analysed as international or global film noir.[26]

Fig. 6.3   Lea Joutseno as the quintessential modern heroine of *Miss Hothead* (1943)

Another cycle that involved both the major and the minor companies started in the late 1930s, when the success of the remake of *The Light Infantryman's Bride* (1938) inspired them to make several nationally charged historical melodramas. Despite certain common themes—all of the films concerned Finnish–Russian relations—there were telling differences in the major studios' entries. According to the scripts, both *February Manifesto* (*Helmikuun manifesti*, 1939) by Suomen Filmiteollisuus and *Activists* (*Aktivistit*, 1939) by Suomi-Filmi were planned to start with a montage sequence cataloguing many of the same historical turning points of Finnish–Russian relations of the late nineteenth and early twentieth centuries: Tsar Nicholas II signing the manifesto that diminishes Finnish autonomy in 1899; activist Eugen Schauman assassinating the Russian governor-general Bobrikov in 1904 (Fig. 6.4). Probably because *February Manifesto* premiered first, Suomi-Filmi decided to cut the opening montage sequence. Otherwise the two films differ considerably. *February Manifesto* aims at a historical cavalcade and a cross-section of all social classes that are united by a common enemy, the Russians, who, in turn, are portrayed as crude stereotypes. Historical events and characters are

Fig. 6.4 Activist Eugen Schauman assassinates the Russian governor-general Bobrikov in *February Manifesto* (1939)

presented in a didactic history-book manner. *Activists* shows at least some understanding for the upper-class Russians, focuses on individuals rather than representatives of social classes, and features two female characters who are not unlike the active young protagonists of the women's films (Fig. 6.5). As a melodrama, *Activists* shows many more nuances and much more subtlety than *February Manifesto*.

After the 1940s, women's genres were more or less put aside and replaced by male-oriented ones, like the crime film, lumberjack film, military farce or war film. Nevertheless, Suomi-Filmi held on to its urban and international characteristics, and never invested in such populist themes as its main competitor.

In terms of style and cinematic expression, differences in studio styles were, especially in the 1930s and 1940s, as apparent as in terms of genres and cycles. The modern and urban thematics of Suomi-Filmi often entailed some stylistic experimentation. Films like *VMV 6* (1936, shot by Erik Blomberg, who was trained in Britain and France[27]) or *And Below Was a Fiery Lake* (*Ja alla oli tulinen järvi*, 1937, shot by the Swedish cinematographer Albert Rudling) displayed sharp contrasts between light and shadow, extreme low angles with the characters shot against the sky (Fig. 6.6),

Fig. 6.5   *Activists* (1939) brings elements of women's film into a historical drama

Dutch angles, staging in depth (especially with fences, curtains, plants or other objects framing the foreground) and other conspicuous techniques. This was a style widely referred to as 'French cinematography', and this was well before the French cinematographers Marius Raichi and Charles Bauer were employed by Suomi-Filmi in 1937 and 1938 respectively. The 'French style'—associated in particular with poetic realism—represented for many the most artistic and innovative that cinema had to offer, while others considered it overblown. The distinguished cinematographer Felix Forsman, who himself had made an educational trip to film studios in Paris in 1937, expressed an ambiguous attitude towards it in the early 1940s:

> The French school of style is—or rather was—a so-called effect style of cinematography: light and shadow, but light as little as possible and shadow as much as possible; high and low angles, diagonal and distorted angles, imagery that is often quite incomprehensible and that bypasses the eye and tries to speak straight to one's instinct.[28]

Forsman referred here probably not only to certain of Suomi-Filmi's more experimental features, but also to the films by two independent

Fig. 6.6   Low-angle shooting with the accordion blocking the characters in *VMV 6* (1936)

directors, Nyrki Tapiovaara and Teuvo Tulio, for whom Forsman had worked. Tapiovaara's *Stolen Death* (*Varastettu kuolema*, 1938)—which subject-wise, interestingly enough, belongs to the same cycle of historical melodramas about anti-Russian activists as *February Manifesto* and *Activists*—takes the assumed 'French style' further than most other films. It is filled with striking angles and compositions, unmotivated camera movements, scenes shot behind fences, curtains or house plants, and fast-cut montage sequences (Fig. 6.7). A prime example is a scene near the beginning that starts with a high-angle shot of two men under a lamp post. It is followed by a relatively fast-cut series of scarcely lit shots from various angles, accompanied by only background music. We see a man, whom we may recognize as an underground activist introduced in the opening scene, followed by two other men, presumably the two from under the lamp post. The activist is carrying some papers, which he hides just before the two other men halt him and frisk him. Meanwhile, we see an unknown woman grab the papers and merge with the darkness.

One can grasp some narrative information from the scene, but it is only later that we get to know who the woman is, why she takes the papers and so on. What is at stake in this scene has at least as much to do with style

Fig. 6.7   An extreme high-angle shot in *Stolen Death* (1938)

itself as with narrative progression. The high angle is justified later, when we learn that it is a point-of-view shot from the arms trader's window, but at the same time it gives the scene a formal structuring principle: we return to this angle several times during the scene, as well as later in the film. The gloomy shadows and the sharp backlights add to the atmosphere and serve the narrative by controlling the amount of information revealed to the spectator and thus heightening suspense, but they also create mysterious and effective compositions that have a value of their own, irrespective of the narrative. Hence, while *Stolen Death* is a narrative film with an—eventually—comprehensible storyline, it does stretch the limits of classical narration much further than is usual with mainstream cinema, relying on what Kristin Thompson and others have called cinematic excess.[29] In contrast to the usual forms of classical film narration, which tend to emphasize intelligibility and keep stylistic details within the boundaries of narration, *Stolen Death* contains elements that are not only 'unfunctional' in terms of narrative flow but may even hinder narrative comprehension.

As a contrast to the more or less striking and excessive 'French style' of some of Suomi-Filmi's and especially Tulio's and Tapiovaara's films, the house style of Suomen Filmiteollisuus was often quite pragmatic and primarily actor and character centred: seamless narrative was the guiding principle. With regard to lighting, high key was preferred to low key and, as is witnessed by those who worked at Suomen Filmiteollisuus, the arc lights at the studios were extremely bright and hot.[30] If the choice of camera angles and movements in *Stolen Death* was motivated by expressive qualities, in a typical Suomen Filmiteollisuus film the main focus was on the characters. The principal function of the camera was to follow the actor; thus, a slight reframing was the most common camera movement. Probably the most innovative cinematic experiment at Suomen Filmiteollisuus was the use of a 'transfocator', a home-developed precursor of a zoom lens; this was also often used in order to emphasize the character's reactions with a quick zoom-in to a close-up of a face.

Besides being the president of Suomen Filmiteollisuus, T.J. Särkkä was also the company's most prolific director and screenwriter, even though he had no experience in filmmaking when he joined the firm. It is perhaps telling that unlike Orko, who started out at Suomi-Filmi by hiring the experienced filmmaker Valentin Vaala as a director, Särkkä relied on Wilho Ilmari, Jorma Nortimo and Edvin Laine, all notable stage directors with no background in cinema. No doubt this contributed to the character centeredness of Suomen Filmiteollisuus. Furthermore, although the majority of Finnish film actors came from the stage, the use of theatre actors at Suomi-Filmi was not as exclusive as at its rival studio; Vaala was particularly noted for his eagerness to 'find' new actors with little or no experience in theatre, whereas Särkkä readily turned to well-known stage actors, preferably from the Finnish National Theatre.

Accordingly, while at Suomi-Filmi a more subtle and restrained acting style was developed, the acting in Särkkä's films is often considered somewhat ponderous and pathetic. As Felix Forsman later described the directing practices at Suomen Filmiteollisuus:

> The director, who sits beside the camera, does not see the image the way the camera does, whether it is a close-up, a medium shot or a long shot. Thus, the director works like on a stage: like it was a long shot all along. This is why the facial expressions of the actors are performed for the third row in a theatre, overblown.[31]

On the other hand, Särkkä's disinterest in technology allowed the cinematographers at Suomen Filmiteollisuus to have more artistic freedom and responsibility than they would have had working with directors with a background in cinema. Indeed, the reliance on technical personnel gives a certain credit to the 'genius of the system': numerous stories recount that Särkkä or Edvin Laine would sometimes be away from the shooting location for hours or even for days, letting the technical crew take charge. This, again, would offer a chance for young aspiring filmmakers like Matti Kassila to show their talent in the post-war years.[32]

RHETORIC OF NATIONAL STYLE

The studio era of Finnish cinema was characterized by highly nationalistic rhetoric, whether the emphasis was on art, politics or money. With the introduction of recorded sound, the marketability of Finnishness grew, arguably, to be even bigger than it was before: hearing your mother tongue on the screen provided for the home markets an attraction with which imported films had a hard time competing. Domestic films dominated—at least relatively speaking—the screen, and especially in the 1930s and 1940s they dominated film-related discourse.

Yet, however nationalistic the film talk was, there was, almost by definition, always a transnational angle to it: especially for a small nation cinema it is probable that it will be constantly weighed and defined in relation to other cinemas. After all, according to the basic semiotic principle, a concept like 'Finnishness' is never defined in and of itself, but rather in relation to other nationalities. This principle was clearly exemplified in the launch issue of *SF-Uutiset*, a magazine devoted not only to showcasing the output of Suomen Filmiteollisuus, but also to promoting national cinema:

> Perhaps the pace [of Finnish films] is not fast in the American manner after all, the characters not refined in the French or English manner, nor the performance sensitive in the Russian manner; still, in spite of this, or perhaps because of this, the films go well with the Finnish character ....[33]

Most spokespersons of national cinema saw national specificity as something collective and subconscious and, hence, unavoidable. Therefore, film production was considered deeply determined by nationality, since these unquestionable national features provided, for good or ill, the necessary framework for production. Such views, however, were not without paradoxes. One was that although Finnish cinema was constantly—and could only be—defined in relation to other national cinemas, Finnishness was at the same time considered as an intrinsic and self-contained quality, as can be seen in this thoroughly essentialist reasoning published in the popular film magazine *Elokuva-Aitta*:

> Film, being the youngest of arts, represents in the most immediate and conspicuous way the national and racial characteristics of the country of its origin. These national features do not arise from national subject matters alone, nor, in the least, from national ideologies; rather, they are something so essential to each country's film production that one could not avoid them even if one wanted to.[34]

Another paradox was that, as Andrew Higson has suggested is typical for discourse on national cinema generally,[35] the critical comments were often both descriptive and prescriptive at the same time: while describing the supposedly Finnish features of the films, the critics simultaneously were most eager to draw boundaries for national culture by pointing out what was and was not appropriate for Finnish films.

What were the characteristics the contemporary critical and industrial discourses attached to Finnish cinema? What was included in and excluded from nationally distinct—although transnationally defined—film style? Three broad themes can be discerned, all of them having as much to do with the supposed national character as with the films the nation produces. One of these themes is tempo (or pace, or rhythm); the other two intertwining themes are taste and plausibility—or decorum and verisimilitude—as discussed by Steve Neale and Frank Krutnik: 'Decorum means what is proper or fitting, verisimilitude what is probable or likely. Both concepts therefore centrally concern the relationship between representations, cultural knowledge, opinion, and beliefs, and, hence, audience expectations.'[36] With regard to national cinema, decorum and verisimilitude are intertwined precisely because they represent the inseparable and mutually dependent prescriptive and descriptive sides of critical discourse.

Taste

Matters of taste or decorum were of importance to discussions on Finnish cinema. Bad taste or lack of decorum was often associated with those features in films that were considered 'international' or 'non-Finnish', be they details in mise-en-scène, character behaviour or actor performance. Examples of such a lack of decorum were found by critics especially in films with a modern, urban and international flavour. These included characters drinking whisky in the 'American' style,[37] smoking pipes while dressed in tails[38] or, indeed, the foreground of the image being filled with furniture, flowers, railings or curtains in the 'French' style.[39] Such details were either regarded as out of place in Finnish films or, alternatively, the critics thought the filmmakers had misinterpreted the codes of behaviour. Thus, a typically paradoxical mixture of feelings of superiority and inferiority was often at stake: the 'foreign' features were either 'impure' and not worthy of pursuing, or out of reach for Finnish filmmakers.

Plausibility

Throughout the studio years, a demand for a certain plausibility was one of the most recurrent themes. The proper realm of Finnish narratives was that of a fairly conventional realism. The norms of decorum consisted in complying with 'good taste', whereas the norms of verisimilitude consisted in keeping to generic assumptions and sociocultural 'public knowledge',[40] and the critics expected both sets of rules to be obeyed.

Stretching the norms of generic or narrative verisimilitude was rather rare, mostly limited to genre parodies like *The Wild North* (*Villi Pohjola*, 1955; a western parody that places the frontier up north) or *Pete and Runt in a Chain Collision* (*Pekka ja Pätkä ketjukolarissa*, 1957; an episodic buddy comedy that parodies Robinson Crusoe films, military comedies and westerns). The critics felt an urge to comment on deviations from sociocultural norms more often than generic norms. For example, a 'champagne farce' in a continental style was not fit for the screen, since it had no equivalent in Finnish reality[41]; a 'German-type' comedy suited the Finns better, because it contained no impossible or tasteless elements.[42]

These sociocultural norms were closely related to and affected by conventional ideas of national character. A classical description—with an obviously prescriptive flavour—of the Finnish character is provided by Zacharias Topelius, an influential historian and author of historical novels, travel books and fairy tales, whose *Maamme kirja* ('The Book of Our Land', 1875) was used as a text book in primary schools until the 1940s. In Topelius' view, national character was a God-given property that was easy to observe but difficult to explain. According to Topelius, Finns were God-fearing, hard-working and stable, hardened and strong, patient, prone to renunciation, vital, calm, brave in war, tough and self-willed, and longing for freedom and knowledge.[43] These characteristics of the Finns were, once again, continually weighed against those of other nationalities, either explicitly or implicitly. Such conceptions of national character evidently contributed to the critics' view of Finnish films: a genuinely Finnish film had to operate within the boundaries of these traits in order to evoke a response in Finnish audiences.

Tempo

These romantic conceptions of national character also led to the third theme of national specificity in critical writings on Finnish cinema: tempo or pace. Most traits described, or prescribed, by Topelius emphasize slowness, patience and modesty. Accordingly, the task set for Finnish films—including comedies—was to look for ways of mediating such traits. Thus, the Finnish style stood in sharp contrast to 'continental' sophisticated films, and especially to Hollywood comedies with 'an atmosphere of skyscrapers, ocean liners, and crowded trains flashing by at lightning speed'.[44] Many shared the view of a critic of the trade journal *Kinolehti* who associated low culture, underdeveloped taste, mass thinking and lack of personality with American culture, whereas 'one seldom encounters a European film that lacks a personal creative element and everything that comes with it: sense of art, psychology, atmosphere and culture'.[45] However, while Finnish views of European film cultures were usually quite unanimous, discussions over Hollywood were often ambiguous, as if the former were something 'old' and 'known', in contrast to the 'new' and 'uncharted' American culture. Hence, traits associated with American culture—speed, technical innovativity, indifference to class boundaries—were both admired and shunned at the same time. This ambiguous attitude is illustrated by the views of the esteemed literary critic Rafael Koskimies, who regarded the American film director as a mere engineer watching over the apparatus and, simultaneously, admitted that such an 'artist-engineer' was a most interesting psychological type who leads our thoughts to the vital question of the relations between art and technology.[46]

In short, suspicions about speed were connected with a belief in a stable national identity, characterized by opposite qualities. Furthermore, speed can be seen as an emblem bringing together a number of ambivalent factors of the modern world. While the Topelian national inheritance was defined by qualities such as male rural culture, peasantry or the middle classes, concentration, consideration and persistence, the modern world of speed, in turn, was associated with female urban culture, the working class, nervousness, temporality and ephemerality.[47] As a modern technology, cinema was, in a sense, pre-determined to the zone of speed. Many contemporary commentators—both defenders and opponents of cinema—believed that films had had an irreversible impact on human experience, and even human perception.[48] The author and playwright Arvi Kivimaa expressed a mediating and ambivalent view:

> It is sometimes claimed that movies have enormously cultivated the theatre audience. People have become visual types. Swift, flashing images—in cinemas, out in the streets, at restaurants—have improved the reception of our eye. This audience is able to grasp a tiny and sparing movement, where once an abundance of grand opera gestures was needed. ... But do the quickening visual advertisements not manifest that our sight is—already!—stultifying in the exuberance of images? Did our innocent grandmothers and grandfathers not observe the world with fresher eyes? Our excitement and passion for life as well as our paralysis is different from theirs.[49]

Against this background, the critics' claims that films should respect the norms of plausibility and decorum and proceed with a smooth rhythm can be seen as endeavours at preserving cinema for the purposes of national culture. A genuine Finnish film should be purified of features pointing in the direction of technology and speed, as much as it should avoid bad taste—or 'impure' elements—and stay within the realm of plausibility. Since it ought to be calm and mild, the pace of narration and the way temporal relations were organized became central questions. Finally, debates over what was considered 'filmic', while being aware of the international discussions on the theme, also had a national twist. A good example is provided by a critic of *SF-Uutiset* who defines one of the essential filmic qualities in a clearly nationalist vein: 'However, the movability of film is not to be brought to its limits. The unity of action must be maintained, and the characters must not be torn to pieces with excessive speed.'[50]

In the last instance, the legitimacy of a national film style was justified in a circular manner. Style was explained by national character, and national character was reflected in the domestically produced films: for the Finns they were 'flesh out of their own blood'.[51] And the ultimate legitimation came from the—as such, not entirely untrue—populist reasoning that since domestic films were extremely popular, they had to have the backing of all social classes. 'The film audience is made of practically all population groups,' wrote Särkkä in 1939, 'in no other way can the success of cinema be explained. The working man and the schoolteacher, the farmer and the bank manager, the housemaid and the professional woman all sit side by side at the cinema, as a grand democracy of the auditorium.'[52]

FOUR MODES OF FILM STYLE

The rhetoric of national cinema obviously emphasized the unity of national style and the homogeneity of culture, in contrast to the potentially distractive international cinema. At its most chauvinist and protectionist, the national rhetoric might go to extremes by claiming that domestic production prevented the Finns from watching 'bad, spiritually worthless foreign films that are not only alien to us, but may even prove dangerous'.[53] These were the words of Särkkä, whose company was not a notable importer of foreign films; otherwise such a statement would not have made commercial sense.

Even if national rhetoric declared unity, the cinematic reality of the domestic output was never quite as unified as the critiques and pamphlets would have liked it to be, as has already been seen with regard to the differences in house styles. In mapping the variety of different approaches to filmic expression during the studio years, four different modes of film style that partly coincide with the studio styles and partly transcend their borders can be discerned. These modes are classicism, theatricalism, pictorialism and narrative avant-garde, and each of these is further exemplified by one director: Valentin Vaala, T.J. Särkkä, Teuvo Tulio and Nyrki Tapiovaara, respectively. As we have seen, Vaala was the backbone director at Suomi-Filmi all through the studio years, from the mid-1930s to the early 1960s, as was Särkkä at Suomen Filmiteollisuus. Tulio, after having an acting career as the 'Finnish Valentino' in Vaala's early films,[54] started as a director for the import company Adams-Filmi and then became an independent filmmaker. Tapiovaara's short career— he died in the Finnish–Soviet Winter War in 1940 at the age of 28—comprised only five feature films, all produced by private funding or by a small independent company. Nevertheless, the lasting reputation of his films and his inspiration for later generations of filmmakers make him much more than a curiosity in film history.

With the possible exception of Tulio, whose idiosyncratic, excessive melodramatic style remained quite unchanged from the 1930s to the early 1970s, there was an element of variety in the work of each of these directors. Both Vaala and Särkkä worked on different genres, from lumberjack and vagabond films to historical films and literary adaptations, and obviously the style of their comedies differs quite significantly from that of their melodramas. Of Tapiovaara's five films, *Stolen Death* was a political thriller, *Juha* (1937) and *One Man's Fate* (*Miehen tie*, 1940) were rural (melo)dramas and adaptations of well-established novels, whereas *Two Henpecked Husbands (Kaksi Vihtoria*, 1939) and *Mr. Lahtinen Takes French Leave (Herra Lahtinen lähtee lipettiin*, 1939) were musical comedies. Although all of these were recognizable genre films, none of them would count as a typical representative of its genre. Rather, as varied as these films are, the idiosyncrasy of Tapiovaara's work lies in the way it synthesizes popular film genres with a variety of modernist and avant-garde devices, inspired by, for example, French Impressionism, German Expressionism, kinetic abstract cinema of the 1920s, Soviet montage cinema (especially Alexander Dovzhenko) and Brechtian theatre.

The basic distinctions between these modes of style can be presented as in Table 6.1, charting different aspects of cinematic expression: lighting, framing, telling/showing, continuity of sound, acting and setting.

Of all Finnish filmmakers of the studio era, Vaala was arguably the one most inclined towards Hollywood. From early on he studied the practices of classical scene dissection in detail and, to take only one example, he was the first Finnish director systematically to favour the shot reverse shot

Table 6.1 Modes of style, their salient features and principal proponents

Classicism Valentin Vaala	Theatricalism T.J. Särkkä	Pictorialism Teuvo Tulio	Narrative avant-garde Nyrki Tapiovaara
Naturalist lighting	Naturalist/dramatic lighting	Dramatic lighting	Poetic/dramatic lighting
Invisible framing	Fourth wall framing	Visible framing	Visible framing
Telling	Showing	Showing/telling	Showing/telling
Continuity of sound	Continuity of sound	Alternation of music and dialogue	Occasional dominance of music
Realist acting	Realist/theatricalist acting	Theatricalist/pictorialist acting	Theatricalist/alienating acting
Naturalist setting	Naturalist/theatricalist setting	Pictorialist/minimalist setting	Naturalist/stylished setting

technique in conversation scenes instead of two-shots. As Matti Kassila, Vaala's apprentice and, arguably, his most important follower as a classical-style filmmaker in the 1950s, wrote in his memoirs:

He applied the Hollywood model in storytelling, visual design, as well as in star cult. He had closely observed how scenes are constructed in Hollywood, how scene dissection, shot scales, framing and continuity are realized, and how information is distributed. In his shooting scripts, Vaala applied exact shot scales (long shot, medium shot, medium close-up, close-up), and he was careful to follow the patterns. It was impossible for him to cut straight from a long shot to a close-up.[55]

According to the classical Hollywood tradition, Vaala aspired to invisible storytelling, where continuity and clarity of image and sound are more important than the quality of any singular composition. The objective in lighting, setting and directing actors was to create a world that appeared plausible by both sociocultural and generic standards, even within the supposedly stylized conventions of comedy or melodrama. Showing/telling goes back to the classical division between mimesis and diegesis, where showing is represented by drama, appearing to the eyes of the spectator as if narrated by no one, whereas telling is represented by epic poetry, explicitly mediated by a narrator. André Gaudreault has considered editing to be the formative ingredient of cinematic narration: while early one-shot films were based on showing (in Gaudreault's terms monstrating) a scene,

view or singular action, editing shots together introduced the act of telling (or narrating).[56] In this sense, Vaala's films that build on relatively fast
editing and classical scene dissection verge on telling much more than, for
example, Särkkä's films that rely on longer takes, two-shots and, occasionally, tableau-like framings.

The theatricalist style of Särkkä—and Suomen Filmiteollisuus more or
less in general—does not necessarily imply static shots. On the contrary,
in addition to the constant reframing and the use of the 'transfocator',
mentioned in the preceding section, camera movements in depth were
common in Särkkä's films. Yet since scene dissection—the use of eyeline
match, match on action and dividing a scene into complementary shots
taken from different angles—was less systematic than in Vaala's work,
Särkkä's films provide a stagey view, not unlike the invisible 'fourth wall'
in illusionist theatre. This impression is further consolidated by the ponderous acting style in Särkkä's films.

In such films as *Song of the Scarlet Flower* (*Laulu tulipunaisesta kukasta*,
1938), *Restless Blood* (*Levoton veri*, 1946) and *Jealousy* (*Mustasukkaisuus*,
1953), Teuvo Tulio developed a distinctively excessive melodramatic style
that was highly influenced by German Expressionism and Czech cinema,
especially the films of Gustav Machatý. Instead of continuity, the focus is
on separate images and compositions. Such pictorialist quality is, perhaps,
most visible in the lyrical and decorative shots of the idyllic countryside
and nature on the one hand, and in carefully framed close-ups of faces on
the other. The dramatic quality of lighting in such close-ups exceeds any
naturalist aspirations, and the expressive centre is in the wide-open eyes
of the character in close-up (Fig. 6.8). The acting in general is highly stylized and non-naturalistic, and in close-ups the actors may even petrify into
expressive poses. The impression of discontinuity is further highlighted
by the abundant use of silent camera. Often these sequences have neither
post-recorded dialogue nor any other sounds that are supposed to be perceived as diegetic, only background music. Thus, the division between
'silent' scenes and dialogue scenes is often extremely sharp.

Finally, the work of Nyrki Tapiovaara may encompass scenes that are
dominated by relatively atonal music (*Stolen Death*), and scenes that blur
the boundaries between fantasy and reality (*Mr. Lahtinen Takes French
Leave*) or between ethnographic film and studio realism (*Juha*). Verging
on different traditions of the avant-garde, his films demonstrate that the
national style during the studio era was anything but a unified notion.

Fig. 6.8   Regina Linnanheimo in an expressive close-up in *Restless Blood* (1946)

NOTES

1. Uusitalo 1994: 83–108.
2. Keto 1974: 64.
3. Honka-Hallila 1996: 464.
4. Bordwell 1985: 301.
5. Neale 1985: 91–5.
6. Williams 1992: 137.
7. Honka-Hallila 1995: 67–8.
8. See Wahl: 2010.
9. See Töyri 1978: 199.
10. Honka-Hallila 1996: 468–9.
11. See Kuusela 1976: 37–42.
12. See Danan 1999: 229.
13. 'Elokuvan suuri kansallinen ja kansainvälinen tehtävä', *Elokuva*, 14/1928, 3.
14. 'Kansallisen filmituotannon nousu', *Suomi-Filmin Uutisaitta*, 4/1938, 3.
15. Quoted in Honka-Hallila 1994: 18.
16. Interview of Erkki Karu, *Helsingin Sanomat*, 27/5/1934.
17. See Ove Finell, 'Till biopublikens trevnad', *Fama*, 4–5/1936, 35.

18. See Staiger 1985: 96–112.
19. Cf. Balio 1993: 85–98.
20. Kääpä 2010: 15–18.
21. See Hake 2002: 118 ff.
22. See Qvist 2010: 119–33.
23. Koivunen 1995: 45–51.
24. Uusitalo 1994: 180.
25. Altman 1999: 59–68.
26. Broe 2014.
27. Töyri 1983: 40–1.
28. 'Elokuvan luo kamera', *SF-Uutiset*, 7/1940, 6.
29. Thompson 1988: 259–62.
30. Töyri 1983: 133–136.
31. Von Bagh and Riikonen 1991: 25.
32. Kassila 2004: 63–6.
33. Pekka Lönngren, 'Minkätähden kotimaisia elokuvia?', *SF-Uutiset*, 1/1935, 8.
34. L.O., 'Elokuva ja kansallisuus', *Elokuva-Aitta*, 3/1939, 54.
35. Higson 1989: 37.
36. Neale and Krutnik 1990: 84.
37. Review of The Bachelors' Ward (Poikamiesten holhokki 1938), *Uusi Aika*, 17/9/1938.
38. -gn, Review of Me and the Cabinet Minister (Minä ja ministeriss 1934), *Hufvudstadsbladet*, 19/3/1934.
39. H. K., Review of A Day as an Heiress (Markan tähden 1938), *Hufvudstadsbladet*, 3/10/1938.
40. See Neale and Krutnik 1990: 83–94.
41. Y., Review of Surrogate Husband (Mieheke, 1936), *Uusi Suomi*, 21/12/1936.
42. Review of The Stopgap (Hätävara, 1939), *Hämeen Sanomat* 2/2/1939.
43. Topelius 1942: 151–2.
44. L.O., 'Elokuva ja kansallisuus', *Elokuva-Aitta*, 3/1939, 54.
45. G. Stjernschantz, 'Näytäntökauden huippukohtia', *Suomen Kinolehti*, 5/1936, 123–4.
46. R. K., 'Näyttelijä, ohjaaja ja filmi', *Valvoja-Aika*, 11 (1933), 104–6.
47. An important source for contemporary Finnish views on phenomena associated with national inheritance and modernity is Kivimies 1937, a collection of debates by young intellectuals. On associations between women, modernity and mass culture in Finland, see Koivunen 1995.
48. Cf. the 'modernity thesis' debate concerning especially early cinema experiences, Gunning 2006, 302–9. For the opposing view, see Bordwell 1997: 139–149.
49. Kivimaa 1937: 88.

50. 'Mitä on filmaattisuus?', *SF-Uutiset*, 1/1939, 6.
51. 'Suomalaisen filmin oikeutus', *SF-Uutiset*, 3/1937, 11.
52. Sulka, 'Lukijalle', *SF-Uutiset*, 2/1939, 3.
53. 'Suomalaisen filmin oikeutus', *SF-Uutiset*, 3/1937, 11.
54. See Kalha 2009: 132–42.
55. Kassila 2004: 47–48.
56. Gaudreault 2009: 101–12.

CHAPTER 7

Exporting Finnish Films

Anneli Lehtisalo

Finnish cinema can be considered a small nation film culture[1] not only because of the limited number of films produced, but it is relatively unfamiliar to an international audience. During the studio era, the Finnish film industry targeted its products mainly at a domestic audience, yet it continually upheld the hope of expanding its markets. Although the film industry did not have the resources to promote its products abroad on a large scale, Finnish feature films were steadily distributed abroad at least from the 1920s.[2] In the late 1930s, the increasing activity of the film industry and tightening transnational networks enhanced the efforts to export films. This chapter examines the major historical trends in the foreign distribution of Finnish films in the studio era.

Although there had been international networks and active business activity between the Finnish and foreign film industries from the turn of the twentieth century,[3] a significant change in foreign distribution occurred in the late 1930s. After the years of the Depression, two of the major Finnish film companies, Suomi-Filmi and Suomen Filmiteollisuus, were operating at capacity by the mid-1930s.[4] Increasing production and the recovering economic situation gave rise to the expectation that the markets for Finnish films would be expanded. The film industry was able to invest more in

A. Lehtisalo (✉)
e-mail: anneli.lehtisalo@kotiportti.fi

© The Editor(s) (if applicable) and The Author(s) 2016
H. Bacon (ed.), *Finnish Cinema*, Palgrave European Film
and Media Studies, DOI 10.1057/978-1-137-57651-4_7

increasing its foreign marketing, and successful efforts at exporting films inspired companies to invest more in production and export.[5]

The rising expectations of finding international markets also gained ground in media coverage of the film industry, and discussions were reopened on the quality and essence of Finnish cinema, which had already circulated in Finnish film magazines before the Depression, in the 1920s.[6] The discussions illuminate how foreign distribution, and the expectations connected to it, were related to the construction of the notion of national cinema. The idea that Finnish films met international standards— that is, that they were exportable—seemed to substantiate the existence of 'Finnish cinema' and set it in its place among other national cinemas.[7] The notion of Finnish cinema was further defined and redefined in public discussions on the distribution and reception of Finnish films abroad.

In the late 1930s, the successful foreign distribution of Finnish feature films was hailed as a mark of a new era for Finnish cinema (Fig. 7.1).[8] According to commentators, Finnish films had reached the level of international film art: 'Among the films of the last season there were several films which convincingly demonstrate that our domestic films have reached an artistic level. As this gradually expands, our country will be ready to make its appearance in the broader international market.'[9]

However, such optimistic anticipations mingled with more sceptical thoughts. The managing director of Suomi-Filmi, Matti Schreck (1897–1946), admitted there were promising prospects in Scandinavian countries, but doubted whether success could be achieved in Central and Southern Europe.[10] According to him the main problem was the Finnish language. Because Central and Southern European countries used dubbing instead of subtitles, it would be too expensive to distribute films there.

Over the years, the language issue was seen as one of the main hindrances to the export of Finnish films. While dubbing was expensive, subtitles were claimed to be distractive.[11] It was not, however, only a question of costs or technical matters. Speech itself was seen as a problematic element in Finnish films, as a major flaw in Finnish cinematic style. Someone under the pseudonym H. Soldan in *Elokuvateatteri* suggested that a film is an international art based on imagery 'understood by all peoples'.[12] Thus, Finnish cinema should adopt such a purely cinematic style. As late as the beginning of the 1960s, the editor of *Kinolehti*, Helge Miettunen, complained that Finnish film style is based on dialogue: 'The dialogue, Finnish dialogue, still has a primary role. Because of this, a dialogue is

Figs. 7.1–7.2 *The Logger's Bride* (1937) attracted audiences in other Nordic countries with its spectacular rapid scenes

Fig. 7.3 (continued)

used to express more than is typical in films produced in other countries.'[13] According to him, one ought to create nationally specific visual ways of expression in order to make films exportable.[14]

Other challenges to the foreign distribution of films were also publicly discussed. Among them were poor resources and the lack of vehicles for international publicity. Someone writing under the pseudonym K.E.P.H. noted in *Elokuvateatteri* that it is no use trying to export films to countries with rich, high-quality production, such as the USA, the UK and France.[15] Producers themselves explained that they could not compete with a foreign film industry that had better resources and technical equipment.[16] Some commentators saw that there is potential in Finnish cinema, but felt that there had not been sufficiently serious efforts to distribute the films abroad.[17] It was also noted that it was difficult to market Finnish films because there were no internationally famous stars or directors, big names who could attract a foreign audience.[18]

Despite these challenges, exporting Finnish films was part of the film business in Finland throughout the studio era, although it was not the primary area of operations. Because of a lack of detailed data, it is difficult to estimate the actual economic significance of foreign distribution for the film companies.[19] Whatever the economic gain, however, in public debates on cinema international distribution was seen as a desirable state of affairs. The exportability of Finnish films was regarded as a proof of quality, and it legitimized the existence of Finnish cinema as part of the international film culture.

THE MAIN TRENDS IN FOREIGN DISTRIBUTION

From 1936 to 1965, at least 448 export transactions were made to export Finnish feature films for commercial theatrical distribution abroad (Table 7.1).[20] The figure is an estimate, because no comprehensive export data exists. The estimate is based on a heterogeneous range of material, for example articles in trade magazines and newspapers, and different archive materials.

Table 7.1 shows the main target countries, the quantity of exported films per country and the number of export transactions.[21] In addition to these countries, there were sporadic sales to Estonia, Chile and Mexico (3 films), the UK, Poland, the Netherlands and Japan (2 films) and Czechoslovakia, Belgium, Liechtenstein, Luxemburg, Italy, Lithuania, Tunisia, Cuba, Bolivia, Peru, Australia and China (1 film).

The number of exported films follows the total number of films produced. This, however, does not indicate that increasing production automatically led to increasing foreign exports. First, exported films were not necessarily recent productions; the films could be more than 10 years old. For example, Suomen Filmiteollisuus sold a 17-year-old film, *Out to Borrow Matches* (*Tulitikkuja lainaamassa*, Toivo Särkkä and Yrjö Norta, 1938), to the Yugoslavian distributor Morava-Film in 1955.[22] Furthermore, circumstances varied over the decades. For example, exports in the late 1930s were based on expanding business activities, whereas after the Second World War foreign distribution was considered a way of sustaining the Finnish film industry, thought to be in crisis at the time.[23] Thus, instead of a causal relation between production and export, it appears that the increase in production and the growing numbers of films exported were both results of the increasing business activity within the Finnish film industry. The active periods in the domestic field gave rise to energetic efforts to find international distribution.

As Table 7.1 indicates, there were few opportunities to export films to the larger European countries, such as the UK, France, Germany, Italy or Spain. Not only was the competition from America and the respective domestic industry too strong, but protective measures in the

Table 7.1   The quantity of films produced in Finland and the number of exported films

	1930–1935	1936–1939	1940–1949	1950–1959	1960–1965	In total
Films produced in Finland	29	61	174	217	85	566
Export trans actions in total	4	47	215	149	53	468
Number of titles exported	3	25	97	68	31	224
Country						*Exported films in total*
USA	1	20	36	30	8	**95**
Sweden	2	11	37	28	8	**86**
Denmark	1	6	42	2	1	**52**
Germany/Federal Republic of Germany	0	0	13	5	9	**27**
Norway	0	4	13	8	2	**27**
Hungary	0	0	18	2	3	**23**
Romania	0	0	22	0	0	**22**
Soviet Union	0	0	0	13	4	**17**
Canada	0	4	0	10	1	**15**
Bulgaria	0	0	11	0	0	**11**
Yugoslavia	0	0	0	10	0	**10**
Slovenia	–	–	7	–	–	**7**
Switzerland	0	0	3	2	1	**6**
German Democratic Republic	–	–	0	2	4	**6**
Brazil	0	0	1	5	0	**6**
France	0	0	1	4	0	**5**
Austria	0	1	2	1	1	**5**
Argentina	0	0	0	3	1	**4**
Venezuela	0	0	0	3	1	**4**
Uruguay	0	0	0	4	0	**4**
Croatia	–	–	4	–	–	**4**
The United Kingdom	0	0	0	1	1	**2**

Source: Material gathered from the Suomi-Filmi Archive (NAI), the Suomen Filmiteollisuus Archive (NAI), the Licence Committee Archive (FBR), the Ministry for Foreign Affairs Archive in Finland (FMA), the Svensk Filmindustri Collections (SFI), the Wive-Film Collections (SFI), the Nordisk Tonefilm Archive (ARBARK) and Finnish and Swedish newspapers and magazines. In addition to the estimated export figure, there are 152 unverified cases, i.e. films that were claimed to have been exported but without enough evidence to support such claims

larger European countries effectively constrained imports from smaller production countries.[24] The target countries for export were mainly other small film cultures, more dependent on imports for their cinemas, or countries to which Finland was oriented through existing cultural or other relations and general political trends. In addition, developments in international film culture, film festivals for instance, offered new possibilities for distributing films outside Finland.

Sweden and other Nordic countries exemplify the significance of long-lasting relations: it was easy to do business with other Nordic countries because of previous business contacts, geographical and cultural closeness and, partly, a common language.[25] Sweden remained the main target for Finnish export activities throughout the studio era regardless of changing political circumstances in Europe. Another region that continued to be targeted for distribution was the location of Finnish emigrants in North America—in both the USA and Canada—although the dominant American film culture eventually squeezed out Finnish films during the 1950s. The notable change in the pattern of exports in the 1950s was expansion of the distribution network, as Finnish films were exported not only to other European countries but also to South America and Asia. This illustrates the increasing internationalization of film culture: the influence of international film festivals, for instance.[26] The dependence on the political climate was most obvious during the Second World War and in the late 1950s, when the politics of the Cold War affected export trends. During the Second World War the Finnish film industry benefited from cooperation with Germany, and after the war the political shift opened up contacts with the Soviet bloc, particularly with the Soviet Union itself.

In the 1930s, Nazi-led Germany wanted to create a 'European' culture that would be dominated by Germany and purified from hostile influences, such as the Jewish community and Bolshevism. The International Film Chamber (IFC, *Internationale Filmkammer*), founded in 1935, was to execute these aims in the field of the cinema.[27] During the Second World War, the outspoken policy of the IFC was to support European film industries against unequal competition from the American film industry by organizing a boycott of Anglo-American films, as well as to back up the film industry in German satellites and occupied countries.[28] Part of the Finnish film industry grasped this opportunity to enhance its business, and established close relations with the German film industry and the IFC. As such, there was nothing exceptional about the contacts with Germany, since the Finnish cultural elite had had traditionally close relations with the German cultural scene.[29] The overwhelming practical concern came to be that from the summer of 1941 onwards, Finland and Germany fought against the Soviet Union as allies. At this point the major argument for cooperation with the IFC was that it guaranteed the supply of raw film to Finland.[30] The situation became heated, as not all film companies in Finland were pro-German, and eventually the disputes concerning the IFC split the Finnish film industry.[31]

Active contacts with the IFC improved the chance of Finnish producers exporting their films within German-dominated areas in Europe. The boycott of Anglo-American films, along with difficulties in transportation during the war, generated a shortage of films in Central European cinemas,[32] and the major companies in Finland, Suomen Filmiteollisuus and Suomi-Filmi, were eager to meet the demand and cooperate with the IFC. Films were mainly exported to German satellites, such as Croatia, Czechoslovakia, Hungary, Bulgaria and Romania, or to occupied Denmark and Norway. There is no precise information about export figures, but it seems that fewer than ten films were exported to Germany between 1941 and 1944.[33] The end of the war cut off connections to Germany. Distribution to the Balkan area, particularly to Bulgaria, continued even after the war, but it ceased by the beginning of the 1950s.[34]

After its defeat in the Second World War, the situation changed radically in Finland. The country had to alter its domestic and foreign policies. Patriotic right-wing organizations were banned, and previously forbidden, underground Communist organizations could participate openly in social activities. In the terms of foreign policy, Finland had to build working relations with the former enemy, the Soviet Union. The situation affected Finnish cultural life as well, including its film culture. The immediate effects were the ban on German and Hungarian films being distributed in Finland, as well as some Finnish films that were considered to be anti-Soviet.[35] These policy changes resulting from political trends did not, however, affect foreign distribution until later in the 1950s.

In the mid-1950s, the relations between Finnish and Soviet film professionals started to strengthen. Authorities and film professionals from both countries initiated Finnish–Soviet film weeks; that is, Soviet films were to be screened in Finland and Finnish films in the Soviet Union. The first week of Finnish films being shown in the Soviet Union was organized in 1956.[36] The main festivities took place in Moscow, but according to the trade magazine *Kinolehti*, films screened during these weeks circulated in the country's cinemas even after the event.[37] In addition, the film production companies Fennada and Suomi-Filmi had chosen to use a Russian colour system, Sovcolor, for their first colour films, which further intensified the cooperation.[38] The colour films *The Vagabond's Mazurka* (*Kulkurin masurkka*, Aarne Tarkas, 1958), *The Young Miller* (*Nuori mylläri/Molodoi Melnik*, Valentin Vaala, 1958) and *The Women of Niskavuori* (*Niskavuoren naiset/Ženštšiny Niskavuori*, Valentin Vaala, 1958) were also distributed in cinemas in the Soviet Union.[39] Later, in 1964, the Finnish–Soviet film week was extended as Finnish films were shown in four cities over the fortnight: in Moscow, Minsk, Tallinn and Leningrad.[40]

The Soviet orientation was in accordance with the official foreign policy and the Treaty of Friendship (Agreement of Friendship, Cooperation and Mutual Assistance, 1948–1992). The treaty concerned not only military affairs, but culture and business as well.[41] Hence, it was no wonder that Finnish officials followed with interest the cooperation between film professionals, and the screenings of Finnish films in the Soviet Union were conjoined with political events, such as official state visits.[42]

The international political situation affected and increased cooperation between Finnish and Nazi German or Russian agents in the field. Although these trends were noticeable in the film industry and in foreign distribution, the international distribution of Finnish films in effect rested on long-lasting contacts with other Nordic countries and certain restricted niche markets.

THE NORDIC CARD

Nordic affiliation was an important factor in exports of Finnish films in two ways. First, Finnish films were mainly exported to other Nordic countries, particularly to Sweden. Exports to Sweden continued steadily from the late 1930s until the Finnish film industry headed into a crisis by the end of the 1950s. Secondly, Finnish films benefited from the international fame of other Nordic films, after Sweden had gained international success in film festivals in the early 1950s.

As Finnish films were mainly targeted at the domestic audience, the 'Nordic card' was not a very notable feature in Finnish film production. In some cases, however, producers combined domestic marketability with Scandinavian interests, as they chose topics that were supposedly appealing to Nordic audiences or made dual-language versions. Swedish–Finnish film versions were relatively easy to produce, as Finland is a bilingual country with Swedish as a second official language.

The young director-producer Teuvo Tulio (born Theodor Tugai, 1912–2000) employed these strategies in some of his productions, but the larger film companies such as Suomen Filmiteollisuus and Fenno-Filmi also resorted to them. Tulio got the idea of making dual-language films after working as an actor in George Schnéevoigt's multilingual film *Fredlös* (1935).[43] Tulio wanted to broaden the market for his films by making both Swedish and Finnish versions and by exporting Swedish versions to Sweden or to other Nordic countries. His production model followed the example of multilanguage productions in other European countries: the two versions were made in immediate succession, bilingual actors were used or some of the Finnish-speaking actors were replaced by Swedish-speaking or Swedish actors, and Finnish versions were then distributed in Finland and Swedish versions mainly in Sweden.[44] Some Swedish versions also premiered in bilingual regions in Finland.[45]

Tulio's first dual-language film was an adaptation of a famous novel by F.E. Sillanpää, *The Maid Silja/ Nuorena nukkunut* (1931), which premiered in Finland in 1937 and in Sweden in 1938. The most intensive period for dual-language versions, however, was after the war. In the late 1940s, Tulio made five dual-language versions,[46] and Suomen Filmiteollisuus and Fenno-Filmi produced one dual-language version each: *The Tracks of Sin* (*Synnin jäljet/Farligt lättsinne*, Hannu Leminen, 1946), *The Northern Express* (*Pikajuna pohjoiseen/Tåg norrut*, Roland af Hällström and Palle Hagmann, 1947).[47] Because a foreign language was no longer an issue at that time—Swedish audiences were used to reading subtitles—it is probable that Finnish filmmakers wanted not only to expand the market with dual-language versions but to use scant resources cost-effectively. For example, according to one article, Tulio made the Swedish version of *In the Grip of Passion* (*Intohimon vallassa/Olof-forsfararen*, 1947) in order to be able to exchange it for raw film.[48] Presumably it was also easier to market a film if it did not need subtitles, at least if the film originated from a minor film producing country.

Various kinds of Finnish films, from historical dramas and romances to peasant melodramas and comedies, were exported to Sweden and other Scandinavian countries. If, however, Scandinavian distribution was planned during a pre-production phase, Finnish filmmakers typically chose topics that were familiar to audiences in other Nordic countries, and thus more marketable. According to Tulio's memoirs, he calculated that a topic based on a novel by F.E. Sillanpää, who had been a candidate for a Nobel prize in literature from the beginning of the 1930s, would appeal to Swedish audiences.[49] Similarly, he filmed Johannes Linnankoski's famous novel *The Song of the Scarlet Flower* (*Laulu tulipunaisesta kukasta/Sången om den eldröda blomman*, 1938) and a Finnish version of a folk play by the Swedish author Henning Ohlsson, *In the Fields of Dreams* (*Unelma karjamajalla/Hälsingar*, 1940). Both films were distributed in Sweden.

Suomen Filmiteollisuus used a similar strategy. In 1943 the company promoted its Nordic trend—that is, its plan to make films from Swedish scripts or topics—in the Swedish trade magazine *Biografbladet*.[50] An adaptation of a novel by the esteemed Selma Lagerlöf, *The Girl from the Marsh Croft* (*Suotorpan tyttö/Tösen från Stormyrtorpet*, Toivo Särkkä 1940), and another adaptation of a Swedish novel by Gunnar Widegren, *Puck* (Hannu Leminen 1942), were mentioned as examples of this trend. Both films also premiered in Stockholm. As late as 1956, Suomen Filmiteollisuus filmed a dual-language version of a novel by the Finnish author Juhani Aho, *Juha* (*Kärlek i ödemarken*, Toivo Särkkä, 1956). This film was a prestige production, the company's first widescreen film in colour.[51]

Andrew Higson and Richard Maltby have suggested that European film culture in the 1920s and 1930s can be comprehended as a series of strands.[52] 'The Americanized metropolitan popular culture' and films based on high culture formed two strands of production that more easily traversed national borders than the strand that relied on provincial or national cultures. Although the strands overlapped, according to Higson and Maltby a clear distinction is observable between the more metropolitan and the provincial strands.[53] In terms of Nordic film culture(s) during the 1930s–1950s, Scandinavian distribution of Finnish films indicates the existence of a regional Nordic film culture of some kind, which easily absorbed more parochial films.[54] When Finnish film producers wanted to make a film especially for Scandinavian markets, they turned to esteemed Nordic literature. It is interesting, however, that the adaptations of *The Song of the Scarlet Flower*, *In the Fields of Dreams*, *The Girl from the Marsh Croft* and *Juha* did not only rest on the literary heritage, but also on the Swedish cinematic tradition. *The Song of the Scarlet Flower* and *In the Fields of Dreams* had already been filmed twice in Sweden: the former in 1919 and 1934, the latter in 1924 and 1933.[55] *The Girl from the Marsh Croft* and *Juha* were also remakes. The first of these adaptations dated from the 'golden era' of Swedish cinema: *The Girl from the Marsh Croft* was directed by Victor Sjöström in 1917, and *Juha* by Mauriz Stiller in 1921.

Stiller also directed the first adaptation of *The Song of the Scarlet Flower*. This recycling of famous cinematic motifs further indicates that a certain idea of Nordic film culture existed at least in Finland, as the Swedish film canon (partly based on Finnish literature) was understood as a shared tradition that appealed to both domestic and Scandinavian audiences.

After the Second World War, the fame of the Swedish cinema once again helped the export of Finnish films. The Swedish *One Summer of Happiness* (*Hon dansade en sommar*, Arne Mattson, 1951) won the Golden Bear at the 1952 Berlinale, and the international success of the film made Swedish cinema famous, along with an image of liberal portrayals of Nordic nature, eroticism and nudity.[56] The image was extrapolated to Nordic cinema in general, which the Finnish film industry was happy to exploit, as Olavi Linnus under the pseudonym Olaus noted in an editorial in *Elokuva-Aitta* in 1955: 'Scandinavian film is famous, Swedes have undertaken valuable work in that respect, which now turns out to be a benefit even for us as we are counted among the Scandinavian countries.'[57]

Nude scenes were not uncommon in Finnish films before the 1950s, but 'daring' scenes—those with erotic love or nudity—became prominent in some films made in the 1950s and the early 1960s. Such films as *The Witch* (*Noita palaa elämään*, Roland af Hällstöm, 1952), *The Milkmaid* (*Hilja maitotyttö*, Toivo Särkkä, 1953), *The Bridal Wreath* (*Morsiusseppele*, Hannu Leminen, 1954), *Blue Week* (*Sininen viikko*, Matti Kassila 1954) and *Preludes to Ecstasy* (*Kuu on vaarallinen*, Toivo Särkkä, 1961) received relatively wide distribution abroad, and they even reached the difficult US market (Fig. 7.2).[58]

Thus, 'Nordic eroticism' partly substituted for the lack of big, internationally marketable names, which caused problems for the export efforts of the Finnish film industry.[59] It could function quite effectively as an attraction for international markets. In addition, it could, in turn, create international fame for Finnish filmmakers and actors, as the case of Anneli Sauli (1932–) demonstrates.[60] Sauli, the actor in the title role in *The Milkmaid*, also had the chance to work in West Germany in the early 1960s. After that, her international fame was exploited in *A Report* (*Raportti eli balladi laivatytöistä*, Maunu Kurkvaara, 1964), a sensational story of prostitution taking place in a harbour. As the independent producer-director of the film, Maunu Kurkvaara (1926–), calculated, the appeal of the star Anneli Sauli together with its daring topic made the film exportable, at least to West Germany.[61]

Fig. 7.4 'Nordic eroticism'—that is, nudity and beautiful nature scenes—was exploited in *The Milkmaid* (1953), earning the film an exceptionally wide distribution abroad

NICHE MARKETS FOR FINNISH-LANGUAGE FILMS

During the studio era, the Nordic countries formed a potential distribution area for Finnish films, but the most reliable markets were in the northern USA and Canada among Finnish emigrants and in northern Sweden, particularly in the area where people spoke the so-called *meänkieli*, 'our language', a dialect based on Finnish. These niche markets were based on audiences that had close connections to Finnish culture and/or the Finnish language. Although the coming of sound typically created obstacles for film export,[62] sound film enhanced the export of Finnish films to these Finnish-speaking areas. Finnish emigrants and Finnish-speaking minorities wanted to hear their mother tongue.[63]

The distribution of Finnish films in northern Sweden was at its height in the 1940s and 1950s. Although there was no actual shortage of films in Swedish cinemas during the war years, the war naturally impeded imports.[64] Finnish films offered convenient padding to the repertoire, as transportation was easier to arrange from a neighbouring country. Although Swedish cinema executives in the major companies, such as Svensk Filmindustri, had rather critical attitudes towards Finnish films and their quality, it seems that Finnish films were considered suitable for the countryside.[65] As a result, the offerings of Finnish films in northern Sweden created a demand for Finnish-language films that continued into the late 1950s. A reason for the popularity of these films in the region might have been the strict language policy in Sweden at that time. This restricted the use of *meänkieli* in public,[66] but screenings of Finnish films offered a public space where the Finnish language was accepted and enjoyed. This could have been an entertaining and even empowering experience for the audience speaking *meänkieli*.

In any case, Swedish distributors in particular looked for Finnish films for cinemas in northern Sweden. For instance, the Swedish film company Nordisk Tonefilm contacted its Finnish business partner Allotria Filmi in 1956 and asked for 'suitable' Finnish films to replace other, already 'used' ones.[67] Finnish films could circulate for considerably longer in small northern cinemas, as the case of *Lovisa, the Young Mistress of Niskavuori* (*Loviisa—Niskavuoren nuori emäntä*, Valentin Vaala, 1946) illustrates: it toured in northern Sweden over 6 years from 1947 to 1954.[68] This indicates that the deals were cost-effective for both the Finnish producers and the Swedish distributors, as film copies could be used for as long as possible and they could provide small but continuous revenues.[69]

The number of premieres of Finnish films in northern Sweden decreased during the 1960s. There might have been fewer films thought to be 'suitable' for the market, as production of Finnish films declined towards the end of the 1950s. In addition, television had started to take its place as a popular form of entertainment.

The American niche market had a longer history than the Swedish one. Already in the 1920s Finnish immigrant businesspeople had imported films into the USA and Canada from their old home country.[70] The late 1930s and the beginning of the 1940s, however, were a heyday of Finnish films among the Finnish settlement in North America (in the USA, particularly in Massachusetts, New York, Michigan and Minnesota, and in Canada, in Toronto). At that time Finnish-American businesspeople showed a growing interest in Finnish films.[71] There were certainly more new films produced, but, importantly, they were Finnish sound films. This offered lucrative business opportunities for addressing the Finnish-speaking cinema audiences in the USA and in Canada. Moreover, Finnish sound films seemed a good way to sustain the Finnish culture and maintain language skills, which made even Finnish officials interested in supporting the export of Finnish films to North America.[72]

Because the US market was dominated by its own domestic film industry, it was not easy to find screen time for films that were especially targeted at immigrant communities such as Finnish-Americans. For instance, the Finnish-American businessman Carl H. Salminen aggressively promoted his first import *As Dream and Shadow* (*Kuin uni ja varjo*, Toivo Särkkä and Yrjö Norta, 1937) in his own Finnish-American newspaper, *Päivälehti*.[73] In an article it was suggested that the Finnish-speaking audience should appeal to cinema owners to screen the film in their local cinemas.[74] The campaign was successful, and Salminen started to import Finnish films in his capacity as a representative for Suomen Filmiteollisuus.[75]

Other Finnish companies exported their films as well, among others Suomi-Filmi, which had its own representatives in North America.[76] Hence, the competition between the major film production companies extended to a new continent.[77] The active export of newly made films indicates that there was also room for this kind of competition in the niche market—after a laborious start. Even films from the minor producers interested distributors in North America.[78] Finnish films were part of an active diasporic culture that at the time offered a wide array of Finnish-speaking entertainment, such as amateur theatre.[79] Films were shown in cinemas, in the special halls of Finnish-American societies and in roadshows in Finnish-speaking areas.[80] Although some films had English subtitles,[81] it is unlikely that the films circulated outside the Finnish-American cultural sphere. However, Nordic immigrant communities might have had a mutual interest in each other's film cultures; at least, Swedish-speaking Finnish-Americans might have enjoyed imported Swedish films.[82]

The Second World War impeded distribution to North America. The number of screenings decreased notably, but the war did not entirely eradicate them. According to advertisements in Finnish-American newspapers, previously imported films circulated in the halls throughout wartime.[83] This illustrates the importance of cultural connections to the old homeland, and the central role that Finnish films had in sustaining them: the films were shown despite the fact that Finland was the ally of the enemy, Nazi Germany.

After the war, imports recommenced. The first 'new' films arrived towards the end of 1945, and in the cinema season 1946–1947 there were premieres of *The Vagabond's Waltz* (*Kulkurin valssi*, Toivo Särkkä, 1941) and *White Roses* (*Valkoiset ruusut*, Hannu Leminen, 1943), the hit films of the early 1940s in Finland.[84] However, just like films imported from Sweden,[85] Finnish films had increasing difficulty finding screen time in local cinemas and they were usually shown in the halls of Finnish organizations that had no proper theatre equipment.[86] The Finnish-American community changed gradually, and one might assume that younger generations were too integrated into American popular culture to be interested in Finnish films made with poorer resources. Hence, there was less demand for Finnish films. Nevertheless, a small niche market for Finnish films in North America existed as long as there were diasporic communities trying to maintain connections with the Finnish language and the old home country.[87]

Generally, many films exported to the niche markets belong to the third strand defined by Higson and Maltby; that is, to the group of provincial films, which Jean-Pierre Jeancolas has called 'inexportable'.[88] Comedies, based on popular plays, and historical films included features that particularly attracted Finnish emigrants and language groups. According to the Finnish-Canadian businessman Lasse Sjöström, who owned a travelling cinema, Finnish immigrants in Canada in the 1950s wanted to see Finnish landscapes and traditional romantic stories.[89] In other words, they wanted to see nostalgic and romantic portrayals of Finland.[90] Yet, if one considers both the North American and the northern Swedish market, the audiences appeared rather omnivorous: in addition to light comedies or musicals, the repertoire included esteemed dramas and literary adaptations. Thus, it seems that Finnish emigrants and minorities had an interestingly diverse film culture, which ought to be studied in greater detail.

ORGANIZING EXPORTS

The foreign distribution activities of the Finnish film industry were not very well organized or specialized. Even the major film companies, Suomi-Filmi, Suomen Filmiteollisuus and Fennada Filmi, were small agents with scarce resources compared to the film companies in major film producing countries. Hence, specialization and differentiation in their organizations were fairly primitive, and many actions depended on managers or chief executive officers (CEOs).[91] This also affected exports. There were no specialized export units, until Suomen Filmiteollisuus founded one in 1954.[92] As the main markets were considered to be domestic ones, efforts to export Finnish films seem to have been rather sporadic and dependent on favourable circumstances.[93]

Manager-led export activities were typical for both major and minor production companies. During their business trips abroad, the managers of Suomi-Filmi promoted their films in person. In the spring of 1937, chief director Risto Orko (1899–2001), CEO Matti Schreck and manager

Nils Dahlström (1907–1978) made an extensive tour in Central Europe in order to acquire foreign films for Suomi-Filmi's cinemas in Finland and to promote their own production, *The Logger's Bride* (*Koskenlaskijan morsian*, Valentin Vaala, 1937).[94] Small producers, such as Erik Blomberg (1913–1996) or Teuvo Tulio, also promoted their films by themselves using their personal contacts.[95] In practice, the major film companies typically handled their own export activities, but minor producers might also rely on the expertise of distribution companies.[96]

In 1954, Suomen Filmiteollisuus founded an export unit and hired the writer and all-round film expert Olavi Linnus (1914–2000) to lead it.[97] The new emphasis on international promotion demonstrates that foreign distribution was now thought of as an essential part of the business. The investment seems to have been worthwhile, since Suomen Filmiteollisuus's distribution increased to countries that had not been previously targeted: Yugoslavia, West Germany, the German Democratic Republic and certain South American countries. Although the marketing might have become more efficient, it did not necessarily signify the end of the old, slightly disorganized modes of operation.[98] Personal contacts and manager-led activities were still important. For example, CEO Toivo Särkkä (1890–1975) continued to do promotion work by himself.[99]

For companies and filmmakers of a minor film producing country, it was challenging to control the distribution of films. Not only was it difficult to guarantee that a distributor could get screen time for Finnish films, as the experiences of Finnish-American distributors illustrate, but Finnish agents had to rely on business partners who did not always prove to be trustworthy.[100] For instance, Teuvo Tulio explained in his memoirs how a German distributor resold Tulio's film to another company, which distributed the film around the world without Tulio knowing anything about it nor getting any revenues from it.[101]

Hence, the Finnish film industry depended on international agents and the circumstances of the international film culture. In some cases, the circumstances were favourable. In 1930, Paramount established an affiliate, Ab Paramount Oy, in Finland, which was to be part of Paramount's Nordic activities.[102] At the end of the decade, Suomi-Filmi intensified its cooperation with Paramount, which exported five of Suomi-Filmi's new productions to Sweden.[103] In addition, Paramount distributed in Sweden Tulio's *Song of the Scarlet Flower* (premiered in Sweden in 1939) and *The Way You Wanted Me* (*Sellaisena kuin sinä minut halusit/ Vägen utför*, 1944, premiered in Sweden in 1945).[104] This was an obvious win–win situation: Finnish filmmakers got an opportunity to distribute their films with the help of Paramount's marketing power; Paramount, in line with its European policy, could get a hold on the seemingly growing Nordic market.[105] During the 1940s, Paramount's interest in Finnish exports faded, and it seems that it did not distribute any Finnish films after *The Way You Wanted Me*, at least in Sweden.[106]

Increasing international networking in the film industry, particularly international film festivals, enhanced the export of Finnish films in the 1950s. The success of *The White Reindeer* (*Valkoinen peura*, Erik Blomberg, 1952) at Cannes in 1953 and Karlovy Vary in 1954 probably encouraged the major film companies to participate actively in festivals, such as at Berlin, Karlovy Vary, Cannes, Locarno, Venice, Moscow, Mar de Plata and Punta del Este. The festivals offered visibility and created opportunities to sell films, thus expanding the potential market area. Successful festival films were sold not only to European countries but also to the Americas.[107] Participation in the festivals of Punta del Este in Uruguay and Mar De Plata in Argentina enabled the distribution of Finnish films in South America.[108] In the 1950s, international film festivals became an increasingly significant route to international markets for Finnish film companies and their films. The vicissitudes of these efforts will be examined in Chapter 15.

NOTES

1. Hjort and Petrie 2007a.
2. Finnish National Filmography 1: passim.
3. Hupaniittu 2013: 113, 129.
4. See Appendix, Fig. A.1.
5. Board meeting 21/5/1937; Annual report 1937, attachment to Company meeting 23/3/1937, SuFiA, NAI.
6. See Seppälä 2012: 152–153, 344–348.
7. Also Laine 1999: 43–45; about film nationalism Andrew 2010: 65.
8. "Koskenlaskijan morsiamella suurenmoinen menestys Skandinaviassa", Suomi-Filmin Uutisaitta 10/1937: 5; "Suomalaisen filmin vientimahdollisuudet rajoitetut", *Helsingin Sanomat* 16/8/1937; "SF-elokuvia ulkomailla", *Suomen Kinolehti* 4/1938; "Suomalainen filmi pohjoismaissa" (editorial), Suomi-Filmin Uutisaitta 5–6/1940: 3, 10. "Ulkomaille" (editorial), *Suomen Kinolehti* 6–7/1938.
9. "Ulkomaille", *Suomen Kinolehti* 6–7/1938.
10. "Suomalaisen filmin vientimahdollisuudet rajoitetut", *Helsingin Sanomat* 16/8/1937; "Suomalaisen elokuvan vientimahdollisuudet", *Suomen Kinolehti* 9/1937: 319.

11. K.E.P.H.: "Koti- ja ulkomaiset elokuvat", *Elokuvateatteri* 9/1942: 4; H. Soldan: "Yleisö ja tuotanto", *Elokuvateatteri* 10/1943: 12; K.E.P.H.: "Kotimainen elokuva tarvitsee suuremman katsojakunnan", *Elokuvateatteri-Suomen Kinolehti* 7/1947: 1–2.

12. H. Soldan: "Yleisö ja tuotanto", *Elokuvateatteri* 10/1943: 12.

13. Helge Miettunen: "Elokuvamme puuttuminen maailmankulttuurista", *Kinolehti* 2/1962: 4–5.

14. Ibid.; also Helge Miettunen: "Elokuvapolitiikan ongelmia", *Kinolehti* 1960/6: 5; "Repliikkejä liian paljon suomalaisessa elokuvassa", *Ilta-Sanomat*, 11/12/1947.

15. K.E.P.H.: "Kotimainen elokuva tarvitsee suuremman katsojakunnan", *Elokuvateatteri-Suomen Kinolehti* 7/1947: 1–2.

16. "Kotimainen filmiteollisuus ponnistelee yhä vaikeuksissa", *Kaleva*, 18/2/1955; Maire Haahti: "Elokuvatuottajat ja suomalainen elokuva", *Kinolehti* 5/1956: 7.

17. Olaus [Olavi Linnus]: "Suomalaiset elokuvat ulkomailla". *Elokuva-Aitta* 1/1955: 3; Kyllikki Markkanen: "Suomalainen elokuva Kanadassa", *Elokuva-Aitta* 6/1958: 25.

18. "Suomalainen elokuva Amerikassa", *Kinolehti* 3/1956: 22; Jaakko Tervasmäki: "Meiltäkin viedään elokuvia", *Elokuva-Aitta* 4/1958: 31; "Suomalainen elokuva saa menekkiä ulkomailla", *Kinolehti* 1/1955; 7.

19. It is probable that profits were not substantial, with the exception of the case of *Tuntematon sotilas* (*Unknown Soldier*, Edwin Laine, 1955), which was an unprecedented international success (Linnus: "T.J.S.", *Turun Sanomat*, 7/4/1991).

20. Many individual films are counted in the figures several times, as they were exported to various countries. The figures also include documentaries that were of feature length (at least 60 minutes). The international co-productions are excluded from the figures, because their distribution formed a special case.

21. The years in the table indicate primarily the date of a premiere of a film in the target country or, if this is not known, the year of sale. If neither was available, the film has been added to the estimate according to its production year. In some cases, it was quite possible that a film was sold to an international distributor but was never screened.

22. "Jugoslavia ostaa elokuvia Suomesta", *Helsingin Sanomat* 12/1/1955.

23. K.E.P.H.: "Kotimainen elokuva tarvitsee suuremman katsojakunnan", *Elokuvateatteri-Suomen Kinolehti* 7/1947: 1–2; Maire Haahti: "Elokuvatuottajat ja suomalainen elokuva", *Kinolehti* 5/1956: 8; Helge Miettunen: "Elokuvapolitiikan ongelmia", *Kinolehti* 1960/6: 3.

24. Guback 1969: 19–20, 22, 23, 24–25; Nowell-Smith 1998: 7.

25. Hupaniittu 2013: 246, 449; Lehtisalo 2013.

26. Andrew 2010: 69–74.
27. De Grazia 1998: 23–24.
28. De Grazia 1998: 24–25; Rep. (pseudonym): "Elokuvan johtoasema takaisin Euroopalle", *Seura* 21/1942: 12–13.
29. Jokisipilä and Könönen 2013: 39–41.
30. Sedergren 1999: 206–207.
31. The situation, however, affected the screening of American films in Finland; see Chap. 17, Fig. 17.3.
32. De Grazia 1998: 24–25; "Parikymmentä kotimaista elokuvaa valmistuu tänä näytäntövuonna", *Aamulehti*, 8/11/1942.
33. "Lähes 50 suomalaista filmiä vietiin viime vuonna ulkomaille", *Aamulehti* 17/1/1944; "Filmitoiminta Saksassa vilkasta", *Suomen Sosialidemokraatti* 20/10/1942; "Suomalaisia elokuvia myyty Unkariin, Bulgariaan ja Kroatiaan", *Aamulehti* 18/4/1942; Olavi Linnus: "Euroopan ovet avautuvat suomalaiselle elokuvalle", *Kuva* 12/1942: 29; Ernst Jerosch: "Suomalaista ulkomailla", *Suomi-Filmin Uutisaitta* 8/1944: 24–25; "Studiossa sattuu", *Suomi-Filmin Uutisaitta* 4/1944; "Suuresta filmimaailmasta", *Suomi-Filmin Uutisaitta* 5–6/1944; "Aktivisti esitetty Kroatiassa", *Uusi Suomi*, 7/11/1942; Suomen Filmiteollisuus and Suomi Filmi, Ff:18, 33, 43–44, 54, 70–71 Export licences 1941–1944, LCA, FBR.
34. "Suomalaiset filmit päässeet taas Balkanille", *Elokuvateatteri—Suomen Kinolehti*, 6/1947: 26; Polaris Film, Ff:143 Export licences 1947, LCA, FBR.
35. Sedergren 1999: 200–202, 252, 259.
36. Mauno Mäkelä's speech at the 1964 Finnish-Soviet film week, act 20/11/1964, 46S Filmit/Suomi, FMA; "Suomalainen elokuvaviikko Neuvostoliitossa", Kinolehti 8/1956: 6–7.
37. "Suomalainen elokuvaviikko Neuvostoliitossa", Kinolehti 8/1956: 6.
38. Uusitalo 1998b, 207.
39. Ibid.; "Niskavuoren naiset", *Kansan Uutiset*, 13/11/1959.
40. Antti Karppinen (FM) to the Embassy in Moscow 23/10 and 20/11/1964, S46 Filmit/Suomi, FMA.
41. E.g. Jalonen 1985: 145–147, 168–169.
42. E.g. "'Loviisasta' NLssa 700 kopiota", *Uusi Päivä*, 3/6/1958.
43. Teuvo Tulio: "Teuvo Tulio. Suomalaisen elokuvan yksinäinen susi", part 6, *Jaana* 9/1974: 86.
44. Tulio: "Teuvo Tulio. Suomalaisen elokuvan yksinäinen susi", part 13, *Jaana* 17/1974: 84, 88; Tulio: "Teuvo Tulio. Suomalaisen elokuvan yksinäinen susi", part 14, *Jaana* 18/1974: 83; Feature films in Sweden 1950–1959: passim; Feature films in Sweden 1940–1949: passim; see Vincendeau 1999: 208–209.
45. Films *Sådan du ville ha mig*, *Kärlekens kors*, *Orolig blod*, Database Elonet.

46. The films *Sellaisena kuin sinä minut halusit/Vägen utför* (*The Way You Wanted Me*, 1944), *Rakkauden risti/Kärlekens kors* (*Cross of Love*, 1946), *Levoton veri/Orolig/Blod* ('Restless Blood', 1946), *Intohimon vallassa/Olof/forsfararen* In the Grip of Passion (1947), *Hornankoski/Forsfararnas kvinna* The Rapids of Hell (Teuvo Tulio and Roland af Hällström, 1949). All in all, Tulio made 16 fiction films, of which seven were dual-language versions.

47. Fenno-Filmi's film was a co-production together with a minor film company, Ab Color-Film Oy, the owner of which, Palle Hagmann, directed a Swedish version. Fenno-Filmi had already made one/dual-language co-production, *Matkalla seikkailuun/Biljett till äventyret* On the Way to Adventure (Yrjö Norta and Gösta Rodin, 1945) with Swedish production company Hamberg Studio.

48. Markku Tuuli et. al.: "Tulio esittää: Mustasukkaisuutta, intohimoja ja synnin hekumaa." *Katso* 10/1973: 15; see also Tulio, Ff:93 Export licences 1945, LCA, FBR.

49. Tulio: "Suomalaisen elokuvan yksinäinen susi", part 6, *Jaana* 9/1974: 86.

50. Olavi Tommila: "Finska filmen arbetar i nordisk anda", *Biografbladet* 2/1943: 8.

51. "Juha laajakankaalla", *Aikamme* 8/1956: 20–22. The anamorphic technique was borrowed from Sweden (Uusitalo, 1998).

52. Higson and Maltby 1999: 20.

53. Ibid.

54. Cf. Soila, Söderbergh Widding and Iversen 1998: 235–236.

55. About the versions of *The Song of the Scarlet Flower*, see Soila 1994.

56. Larsson 2010: 216; Furhammar 1991: 216.

57. Olaus [Olavi Linnus]: "Suomalaiset elokuvat ulkomailla". *Elokuva-Aitta*, 1/1955: 3.

58. "Münchenin varhaiskevättä", *Satakunnan Kansa*, 1/6/1963; "Mirja Mane saanut kutsun Hollywoodiin", *Helsingin Sanomat*, 19/1/1954; "Kotimainen filmiteollisuus ponnistelee yhä vaikeuksissa", *Kaleva*, 18/2/1955; Warren M. Geoffrey: "The Milkmaid Very Poorly Made Picture", *Los Angeles Times*, 13/6/1958; Reino Aarva (Embassy in Bern) to FM on the exhibition of *The Bridal Wreath*, 20/1/1961, 19G Filmit, FMA; "Suomalaisia filmejä ulkomaille", *Jyväskylän Sanomat*, 12/1/1955; "First Finnish Features for Britain", *Kinematograph Weekly*, 5/5/1955; "'Kuu' myyty 30 maahan", *Uudenmaan Sanomat*, 17/1/1963.

59. "Suomalainen elokuva Amerikassa", *Kinolehti*, 3/1956: 22; Tervasmäki: "Meiltäkin viedään elokuvia", *Elokuva-Aitta* 4/1958: 31.

60. E.g. "Suomalainen elokuva saa menekkiä ulkomailla", *Kinolehti*, 1/1955: 7.

61. Interview with Maunu Kurkvaara, 19/3/2013.

62. E.g. Garncarz 1999: 251.

63. E.g. Nygård 1997: 89–90.

64. Furhammar 1991: 163–164.
65. Inspection 12/10/1937, ...*och under låg en brinnande sjön* and Inspection 10/12/1940, *Guds storm*, Film inspections 8000-8399 and 9200-9599, SFC, SFI.
66. E.g. Andersson and Kangassalo 2003: 108, 122.
67. Gösta Hammarbäck to Allotria Film 12/4/1956, 2294/E/2/17 Foreign correspondence, NTA, ARBARK.
68. Revenues from *Lovisa*, Swedish films 127, Film incomes 225, WFC, SFI.
69. Also Hammarbäck to Allotria Film 12/4/1956, 2294/E/2/17 Foreign correspondence, NTA, ARBARK.
70. Nygård 1997: 23, 27, 29.
71. Nygård 1997: 55; Ilmari Kääriäinen (Consulate in New York) to FM 26/2/1937, 19G Filmit, FMA.
72. Kääriäinen (Consulate in New York) to FM 26/2/1937, 19G Filmit, FMA.
73. "Kuin Uni ja Varjo" (advertisement), *Päivälehti*, 10/3/1938; "Ester Toivonen...", *Päivälehti*, 19/3/1938; "'Kuin Uni ja Varjo' Vista teatterissa" (advertisement), *Päivälehti*, 13/4/1938; "'Kuin Uni ja Varjo' -filmillä Suuremmoinen Menestys", *Päivälehti*, 19/4/1938.
74. "Kuin uni ja varjo", *Päivälehti*, 25/3/1938.
75. E.g. "Nummisuutarit Ironwoodissa!" (advertisement), *Päivälehti*, 20/1/1940.
76. Nygård 1997: 56–60.
77. The Finnish-American distributors were, however, not entirely loyal to their Finnish companies, since they could exhange imported films with their colleagues (see Nygård 1997: 63–64).
78. E.g., Do the Work and Learn to Play/*Tee työ ja opi pelaamaan* (Kalle Kaarna, 1936), a film by small film company Elokuvatuontanto Oy, was exported to the USA.
79. Kero 1997: passim.
80. Nygård 1997: 75, 80.
81. E.g. "Kuin Uni ja Varjo" (advertisement), *Päivälehti*, 26/3/1938.
82. Nygård 1997: 40–45; about Swedish film culture in the USA, see Wallengren 2013.
83. E.g. "Heimo Haitto kuvassa 'Pikku pelimanni'" (advertisement), *New Yorkin Uutiset*, 12/9/1942; "Alekisi Kiven kuolematon huvinäytelmä valkokankaalla 'Nummisuutarit'" (advertisement), *New Yorkin Uutiset*, 2/3/1943, "Myyjäiset Työveäentalon rahaston hyväksi: 'Tulitikkuja lainaamassa'" (advertisement), 30/11/1944; "Rykmentin Murheenkryyni Lyric teatterissa" (advertisement), *Raivaaja* 20/3/1945; "Työväentalossa: 'Helmikuun manifesti'" (advertisement), Raivaaja 28/5/1945.
84. E.g. "O.Y. Suomen Filmiteollisuus (SF) esittää Kulkurin valssin" (advertisement), *New Yorkin Uutiset* 13/8/1946; "O.Y. Suomen Filmiteollisuus (SF) esittää äänielokuvan 'Valkoiset ruusut'" (advertisement), *New Yorkin Uutiset* 17/9/1946.

85. Wallengren 2013: 106.
86. H. Ramo: "Suomalaiset elokuvat", *New Yorkin Uutiset*, 10/12/1954; "Suomalainen elokuva Amerikassa", *Kinolehti* 3/1956: 22.
87. Sundström 1998; see Iordanova 2010: 33.
88. Higson and Maltby 1999: 20; Jeancolas 1995: 141.
89. Kyllikki Markkanen: "Suomalainen elokuva Kanadassa", *Elokuva-Aitta*, 6/1958: 25–26.
90. See Wallengren 2013: 104, 125, 131; Jeancolas 1995:142.
91. About the Finnish studio system, see Laine 1999: 128–132.
92. As Suomi-Filmi actively imported foreign films, it may be that its import unit also dealt with exports.
93. Also Olaus [Olavi Linnus]: "Suomalaiset elokuvat ulkomailla", *Elokuva-Aitta*, 1/1955: 3.
94. Board Meetings 21/5/1937, SuFiA, NAI; see also Inspection 17/11/1936, V.M.V.6, Film inspections 7200-7599, SFC, SFI.
95. Inspection 10/12/1940, *Guds storm*, Film inspections 8000-8399 and 9200-9599, SFC, SFI; Tulio: "Teuvo Tulio. Suomalaisen elokuvan yksinäinen susi", part 14, Jaana 18/1974: 85–87.
96. E.g. Suomen Filmiteollisuus, Suomi Filmi and Polaris Film, Ff: 18, 33, 43–44, 54, 70–71, 91, 120, 143, 149, Export licences 1939–1947, LCA, FBR.
97. Olavi Linnus (Suomen Filmiteollisuus) to Gösta Hammarbäck 18/2/1954, 2294/E/2/11 Foreign correspondence, NTA, ARBARK.
98. About the distribution problems with Nordisk Tonefilm, see letters 1–14/10/1955, 12/4/1956, 2294/E/2/14, 2294/E/2/17 Foreign correspondence, NTA, ARBARK.
99. E.g. I. L-s: "Kuu on vaarallinen", *Suomen Sosialidemokraatti* 18/10/1962.
100. Jorma Laukkanen (Suomi-Filmi) to Judical section in FM 28/5/1957, 19G Filmit, FMA.
101. Tulio: "Teuvo Tulio. Suomalaisen elokuvan yksinäinen susi", part 14, *Jaana* 18/1974: 85–86.
102. "Paramount Suomessa täyttää 20 vuotta", *Elokuvateatteri—Suomen Kinolehti*, 4/1950: 26.
103. Board meeting, 21/5/1937, SuFiA, NAI; Feature films in Sweden 1930–1939: passim; Feature films in Sweden 1940–1949: passim.
104. Teuvo Tulio was friends with Carl P. York, CEO of Paramount's Scandinavian unit (Tulio: "Teuvo Tulio. Suomalaisen elokuvan yksinäinen susi", part 14, *Jaana* 18/1974: 86–87.).
105. About Paramount's policy, see Higson and Maltby 1999: 10–11.
106. Feature films in Sweden 1940–1949; Feature films in Sweden 1950–1959.
107. E.g. "'Valkoinen peura' Suomen symbolina tämän hetken Cannesissa", *Uusi Suomi*, 25/4/1953; "'Nukkekauppias' myyty USA:han ja Kanadaan", *Uusi Suomi*, 15/3/1955; "'Tuntemattoman' voittokulku", *Vapaa Sana*,

28/7/1956; Risto Hannula: "'Ryysyrannan Jooseppi' ja 'Elokuu' Lyypekin pohjoismaisilla filmipäivillä", *Kinolehti*, 4/1959: 16.

108. E.g. "Pelicula finlandesa al festival", *Accion*, 8/12/1954; Leikkaaja (pseudonym): "Filmipaloja", *Suomen Sosialidemokraatti* s.d. 1955, Scrapbook no. 81, SFA, NAI; P. (pseudonym): "Nina, Erik ja Särkkä lentävät Argentiinaan", *Helsingin Sanomat*, 10/2/1960.

PART III

New Waves: 1960–1980

CHAPTER 8

Trade and Diplomacy Between East and West

Henry Bacon

The election of Urho Kekkonen as the President of Finland in 1956 consolidated the country's political position between East and West. He emerged from the Agrarian Leagues (the Centre Party after 1965), but he succeeded in getting across an image of himself as the only political leader able to maintain favourable relationships with the socialist Soviet Union (USSR). His presidency lasted for 26 years, for the most part through democratic procedures: four times by elections and once by the enacting of an emergency law. Although Finland had to respect the Treaty of Friendship, Cooperation and Mutual Assistance with the USSR, it was also able to maintain political, commercial and cultural relationships with Western countries and to proclaim its neutrality in global political affairs. In many ways things worked out remarkably well. Finland was the only country with a major land border with the USSR (1340 km) that was able to maintain fully working democratic institutions, despite a degree of stagnation and political manoeuvring in certain aspects of the country's foreign relationships. Finland gained prestige as a mediator between East and West, a balancing act that culminated in its hosting of the Conference on Security and Co-operation in Europe in 1975.

H. Bacon (✉)
Film and Television Studies, University of Helsinki,
Helsinki, Finland
e-mail: henry.bacon@helsinki.fi

© The Editor(s) (if applicable) and The Author(s) 2016   141
H. Bacon (ed.), *Finnish Cinema*, Palgrave European Film
and Media Studies, DOI 10.1057/978-1-137-57651-4_8

Economically Finland benefited enormously from its bilateral trade with the USSR, which provided it with both access to raw materials and a huge market for the goods it produced. By the 1980s about one-quarter of Finland's foreign trade was with the USSR. At the same time, trade relationships with the West were developed, and in 1962 Finland became an associate member of the European Free Trade Association (EFTA), thus beginning the nation's participation in European economic integration. In 1973 Finland made a free trade agreement with the European Economic Community (EEC, the present European Union), which caused fierce ideological debate as it consolidated the country's economic ties with the capitalist West. Almost throughout this period economic growth was steady, and Finland was transformed from a primarily agrarian country to a modern industrial state with an ever larger urban population.

Political and ideological tensions were felt very strongly both in the sphere of domestic politics and in cultural life. Since the mid-1960s the moderate right-wing National Coalition party had not been able to dream of participating in the government during Kekkonen's presidency, and the main line of policy was the building of a welfare state under the leadership of centre and left-wing parties. Yleisradio, the national radio and television broadcasting company, was supposed to adhere to a policy of political impartiality, but many conservative-minded citizens complained about the large number of clearly propagandistic programmes about the USSR. On the other hand, some left-wing intellectuals were appalled by the US popular culture that they thought was flooding in through television into decent Finnish homes. After Rouben Mamoulian's *Silk Stocking* (1957) was broadcast on New Year's Eve 1973, even parliament debated whether this was an infringement of Finnish foreign policy. This was obviously an overreaction even in the ideologically tense context of the Cold War. In terms of international connections, Finnish broadcasting policy was another instance of mediation: Yleisradio was a member of both the Western European Broadcasting Union and the Eastern International Radio and Television Organization, and being the only country thus positioned served as a channel of programme exchange.

It was no doubt true that Finland was acquiring a taste for consumer culture, with the West and definitely not the East showing the way. Western popular culture prevailed also in the music and film industries. Anglo-American pop and rock music was a defining feature of youth culture, and almost half of new films came from the USA; the number of Soviet films was only about one-tenth of that amount. Yet in many fields of cultural life the leftist bias was quite dominant. Prominent artists saw it as their mission to participate in a worldwide struggle against capitalism and imperialism in their various forms. In some quarters the degree of political commitment became a major criterion of good art. This would at times take the form of adopting a strong anti-American, pro-Soviet stand, but the most important point was to show the way towards progressive social policies. Film culture became one of the major battlegrounds of the cultural political struggle. This was partly because by the turn of the 1960s the Finnish studio system had come to an abrupt end. As elsewhere, television was recognized as a major enemy of the film industry, although at first it was thought that it could not seriously compete with the big screen. However, an equally important challenge lay in the enormous social and cultural changes that were taking place in Finnish society. The studio system was too stuck to its old formulas and thus unable to respond. Popular music cavalcades with the thinnest of plots emphasizing musical numbers helped financially, but did little to develop a cinema that would relate to the transformation Finnish society was experiencing.

Out of this situation a new generation emerged, young individuals aspiring to careers in filmmaking, acutely aware of a new kind of modernist and often politically conscious cinema that was emerging in Europe. They soon came to the conclusion that the structures of film production had to be completely revised if there was to be a Finnish cinema at all. Subsidized domestic film production began to be seen as a crucial dimension of the welfare state. A decade of fierce debates fired by political passions eventually led to the creation of a system of state subsidy and the establishment of the Finnish Film Foundation in 1969.

Whereas throughout most of the studio era the film industry had to a significant extent participated in the project of nation building and the formation of a national identity, in the new situation film was seen as an artistic enterprise that was to create awareness of the social and cultural changes that were taking place on the national as well as the international level. Film was also to participate actively in the political controversies of the day, giving rise to suspicions about whether the system was, in effect, supporting certain, mainly left-wing ideologies. One main problem was that there was a significant disruption of the established tradition of filmmaking. Only three major directors who had started in the big studios, Edvin Laine, Matti Kassila and Mikko Niskanen, were able to continue their careers in the new situation and to varying degrees to absorb some of the influences that the European New Waves offered. Newcomers often started their own production companies, some of which were doomed to disappear quickly, while others provided at least slightly more continuous production conditions. This was a familiar pattern for independent producers, but now there were no big studios to ensure the continuation of film production. Remarkably, both the few slightly older filmmakers as well as the newcomers were able to embrace the New Wave influences in quite personal ways and make them serve their social, political and existential concerns.

The system of state subsidy gave a number of filmmakers considerable artistic freedom, and occasionally they were successful at international film festivals. Yet the liberation also meant that there was little pressure to take into account audiences or invest in marketing the films. Meanwhile, many of those making popular comedies had to make the near desperate attempt to rely on box-office receipts with an audience that was much smaller than in the heyday of the studio system. This division led to the basically unhealthy situation in which the vast majority of the public was not interested in what was being offered as the national film culture. The all-time low point since the establishment of Finnish production companies came in 1974, when only three Finnish films were premiered. In retrospect, many commentators have blamed the subsidy system for being overpoliticized and offering filmmakers the possibility of fruitless self-indulgence. The system could only continue because of the political stagnation, which was not conducive to changing ideologically motivated structures.

The political system that President Kekkonen epitomized was not significantly altered while he was still in office. Symptoms of his deteriorating physical and mental condition were already apparent in the early 1970s, but they were not publicly acknowledged until 1982, when he finally had to resign. Things started quietly changing during Mauno Koivisto's presidency (1982–1994). These developments were partly made possible by the changes that were taking place in the Soviet leadership under the premiership of Mikhail Gorbachev. The policy of openness and transparency (*glasnost*) as well as restructuring (*perestroika*) gave more room for policymaking in neighbouring countries too. The real fundamental change took place after the collapse of socialism in Europe in the autumn of 1989 and the dissolution of the USSR in 1991, following which Finland was very quick to submit an application for membership of the European Union.

CHAPTER 9

The Finnish New Wave as a Transnational Phenomenon

Pietari Kääpä

In 1961, the young critic and vocal cultural commentator Jörn Donner published an article that laid out the rhetorical scope of Finnish film activism, 'Finnish Cinema in Year Zero'.[1] Donner's scathing challenge to studio-era filmmaking takes aim at what he sees as the complacency and commonplace commercialism of domestic cinema. In the eyes of critics like Donner, a new form of cinema was necessary to rebuild the relevance of film culture for changed times, where stoic historical productions or comic folk tales were not enough. A new type of cinema was needed not only to represent daily realities but also to correspond to advances in the cinematic arts. Donner is not writing in a vacuum, as his words echo in many ways the central manifesto of the Nouvelle Vague by François Truffaut, 'A Certain Tendency of the French Cinema'.[2] Both share the aim of challenging the stagnancy of the domestic film culture by engaging in lofty aggressive rhetoric and plans to remodel the politicized significance of cinema.

Any attempt at assessing the dynamics of the New Wave of Finnish cinema of the 1960s must take into account several other film cultural movements that comprised the New Wave. The French *Cahiers du cinéma* generation of critics/producers were reacting against what they perceived as the stagnant bourgeoisie values and means of expression of

P. Kääpä (✉)
University of Stirling, Stirling, Scotland
e-mail: pietari.kaapa@gmail.com

© The Editor(s) (if applicable) and The Author(s) 2016
H. Bacon (ed.), *Finnish Cinema*, Palgrave European Film
and Media Studies, DOI 10.1057/978-1-137-57651-4_9

145

the 'Tradition of Quality'. The Nouvelle Vague was enabled by substantial transformations in the cultural, political, economic and social structures of post-war France. Richard Neupert's incisive study[3] characterizes this era as a time of anxiety and opportunity, as conservative structures and the role of the state in cultural management were challenged by criticism of French colonialist politics and student movements, among a range of factors contributing to social upheaval. In this 'rebellion', initiated by cinéastes such as Jean-Luc Godard and Truffaut, the Nouvelle Vague took aim at linear narratives, protagonists with clear purpose, the suture of classical style, and conservative ideological structures that dominated traditional cinema. Furthermore, the Left Bank movement, with novelists and artists such as Alain Grille-Robbe and Chris Marker, used abstraction and extreme stylistic innovations to push the medium's abilities in realizing subjective states.

The Nouvelle Vague was a product of its time and place, but it was also a transnational phenomenon from its inception. Inspired by the shooting methods and style of Italian Neorealists, Eisensteinian montage, existential art movements both domestic and international, as much as by 'auteur' films produced in Hollywood, the French New Wave was a part of an international network as it was a reaction against domestic film politics. Even as these developments took place in France, András Kovács'[4] work notes that variations on New Wave film culture were simultaneously appearing in other cultural contexts, with British filmmakers drawing on a history of Free Cinema realism and Czech directors utilizing irony and subversion to explore the official history of life behind the Iron Curtain. The New Wave as a film cultural movement clearly has its emergence as well as its operations immersed in both domestic and international cultural production. Unravelling the role of Finnish cinema in these complex networks of adaptation and innovation necessitates the adoption of a transnational approach, as this can productively illuminate the place of a small nation film culture in such international movements.

THE FINNISH NEW WAVE AS A TRANSNATIONAL PHENOMENON

As much as the international New Waves were characterized by a complex cross-pollination of influences, so the flow of cultural influences to Finnish cinema is not to be underestimated. The emergence of the New Wave in Finland was premised on similar structural factors to those of the Nouvelle Vague, including wide-ranging social transformations, such as urbanization and changes in lifestyles, as well as increased industrial factors such as the role of television in altering viewing habits.[5] To respond to these social and cultural transformations, innovative production strategies were already shaping among Finnish film practitioners. Maunu Kurkvaara is often considered the first of the Finnish New Wave directors, having started out in 1955 with the film *The Island of Happiness* (*Onnen Saari*), but it was not until the early 1960s that he engaged in the type of production that characterizes cinematic modernism. His most significant contributions to the Finnish New Wave—*Darling* (*Rakas*, 1961) and *The Feast of the Sea* (*Meren Juhlat*, 1963)—would fit neatly with their more international counterparts, characterized as they are by narratives about young individuals struggling with the world, and themes such as loneliness and alienation, all conveyed in an innovative and often even abstract visual style that challenges the narrative logic of mainstream cinema.

He was not alone by any means, as others came similarly from the arts world, including Eino Ruutsalo. Some came from film schools (Mikko Niskanen), some from the theatre (Jaakko Pakkasvirta), and, while they all had idiosyncratic approaches and perspectives on cinema's artistic role, they often produced films that share much with their international counterparts. These include narratives focused on city youth (Mikko Niskanen's *Skin Skin/Käpy selän alla*, 1966), alienation (Jaakko Pakkasvirta's *The Green Widow/Vihreä leski*, 1968), the experience of growing up (Maunu Kurkvaara's *Red hair/Punatukka*, 1969); Erkko Kivikoski's *This Summer at 5/Kesällä Kello Viisi*, 1963), class differences (Risto Jarva's *The Worker's Diary/Työmiehen päiväkirja*, 1967), manifestos (Maunu Kurkvaara's *Rat War/Rottasota*, 1968). New Wave influences also filtered into more commercial cinema (Matti Kassila's Inspector Palmu series, 1960–1969), while New Wave directors experimented with popular forms (Maunu Kurkvaara's *A League of Millions/ Miljoonaliiga*, 1968). While Finland did not see such clear divisions between the approaches of its practitioners as those of the Nouvelle Vague's different banks, it is best to consider the Finnish New Wave as a complex set of intertwining interests, rather than as a monolithic movement.

INTERNATIONAL COLLABORATIONS

Understanding the New Wave in terms of diversity helps lay the groundwork for our discussion of the New Wave as a transnational phenomenon. However, before we make the case for this, we illustrate some of the ways in which Finnish New Wave cinema was integrated with international New Waves. Chief among the New Wave cohort, Jörn Donner and Risto Jarva were heavily involved in international collaboration with productions such as *To Love* (*Att älska*, 1964) and *Night or Day* (*Yö vai päivä*, 1962), respectively. The former was Donner's second film in Sweden with the production company Sandrew, as he had decided to move to new pastures following his disenchantment with Finland's cultural state. *To Love* is largely faithful to conventional classical style, comprised as it is largely of conventional medium and close-up shots. The narrative focusing on the estranged relationship of a young couple was a key thematic trope of the New Waves, but the main noteworthy aspect of this film, from a transnational point of view, is Zbigniew Cybulski's presence. By situating the iconic star of one of the precursors to the international New Wave movement, Andrzej Wajda, in a film set in Sweden directed by a Finnish-Swedish cinéaste, a dynamic form of interaction between Finnish cinema and a distinctly international film cultural movement begins to emerge.

Another, arguably more productive, indication of the international scope of the Finnish New Wave can be detected in Risto Jarva's *Night or Day*, which focuses on a group of ethnographers visiting Finland. The film is a highly deconstructive exploration of Finnish cultural and national identity in ways that emphasize the constructed aspects of these notions. All aspects play out as if in a caricature of a tourist film, where voiceover narration self-consciously (and self-reflexively) points out the limitations of these characteristics. Such a distanced exploration of Finnish culture from a faux-external perspective is not uncommon for New Wave cinema, which the use of documentary-type stylistic devices (from direct address to location shooting) and lack of a linear narrative further emphasize. Even if the film lacks some of the trademarks of the Nouvelle Vague, its approach to Finnish culture (and its contribution to film politics in Finland) is best understood as a provocation challenging taken-for-granted notions of how Finnish identity could or should be expressed cinematically.

While these two films are both examples of some of the experimental tendencies of the New Wave and also show the ways in which international collaboration challenges the structures of domestic film cultures as well as connecting them to external cultural movements, this sort of explicit internationality is only one aspect of the transnational dimensions of the New Wave in Finland. While the history of the New Wave has been covered by Kari Uusitalo,[6] Sakari Toiviainen[7] and others, there are parts of this history that need elaboration. If the notion of transnational is taken to refer to changes that take place within domestic film cultures as a response to international exchange and cross-border flow of cultural influences, many patterns correspond to this throughout the history of the New Wave. For example, film historians have a tendency to compare Finnish films derisively against their international counterparts. This is especially evident in the film criticism of the era, with many of the reviewers discussing, in particular, the films of Kurkvaara and Ruutsalo in terms of their debt to the Nouvelle Vague as well as to other respected directors such as Michelangelo Antonioni. Henry G. Gröndahl is just one of these voices when he suggests that 'if it is necessary to discuss a "new wave", it is Ruutsalo and Kurkvaara who are to date mostly responsible for it'.[8] While more negative views focused on the lack of purpose in these 'Nouvelle Vague approximations' or on an overall lack of technological ability, it is clear that critics saw the Finnish New Wave as a transnational enterprise, even if they never used the term. To explore this complex network of exchanges and adaptations further, I now turn to issues of film style as a concrete manifestation of many of the key New Wave approaches.

THE STYLE OF THE NEW WAVE

Even though I focus on the style (or rather the styles) of the Finnish New Wave, it is not my intention to provide an exhaustive list of its relationship with other New Waves. Due to considerations of length, I focus predominantly on the most commonly discussed stylistic innovations of the Nouvelle Vague, which include formalist aspects that fragment the classical continuity and narration styles. Occasional discussion of the works of the Left Bank movement will also be included, even if many of the Finnish case studies covered here come nowhere near the experimentalism of these works. While the Nouvelle Vague is certainly a stylistically and ideologically diverse movement, in this discussion of the Finnish New Wave I will concentrate predominantly on subversions of classical continuity, as these are the types of challenges mostly envisaged by Finnish producers.

As authors such as Naomi Green,[9] Richard Neupert,[10] Ginette Vincendeau and Peter Graham[11] and Chris Wiegand[12] forcefully argue, most areas of the classical system were designed to give the impression of a continued cinematic reality, whereas Nouvelle Vague filmmakers used a group of techniques inspired by a range of fictional and documentary movements from around the world, including inspirations as varying as the documentaries of John Grierson through to early Italian Neorealist film. These include jump cuts, fast editing, narratively unmotivated shot lengths, direct gaze and so on, which direct the spectatorial attention to the construction of the cinematic diegesis. For constructing an impression of freewheeling realism, the emphasis on real locations and outdoor shooting, the use of handheld cameras and location sound recording, natural lighting and improvised dialogue provided the essential materials.

These techniques were heavily mobilized in the Finnish New Wave. As was the case with the Nouvelle Vague rebellion against the Tradition of Quality, the Finnish New Wave was largely constructed as a reaction against the golden age of Finnish cinema. In focusing on the stylistic content of Finnish New Wave films, it is imperative to remember that the formation of the final products was a combination of film politics and cultural dialogue. First of all, the collapse of the studio system and contemporaneous technological innovations enabled the 'liberated' style identified in the films. Especially towards the end of the 1960s, cultural politics increasingly favoured 'artistic' cinema, and the New Wave's innovative styles certainly met these objectives. The continuity style of the studio era was clearly the benchmark to be deconstructed by the antagonistic perspectives, and it is precisely this unravelling of conventions that can be productively inspected through the analysis of style. Style is also useful for exploring the transnational dimensions of these films, as it provides a concrete register for understanding how Finnish producers integrate and interact with the transnational flow of culture. As many of the preceding chapters of this book point out, transnational is not only a concern that focuses on exploring the concrete movements of individuals and cultural elements across borders. It is a much more complicated idea concerning the transformations that cultures undergo as a result of these moves—and it is these transformations that this chapter aims to explore.

In view of the fact that Finnish New Wave directors acted as part of a multipolar, rhizomatic network of influences flowing from one different culture to the next, listing out a range of particular influences and inspirations is not the most appropriate way for assessing the transnational influences of style on the Finnish New Wave. For one, the directors of the films will often deny such modes of influence, especially as the film culture of the time was heavily auteur based, and, as such, artistic credibility was a key commodity. While questions of influence and inspiration are relevant, they are also difficult to prove. A better way to conduct this analysis is to explore similar modes of effect and how they are communicated stylistically, as well as those moments that differ from the norm. The focus is on stylistic moments that stand out from the general construction of an immersive cinematic diegesis; that is, a filmic world not unlike that of main-stream cinema, where the aim is for the spectator to identify with the world presented. Even within the experimentalism of much of the Nouvelle Vague, certain moments stand out, whether these are the jump cuts of Godard or the long takes of Antonioni. My focus is on similar instances in Finnish cin-ema, which enables us to evaluate similarities and differences in the ways in which such ideas are contextualized within the films. Accordingly, the aim is not so much to note the various references and influences from other films, but to take up those moments that exceed the already fragile narrative con-structions of the New Wave films. Through this, the purpose is to evaluate how stylistic transgressions are simultaneously domesticated versions of an international New Wave as well as specific responses to changes in domestic film culture. To these ends, I turn to the concept of cinematic excess.

EXCESS AND NEW WAVE FILM CULTURE

In theorizing the concept of excess, I draw on the work of Kristin Thompson. For her, the concept of excess is a way to analyse the shatter-ing continuity of the narrative world. In such instances, style becomes a way of revealing the film as the construction that it is, instead of serving simply as a portal to the diegetic world:

> The minute a viewer begins to notice style for its own sake or watch works which do not provide such thorough motivation, excess comes forward and must affect narrative meaning. Style is the use of repeated techniques which become characteristic of the work; these techniques are foregrounded so that the spectator will notice them and create connections between their individual uses. Excess does not equal style, but the two are closely linked because they both involve the material aspects of the film. Excess forms no specific patterns which we could say are characteristic of the work.[13]

Excess can refer to scenes that have a specific function within the film's story, but most often they are instances that are part of revealing the extraneous world outside of the film. Thus, excess can refer to laying bare the cinematic means of narration and the need to fragment the illu-sion of a cohesive world. These interruptions are often done in relation to accepted, antecedent stylistic forms, as otherwise they would not be noticed. Inherent in this conception is a normative way of doing things, conventional norms that excess exceeds.

For Thompson, the implications of excess are to do with highlighting potentially subversive elements that refuse to conform to the structures expected of commercial products or suturing the viewer into assimilating the ideological connotations of conservative narratives. For many of the authors who have taken up the concept in very different contexts from Finnish cinema, excess operates as a political project. They discuss areas such as minority identities[14] or the inherent materiality of the cinematic apparatus,[15] where elements can literally exceed the diegetic world in moving specific political questions to the foreground. Simultaneously, excess is very useful as a way of characterizing the deconstructive activity of the New Wave films explored here. If classical narration is 'a struggle by the unifying elements to contain the diverse elements that make up its whole system', many of the key Finnish New Wave films by definition lay bare and challenge this struggle in the continuity of the studio era.

The use of jump cuts in a key text such as *Breathless* (*À bout de souffle*, 1960) can, first of all, illustrate the relevance of excess. The famous scene of Michel (Jean-Paul Belmondo) and Patricia (Jean Seberg) on a car ride along the Champs-Élysées fuses dubbed voiceover with over-the-shoulder shots of the characters. The whole scene is premised on seemingly unmotivated jump cuts focused on Patricia. Whether these are to do with fragmenting notions of linear time and space or to indicate the constructed nature of the narrative, they draw considerable attention to themselves as formative devices that fragment both classical continuity and the diegetic world building of the Tradition of Quality cinema. While jump cuts are applied throughout the film, their use within this scene can be considered excessive in terms of the whole film, as the entire scene seems to be premised on their use. And as they serve very little real narrative function, they accordingly reveal to us the key means by which these filmmakers were challenging norms and providing their own visual language.

Indeed, one could ask whether the New Wave was not an excessive form in its very inception, considering all the stylistic devices fragmenting narratives and countering unity. Yet simultaneously, such a question leads to another pertinent question: how and why are we defining something as excessive? Indeed, while the very concept of excess can only work when it is feasible to identify a clear normative structure that can be exceeded, these 'normative' structures are key to understanding the analytical potential of the excessive moments. The Nouvelle Vague, with its diverse strands, evoked a clear difference in comparison to mainstream cinema, but internally, as a cinecultural structure, is it possible to identify similar transgressions? This is especially difficult with films such as Alain Resnais's *Hiroshima Mon Amour* (1958) and *Last Year in Marienbad* (1961), which arguably make avoidance of conventions and experimentalism their main intention. All aspects of these films play on repetition and abstractions that question individual memory and temporality. Both films are only excessive in the way Thompson defines the notion if contrasted against conventional narrative cinema. Internally, they have their own sets of rules, regardless of how disparate they may be, and excess would need to be something that fractures these audiovisual and narrative parameters. Without persisting too much with the implications of these experimental films, excess here would seem to require resorting to conventional narrative and visual conventions.

TRANSNATIONAL APPROACHES TO EXCESS

While excess as a means of analysis has multiple implications according to the types of New Wave films to which it is applied, its relationship with transnational analysis of film culture needs further elaboration. The most relevant method in this respect is the positioning of specific films as part of international film culture movements. If, in the context of the Chinese mainstream, excess is a way to indicate a romantic tone that may be missing from the immediate context of the protagonists, other commentators see the global art cinema as focusing on 'imperceptibly slow, discontinuous montage and shot sequences'.[16] Such formal modes inextricably position the films as alternatives to mainstream commercial cinema. As with the Left Bank films, the use of such conventions is not excessive within the confines of the particular film movement. Regardless, the ways in which these conventions are used vary in extent and impact, especially as one of the main principles of excess is that aspects that qualify as excessive should not form a unified whole. For the New Waves, formative innovations were a way to rebel against and emulate, to draw from and differentiate against dominant conventions in the domestic film culture.[17] The ways in which these innovations travelled and integrated with stylistic and formalist modes of other New Wave cinemas allow us to investigate how specific national film cultures interconnect with an international film cultural movement. By comparing the use of a specific stylistic device in its domestic context with its use internationally, I can formulate a method of exploring the transnational dimensions of the Finnish New Wave.

The purpose of this discussion is not to identify the use of cinematic devices as being inspired by or copied from their international counterparts. Rather, these are considered instances that show that Finnish directors position themselves as part of the cinematic modernism sweeping different parts of the world. These instances are significant in providing the films with a unique style and form of expression created by their idiosyncratic directors. This is precisely why I focus on the excessive connotations of only certain stylistic devices. While it is necessary to be mindful of the heterogeneous styles of the New Wave films—for example, early Godard such as *Breathless* is distinctly 'tamer' in terms of style than *Weekend* (1967)—discussing the transnational dimensions of Finnish New Waves takes place through four specific formative repetitions. These include such explicit formative devices as shattering the frame, wandering shots of individuals moving through liminal spaces, pop culture evocations that break the narrative continuity, rhetorical manifestos that halt the narrative, and ambivalent conclusions that leave the films open to interpretation.

All of these instances provide the films with certain differences from the texts of the Nouvelle Vague and distinguish the idiosyncratic means through which Finnish filmmakers of the era responded to changes in domestic and international film culture. This is also where the transnational works as a useful tool: a jump cut in the Finnish context does not function like a jump cut in *Breathless*. Trying to manage the whole breadth of Finnish New Wave cinema is simply not practical in the space available, but focusing on stylistic excesses helps to linearize this diversity somewhat, while retaining an appropriate level of comparison with the Nouvelle Vague as well as other New Waves.

Shattering the Frame

One of the most celebrated interventions of the Nouvelle Vague is the jump cut, a stylistic device often associated with fragmenting narrative continuity. The use of jump cuts in *Breathless*, already discussed, is one of the most impressive instances of this stylistic device, with Richard Raskin suggesting that it is able to evoke 'the involvement of the audience less in a narrative than a sensation or an experience'.[18] In Godard's film, Patricia's voice and music suture over potential lapses in narrative consistency and allow the film to create the necessary sensory immersion, even as they allow us to follow the narrative of this doomed romance. The stylistic mode positions the film as part of a reinvention of cinematic language and a form of rebellion against the Tradition of Quality in French film culture.[19]

What does the jump cut imply for Finnish cinema? Jump cuts are a significant part of the vocabulary of the Finnish New Wave and are used in experimental films like *Summer at Five O'Clock* (*Kesällä kello viisi*, Erkko Kivikoski, 1963) as well as more commercial productions like the Inspector Palmu series, albeit in much more moderated ways. The presence of the jump cut in these films presents a spectrum of roles for the device, from modernist innovation to presenting more mainstream texts with an aura of tapping into cultural innovation. In this chapter, the focus is on instances of the jump cut that can be considered excessive. While jump cuts have a variety of uses and applications, their relevance for a transnational study lies in revealing not only the extent to which Finnish directors of the time were cognizant of international cultural movements, but also ways in which these directors innovated with these cinematic devices to distinguish the films they produced from other New Wave films.

Even as the New Waves are part of a transnational movement, being as they are premised on reactions against domestic film culture as well as responding to more international artistic stimuli, their use of stylistic devices contributes considerably to the rhetorical development of national cinema. By this I mean that the conscious use of experimental stylistic devices is one of the ways in which these films construct their claims to social and artistic relevance. With the increased importance of various governmental support mechanisms, eventually culminating in the establishment of the Finnish Film Foundation, such concerns were an increasingly vital part of any film that aspired to receive this all-important support. Interestingly, it seems that the use of style, especially when it comes to notable, excessive uses of that style, can be especially revealing in its cultural political implications. To explore this idea and its transnational implications further, I focus on two examples in which the jump cut works as a rhetorical device: Maunu Kurkvaara's *Here You Are Today* (*Tänään olet täällä*, 1966) and Mikko Niskanen's *Skin Skin* (*Käpy selän alla*, 1966).

Tänään olet täällä invites a transnational interpretation, as its narrative is focused on a cosmopolitan group of individuals in Spain. The film problematizes Finnishness as most of these travellers are Finnish and the film contains flashbacks to northern Finland, captured in heavily exotic ways; the characters are constantly on the move, unable to find solace in either Spain or Finland. By framing the notion of Finnishness in relation to a world in flux, the film emphasizes uncertainty and restlessness, both of which are frequently characterized as key tenets of New Wave cinema from Resnais to Antonioni. The oscillation between home and away consolidates this sense, as the characters all evoke their uncertain liminality with comments such as 'when wandering in the world, the place where I am does not matter'.

To reflect this sense of liminality, Kurkvaara draws on his interests in painting and artistic modernism, even as he does not profess to being inspired by any other contemporary filmmaker. The stylistically most intriguing scene takes place when one of the Finnish characters in the film, Sole (Sinikka Hannula), receives news that her husband has died. In a film that rarely fragments the conventional logic of narrative cohesion, except for a few seemingly unmotivated flashbacks, Sole's moment of realization stands out. Starting out with a static shot of her sitting on a sofa, the camera soon follows her dazed walk to a balcony. An over-the-shoulder shot cuts to an external shot of the building from street level and soon goes back to medium close-ups of her face in her disassociated state. The use of atonal music contributes an alienating quality to the scene as the film cuts to different angles of the house and the balcony.

The scene in itself is not unusual in either content or style, but then Kurkvaara cuts to an exact repeat of the same shot pattern, only extending its culmination with a few additional shots of Sole. Since the film repeats the same pattern a third time, again only with a slight extension, the style of the film is very clearly entering the realm of excess. A repetition such as this calls attention to the form of the film and can be reinterpreted in many ways. Kurkvaara tells the story of a projectionist who cut the repetition out, having mistaken it for a misprint. Others see it, and the film as a whole, as a clear case of modernist inspiration, of innovating with cinematic form, but ultimately not signifying much at all.[20] For this chapter, the scene is most intriguing as it indicates a moment of excess that has a distinct transnational dimension. Indeed, it would not be too difficult to draw parallels with the scene's tone and *Last Year in Marienbad*, for example, evoking as they both do subjective states of mind through abstract form. Yet rather than considering this as a case of direct inspiration from an international counterpart, this scene of excess is best understood as an indicator of innovative strategies in the Finnish film culture of the era, and of its director in particular, for whom a scene of such a nature would have been an instance of idiosyncratic artistic innovation. Thus, the repetition is an indicator of the transnational dimensions of Finnish cinema, where such innovative formative choices transcend cultural boundaries and are best understood as part of international film culture, even as they indicate Finland's part in this movement.

An Excessive Challenge to National Romanticism

In contrast to Kurkvaara's deliberately ambiguous formal experimentation, Mikko Niskanen's innovative but more traditional *Skin Skin* provides a clear case for assessing the national dimensions of excess. The film came out at the tail end of the 'liberated' experimentalism of the Finnish New Wave (much of the late 1960s and early 1970s was devoted to more political activist fare). Premiering after such notable, if rarely seen, films as *The Feast of the Sea* and *Five O'Clock at Summer* that had, according to the critics, consolidated a clear Finnish version of the New Wave, *Skin Skin* attracted an audience of over 700,000 on its domestic release. The director had already incorporated innovative formative techniques into his otherwise conventional war film *Commandos* (Sissit 1963), but in this tale of four city youths who venture into the countryside for a romantic sojourn, nature scenery, youth culture, contemporary politics and New Wave experimentalism combine to impressive effect. The majority of contemporary domestic films, including those of the New Wave, had struggled to find audiences, and thus the use of popular cultural idioms alongside the challenging form of the film drew attention from both critics and audiences.

Arguably the most invigorating instance of stylistic excess emerges in the culmination of *Skin Skin*. After a night of heavy drinking, the two couples' trip culminates as they face hard truths about their lives. This is the end especially for Timppa (Pekka Autiovuori) and Leena (Kirsti Wallasvaara), since Leena considers breaking off the unhappy relationship. As she walks off into the forest, she turns to gaze directly at the camera. A set of jump cuts captures her gaze from a variety of distances, from long shots to close-ups. This is a technique reminiscent of Truffaut's famous conclusion to *400 Blows* (*Les quatre cents coups*, 1959), where Antoine, the protagonist, turns to gaze at the camera while the shot freezes on his uncertain expression. As with this evocation of uncertain adolescence, *Skin Skin* suggests the transient state of the contemporary generation even as it draws considerable attention to itself as a cinematic construct. By consciously breaking the illusion of the fourth wall, the central theme of the film—reformulating the implications of national romanticist narratives—comes forth in a powerful way. When Leena is framed in the centre of the image against the forest background, the multiple perspectives embodied by the jump cuts signify all the different alternatives that emergent generations may bring to envisioning the metonymic relationship between nature and nation, and its significance for such collective imaginaries (Figs. 9.1–9.12).

The visceral use of jump cuts stands out from the already innovative content of the film and allows us to note the ways in which excess operates as a transnational phenomenon. If the transnational is a means of challenging constrictive national imaginaries, the use of the jump cut in *Skin Skin* works at two levels: the cuts both indicate a generational reappraisal of national culture, as well as, crucially, that this generational challenge is made through the means of an international cultural movement. The point is not to argue that Niskanen may have been inspired by Truffaut's use of similar formative conventions in his coming-of-age tale. While the scene certainly fulfils a similar function as *400 Blows*' culmination, indicating the ambiguity and uncertainty of the lives of its protagonists, it also functions in excessive terms to draw attention to the constructedness of national imaginaries in the context of Finnish cinema. As such, it emerges as a transnational stylistic contribution, indicating both the ways in which the Finnish New Wave was immersed in international cultural exchange and the ways in which these were adopted by the dynamic development of the domestic film culture.

WANDERING SHOTS AND ANY-SPACES-WHATEVER

If jump cuts were conceptualized—and, to a large extent, interpreted—as concrete confrontations to the narrative continuity of mainstream cinema, other stylistic means employed by the New Waves present alternative methods for representing disenchantment and the politics of transformation.[21] For this discussion of stylistic excess, shots of individuals wandering across empty industrial and natural landscapes offer an alternative way to consider Finnish cinema's correlation with the international New Waves. These shots can be considered excessive in relation to their length and the narrative functions they occupy, especially as they often self-consciously draw attention to themselves. Gilles Deleuze has discussed such spaces in the works of Michelangelo Antonioni, and calls the represented spaces 'any-spaces-whatever'. Such spaces are interchangeable and have the capacity to embody a sense of alienation as well as ideological significance. In characteristically flamboyant terms, Deleuze identifies them as 'deserted but inhabited, disused warehouses, waste ground, cities in the course of demolition or reconstruction', before going on to describe the actions that take place in these any-spaces-whatever, where 'a new race of characters was stirring, a kind of mutant: they saw rather than acted, they were seers'.[22]

Figs. 9.1–9.6 The concluding climax of *Skin Skin* (1966). Each capture here represents an individual shot, edited together to provide a complex view of one of the main protagonists of the film (© FJ-Filmi, Finnkino)

Figs. 9.7–9.12 (*continued*)

While this argumentation may follow its own convoluted logic, there is a clear point being made here. These seers are typical protagonists of international New Wave cinema, the Antoine Doinels who wander through an alienating world of conventions and norms, or the disillusioned housewives whose experience these films aim to capture. The spaces are fluid, unstable tabula rasa, like the industrial wastelands, 'deserts', that Antonioni's protagonists attempt to navigate, or the end of the road as a new beginning that Truffaut's protagonist discovers on an empty beach. Finnish New Wave films of the era also capture such confused seers wandering through these fluctuating, transmuted spaces, be they construction sites (Jarva's *A Game of Luck/Onnenpeli*, 1965, discussed later), city centres (Jörn Donner's *Here Begins the Adventure/Här börjar äventyret*, 1965, also later), the countryside (*Skin Skin*), the beach (*The Feast of the Sea*) and so on. All of these spaces have lost some aspect of their original meaning, being as they are in a state of reconstruction, much like the cultural politics of the era that many of these films try to recapture.

To illustrate how these empty spaces connect with our arguments about transnational excess, I focus on *The Feast of the Sea*, one of the most complex works by Kurkvaara. The narrative chronicles a chance encounter by two former lovers, Sini (Sinikka Hannula) and Jaska (Jaakko Pakkasvirta), and their ensuing reconnection. In its own right, as with many of Kurkvaara's productions, the narrative needs no correlation with the nation, being as it is premised on universal themes also familiar from films by Federico Fellini or Michelangelo Antonioni, among others. Furthermore, the style of the film correlates with the stylistic conventions of the more experimental style of Antonioni, with abstract dialogue and causal order designed to reinterpret narrative continuity. Yet what makes this film particularly illustrative is a key scene on an island in the Helsinki archipelago, a scene where excess comes to play a key role.

The sea and sailing are key themes in Kurkvaara's work and reflect a sense of liberation and in-betweenness that characterizes his works. They feature lengthy scenes in these liminal areas, which capture the uncertain state of mind of the protagonists as well as reflect Kurkvaara's position as a maverick artist. However, in *The Feast of the Sea*, the elopement of the two protagonists to a desolate island is captured in a way that can best be described as excessive, even in the framework of experimental New Wave cinema. As they fool around on the sparsely scattered rocks, the cinematic world is governed by alienation effects that capture more the feeling of elopement rather than a clear narrative, including extreme close-ups and shots of the couple walking away from the camera. The use of Unto Meriläinen's dissonant music makes these already elusive scenes appear strange, as if the convalescence between the two has somehow been distorted. Kurkvaara's use of colour complements this approach, with deep hues and the use of reflective surfaces that emphasize the environment as well as the isolation.

Perhaps the most intriguing of the scenes on the island takes place when Sini seemingly sleepwalks across the rocks to the sea. The scene lasts for several minutes and completely disrupts the already fragmented narrative, as we see her journey across the rocks with alternating shots from behind, from a distance, of her feet, as well as close-ups of her face, all with the turbulent sky and the sea in the background. The scene is certainly excessive even within the confines of the any-spaces-whatever of the New Waves. Much like the other cases of stylistic excess covered earlier, the scene is telling in its relation to transnational Finnish film culture. For one, this is a case where a culturally specific location—an island off Helsinki—becomes a space for subjective introspection, a space that is inhabited by seers struggling to make sense of their surrounding society. Even as any specific influences on Kurkvaara of such any-spaces-whatever in Antonioni's cinema, for example, are difficult to prove, the scene corresponds to stylistic patterns in international New Wave film culture. As a case of stylistic excess, the scene can be illuminatingly placed in relation to transnational exchange, since it, once more, indicates how Finnish New Wave directors operated within an international cultural norm, producing their own visions of these norms. Yet crucially, this is a scene that maintains its own stylistic parameters, refusing to reproduce a simple copy or approximation. Instead, it is a case of stylistic innovation within the wider parameters of an international movement.

POP CULTURE

If stylistic instances such as jump cuts and wandering shots emphasize the transnational dimensions of the Finnish New Wave, other modes in New Wave cinema warrant further investigation, including the role of popular culture. What I have in mind, specifically, is the use of contemporary popular music as a transnational cultural signifier. In Finland, the films of Erkko Kivikoski (*The Unruly Brothers/Kesyttömät veljekset*, 1969), Mikko Niskanen (*The Girl of Finland/Lapualaismorsian*, 1967), Matti Kassila (*The Stars, Inspector Palmu/Tähdet Komisario Palmu*, 1962) and

Maunu Kurkvaara (*Saturday Games/Lauantaileikit*, 1964) use music as a counterpoint to their rebellious themes. Kurkvaara's *Saturday Games* is a case in point, being as it is part of a cycle of popular *Schlager* films of the era, in which contemporary stars would perform songs premised on flimsy narratives. While the film is missing key aspects of New Wave thematology and stylistic form, its embrace of youth and pop culture reminds us that the New Wave is not only about experimentalism and art, but also about the experiences and perspectives of an emergent generation.

As a particularly useful case study, Jarva's *A Game of Luck* crystallizes many of the themes of liberation and detachment that characterize New Wave film culture. Much of the narrative focuses on a love triangle between Leena (Kirsti Wallasvaara), Jussi (Jaakko Pakkasvirta) and Telle (Eila Pokkinen), a threesome at a turning point in their lives between taking on adult responsibilities and continuing their youthful ways. The theme of the autumn of youth is reflected in a wider concern over social changes, since the film chronicles the disappearance and transformation of traditional Finnish culture by focusing on the reconstruction of Helsinki as part of a modernist drive for functionalist buildings and a more stream-lined society. The focus on social reconstruction is part of Jarva's idio-syncratic fascination with the diverse existential modes engendered by transformations in (and of) the cityscape as well as the lifestyle of those who inhabit it. However, the focus also fits the thematic preoccupations of the New Waves' cinematic modernism in that it largely aims to capture how history and contemporary realities intertwine.

The way in which the film localizes the wanderings and existence of young individuals warrants a transnational inspection in its own terms, especially as the film also echoes certain narrative points from Truffaut's seminal *Jules et Jim* (1962). If the transnational has so far emerged as a productive way of exploring the complex dynamics of cultural flow and domestic innovation that characterize the Finnish New Wave, *A Game of Luck* takes this discussion further by combining many of the thematic areas already addressed. Sakari Toiviainen, for example, sees the film as a case in point: 'In approach and spirit, *A Game of Luck* is part of the new wave tribe, a fruit of the developing awareness and aesthetic rad-icalism of the 1960s as well as a rudder for societal radicalism.'[23] This combination of New Wave thematology and nation-specific forms of social radicalism is well exemplified by a scene on Suomenlinna island off Helsinki. A photo shoot of Telle modelling in the tunnels of the castle turns into an impromptu party when one of the group starts to perform a contemporary song written by Kaj Chydenius, a leading figure in the socially critical 'chanson' movement. The song disrupts the narrative since it is alternatively performed straight to the camera or in cuts to close-ups of the protagonists dancing in the barely lit tunnels. The scene has two functions, both to capture the exuberance of youth as well as to play with contemporary aesthetic norms.

An upbeat rock song soon interrupts this performance, and all the youths explode into wild dancing. Jarva captures this and especially the intimacy between Jussi and Telle with handheld cameras and close-ups. The combination of diegetic music, handheld cameras, natural forms of lighting and close-ups provides the scene with a different aura than other similar dance performance scenes, including films such as *The Unruly Generation* (*Kuriton sukupolvi*, 1957), Matti Kassila's take on famed author Mika Waltari's play, which features a scene where the young people perform a jitterbug dance, much to the horror of their elders. In Jarva's dance scene the main focus is on camera style, as the freewheeling camera and extreme close-up editing emphasize the sexual attraction between Jussi and Telle.

The length of the scene, including its use of a range of musical performances, makes it a clear case of cinematic excess. As with the earlier examples of formative constructions used for consolidating cultural connections, *A Game of Luck* both indicates its close relationship with cultural innovation and constructs a form of dialogue between international and domestic New Wave film cultures. Indeed, Antti-Ville Kärjä suggests that films of the era featuring popular songs in a key role occupied an awkward position, since they were both popular culture with a distinct youth element as well as part of modernist cinema; that is, they were art cinema.[24] *A Game of Luck* exemplifies this potential contradiction given that much of the narrative operates more along the lines of the ambiguous modernism of Godard or Kurkvaara, and it is only this scene of excess that fractures this impression. Yet it is precisely the confrontational collision that makes the scene rewarding, allowing it to stand out from the rest of the film. By drawing attention to its stylistic excesses, the scene's place in the film highlights the notion that Finnish productions of the era were a bricolage of multiple elements, composed in a transnational matrix. Instead of unproductively arguing for an external influence on Finnish cinema or insisting on authentic domestic cultural genius, it is best to understand at least some aspects of this innovative era as a form of negotiation between international norms and domestic inspiration.

RHETORICAL MANIFESTOS

Having discussed transnational stylistic and thematic variations in Finnish New Wave cinema, this chapter now addresses a key part of the Nouvelle Vague's ideological operation: its need for political engagement. Endemic in much of the Nouvelle Vague's political aspirations was the need to reveal and challenge cinema's capitalist entertainment principles, as well as to take part in the radical politics of the era.[25] The result was films such as Godard's agit-prop productions *La Chinoise* (1967) and *Weekend* (1967). These films were laden with aggressive arguments against the Vietnam War and bourgeois complacency. Their style follows extreme experimentalism with long shots, allegorical symbols, lack of clear narratives, as well as manifestos delivered to the camera. Of all the examples mentioned in this chapter, excess characterizes these works comprehensively.

In Finland too, directors such as Mikko Niskanen and Maunu Kurkvaara provided politicized contributions to contemporary debates with *The Girl of Finland* and *Rat War* (*Rottasota*, 1968), respectively. In this section, I focus on *Rat War*, as it operates clearly in the transnational tradition of the international New Wave movement's explicitly political turn, whereas Niskanen's film is more playful in its intertextuality and its modes of expression. Kurkvaara's film combines different areas of its director's stylistic aspirations since it plays homage to a range of genres, from disaster tales to science fiction, as well as more socially focused exploration of the corruption of power and a Nouvelle Vague—inspired tale of a young couple's predicament.

Rat War opens with an intriguing stylistic gimmick, when a young couple, the son and daughter of powerful politicians, venture into the cinema. Positioned as part of the audience, we watch a manifesto unfold concerning all-encompassing ecological catastrophe, which the film integrates with class politics and the destabilizing forces of capitalism. Starting with what seems like 8 mm documentary footage of a city, the screen soon expands into a full-screen shot of a stadium. A voiceover explains the moralistic tone of the film, including political corruption, technological progress, consumerism and the impact of increased pollution. To emphasize this sense of a world gone wrong, toxic slime seems to be overtaking the cities while bodies wash up on the shore. The apocalyptic tone of the film contrasts with advertisements featuring politicians promoting a laundry detergent that 'puts the sun in a box'. The depictions reach fever pitch when mist overtakes the capital city, while organ music counterpoints humanity's doom and a voiceover pontificates that 'the earth had now reached the state it was in a million years ago'.

In an unexpected reversal, Kurkvaara cuts to the young couple leaving the cinema in downtown Helsinki, discussing the role of governmental control in wars. The apocalyptic scenario had been a film they were watching, and it has now motivated these activist young people to discuss individual responsibility in a state of democratic deficit. The rest of *Rat War* does not significantly differ from the conventions of the era, as it uses a somewhat understated audiovisual style to capture the couple's attempts to rebel against society. Although occasional flourishes are present, such as the blank façades of suburban housing accompanied by abstract score music, it is ultimately left to the film within a film to provide the case of excess.

What does this visually impressive short film tell us about transnational connectivity? For one, the section is certainly out of place in the context of *Rat War*. Critics noted this too, with Pertti Lumirae, for example, stating that the film 'contains so many ingredients that even a capable director would have struggled to keep them in some kind of clear order'.[26] While other New Wave film makers had also used science fiction conventions— Truffaut's *Fahrenheit 451* (1966) and Jindřich Polák's *Ikarie-XB1* (1963)— Kurkvaara seems to draw more from contemporaneous ecological writing by Paul Ehrlich (*The Population Bomb*, 1968) and Rachel Carson (*Silent Spring*, 1962), among others, to construct a pointed political contribution along the lines of Godard's experimental works already discussed.

The short film is novel in its use of spectacle, a mode that had not been much attempted in the confines of the domestic film culture. As the arguments and style of *Rat War* are mostly based on imported visual conventions and thematic ideas, the placement of these ideas within Helsinki, and Finnish society in general, positions it as a transnational text. Through this, the film continues a dialogic approach to the New Wave, where influences and appropriations work both locally and globally. As the scope of the arguments as well as their cultural origins gesture well beyond the confines of Finland, the film balances the competing pulls of localization and the planetary implications of environmental messages. With this, both the formative aspects of the film as well as its thematic content swing between different poles in a way that is best made sense of through transnational analysis. The excessive role of the short film in the context of the main feature certainly positions the whole of *Rat War* as a very unusual piece of domestic cinema, indicating how films of the period were, again, integrated into the transnational flow of cultural influences even as they contributed much to international, even planetary, discussions over significant topics such as environmentalism. While many critics found the film unsatisfactory, and it has essentially disappeared, its participation in the transnational dynamics of Finnish New Wave film culture forcefully underlines the need to consider the New Wave as inherently a transnational phenomenon.

OPEN-ENDED CONCLUSIONS

To wrap up this discussion of New Wave film culture as a transnational enterprise, I finish by discussing a frequent feature of New Wave cinema, the open-ended or abstract conclusion. The importance of the conclusion was already noted in the case of Truffaut's seminal *400 Blows* as well as Niskanen's 'variation' of it in *Skin Skin*, but other types of formative excess also breach the confines of the cinematic diegesis, drawing attention to the film as both part of an international film cultural movement and a Finnish variation of its parameters. One such example is Jörn Donner's Swedish-language *Here Begins the Adventure* (*Här börjar äventyret*, 1965). The narrative of the film focuses on a Swedish woman, Anne (Harriet Andersson), who travels to Helsinki and becomes embroiled in a love triangle of sorts with an old flame, Tauno (Matti Oravisto), and her lover from Paris. The film captures her uncertain, dislocated state of mind with lengthy shots of Tauno and Anne walking the streets of Helsinki and musing about architecture and the human condition.

In this respect, much of the film aligns with the Deleuzian time images that, for him, characterize the ambiguity of the art cinema of the era. Through these long, existential explorations, Helsinki takes on qualities of the any-spaces-whatever, supporting more the cinematic recreation of subjective states than any clear architectural cultural memory. The ways in which the film contrasts Helsinki with its two protagonists are highly intriguing, as the architect is a typical doer, an actor of classical narration that would make the narrative progress. However, instead the focus is on the seer, the cosmopolitan in Finland who sees Helsinki through a different set of eyes and uses these to rethink her normative links to culturally located space. To capture a sense of uncertainty and confusion, Helsinki emerges as a space in transition, a way to capture a transnational sense of alienation.

Throughout, there are few clear indicators of the type of formalist experimentation of the Nouvelle Vague besides a few jump cuts and other such indicators of experimental tactics. Instead, the focus is squarely on an aesthetics of spatial displacement that characterizes many of the key films of the era in their refusal to abide with the mannerisms of classical narration.

Such moments are important in making felt the transnational connotations of the film, with Martti Savo describing the film as Antonioniesque.[27] This disassociated perspective captures the director's distanced outsiderness from Helsinki as a tangible geocultural location as much as it is part of connecting the film with the international New Wave cinemas. On another level of excess, the film culminates with a lengthy shot of the archipelagos outside Helsinki as the sun washes over the sea. The visual qualities of the shot are stunning, but what is even more impressive is that the scene holds the spectator for several minutes and provides an apt conclusion to the film's narrative, focusing on the future of its two uncertain protagonists.

While ambiguous conclusions proliferate in Finnish New Wave cinema, including works such as Risto Jarva's *The Worker's Diary* (*Työmiehen päiväkirja*, 1967) and Kurkvaara's *A League of Millions* (*Miljoonaliiga*, 1968), the conclusion of Donner's film provides a clear illustration for considering stylistic choices in a transnational framework. It combines many of the elements discussed throughout this chapter into a single excessive moment. Thus, it employs artistic means that had been developing in the international sphere to capture something very locally specific—arguably, Donner's disenchantment with Finnish culture. As such, it exemplifies the way the New Waves were formed in relation to an international exchange of means of expression even as national specificity maintained a significant role in the formation of the various New Wave styles. The directors of the Finnish New Wave innovated with form in response to changes in domestic culture and thus contributed to the dynamic dialogue between international and Finnish New Wave film cultures—a truly transnational process.

NOTES

1. Jörn Donner, "Suomalainen elokuva vuonna nolla," *Studio 6* (1961).
2. Truffaut 1954.
3. Neupert 2007.
4. Kovács 2008.
5. see Toiviainen 1975; Uusitalo 1984a, b; Honka-Hallila et al. 1995 and Pantti 2000.
6. Uusitalo 1984a, b.
7. Toiviainen 1975.
8. Henry G. Gröndahl, "Rakas..." *Hufvudstadsbladet*, 25/11/1962.
9. Green 2007.
10. Neupert 2007.
11. Vincendeau and Graham 2012.

12. Wiegand 2012.
13. Thompson 2001: 55.
14. Melgosa 2010.
15. Bozak 2012.
16. Rai 2009: 17.
17. Neupert 2007.
18. Raskin 2007.
19. Neupert 2007.
20. Erkka Lehtola, "Tänään olet täällä", *Aamulehti*, 18/9/1966.
21. Neupert 2007.
22. Deleuze 2005: xi.
23. Toiviainen 1983.
24. Kärjä 2005.
25. Neupert 2007.
26. Pertti, Lumirae, "Rottasota", *Päivän Sanomat* 9/4/1968.
27. Martti Savo, "Täältä alkaa seikkailu" *Kansan Uutiset* 19/12/1965.

CHAPTER 10

Popular Modernism

Kimmo Laine

The launch issue of the film journal *Filmihullu* in 1968 featured an interview with the comedian and filmmaker Pertti 'Spede' Pasanen, conducted by Marja-Leena Mikkola. The interviewer, a young leftist author and screenwriter of the seminal New Wave film *Skin Skin* (*Käpy selän alla*, 1966), was intrigued to hear that Pasanen mentioned Jerry Lewis as one of his influences:

Mikkola: Jerry Lewis, that's fascinating. Do you mean that you are interested in his ideology, the incredibly cunning and funny critique of American society, or mostly in his performative skills?

Pasanen: Mostly his performative side and his comic art, the way he uses his face, his limbs and his whole body.

Mikkola: Have you no interest in Lewis's conceptual side?

Pasanen: Yes, of course, but as I mentioned, we try to foist some social critique into here and there; that is not fundamental to our work. Our starting point is that harmless entertainment like ours is needed too.[1]

Filmihullu was highly influenced by the French *Cahiers du cinéma*, whose enthusiasm over Jerry Lewis was well known. *Cahiers* had published a special issue on Lewis at the turn of 1967–1968, and his debut film

K. Laine (✉)
Film Studies, University of Oulu, Oulu, Finland
e-mail: kimmo.laine@oulu.fi

© The Editor(s) (if applicable) and The Author(s) 2016
H. Bacon (ed.), *Finnish Cinema*, Palgrave European Film
and Media Studies, DOI 10.1057/978-1-137-57651-4_10

as a director, *The Bellboy* (1960), was to be included as an example of a 'category c' film, in which 'the content is not explicitly political, but in some way becomes so through the criticism practiced on it through its form', in Jean-Luc Comolli and Jean Narboni's key article 'Cinema/ Ideology/Criticism',[2] translated in *Filmihullu* in 1970. One could assume that the notion of interviewing Pasanen in the first place stemmed from the wish to find in domestic popular comedy some of the self-reflexive potential that *Cahiers* placed in Lewis or Jacques Tati. Although Pasanen later proved both politically and aesthetically conservative—in the 1970s and 1980s he often attacked political film culture and art cinema as well as the film subsidy system—at the beginning of his film career he had indeed not been worlds apart from the New Wave cinema. His first directing credit (*The X-Baron/X-Paroni*, 1964) was shared with Risto Jarva and Jaakko Pakkasvirta, two central figures of the Finnish New Wave, and he played a dramatic role in *Silver from Across the Border* (*Hopeaa rajan takaa*, 1963), the third part of Mikko Niskanen's modernist-influenced war trilogy.

Pasanen's early career, as well as *Filmihullu*'s early interest in his work, is a reminder of the historical overlap between popular, studio-based film and modernist cinema in the 1950s, 1960s and 1970s. The emergence of Finnish New Wave cinema has often been written about in terms of either rupture or continuity. As with many other modernist movements, the filmmakers and critics of the new generation not only experienced but also manifested a break with the past, as was seen in Chap. 9. The cinematographer and director Lasse Naukkarinen highlighted the break on a personal level in a 1972 interview:

> I have never had anything to do with any Finnish Film tradition. When I became interested in the cinema the 'new' Finnish cinema had already been born and I have always worked in it. Of course I have seen a lot of traditional Finnish cinema but I was never specially interested in it and I doubt if it has had any influence on me.[3]

Some later film historians, on the other hand, have questioned the totality of rupture.[4] In this chapter, the perspective is somewhat different. Instead of ruptures and continuities, the relation between popular cinema and modernist cinema is seen from the vantage point of simultaneity and overlap. As Pietari Kääpä noted in Chap. 9, New Wave influences filtered into popular cinema, while New Wave directors experimented with popular forms. The focus is now especially on the former theme, which is exposed from different perspectives: the mode of production, authorship and intermediality.

As with Pasanen, there is often, if not always, an element of comedy involved in popular modernism. There is clearly a two-way relationship between modernist and comical devices. On the one hand, some popular comedies might in particular historical circumstances come close to cinematic modernism, as can be seen in the praise given to Jerry Lewis by French modernist circles in the 1960s. On the other hand, not all forms of modernist movement lack the touch of comedy. A case in point is the early and mid-1960s work of Jean-Luc Godard, noted for his experiments with narrative conventions, popular genres and film sound. Whatever is involved in, for instance, the 'action scenes' of *Pierrot le fou* (1965), or the 'one-minute' total silence in *Band of Outsiders* (*Bande à part*, 1964), nuances of comedy can hardly be overlooked. In Godard, such playing with aesthetic rules is usually considered experimental—exploring the limits and foregrounding the conventions of cinematic narration—rather than comic. In the popular modernist films discussed here, aesthetic transgressions are more likely to serve the narrative goals of the film, to keep us in suspense or to make us laugh. Often the difference is a matter of degree rather than of kind.

The filmmakers discussed in this chapter include in particular Matti Kassila, Aarne Tarkas, Mikko Niskanen, Jörn Donner and Spede Pasanen (and also Jukka Virtanen and Ere Kokkonen, who were among the creative forces who worked for Pasanen). Niskanen, although later an essential New Wave figure, is included mainly because of his early films made for the major studios, and Donner because of his penchant for sensationalism and his double role as a director and producer.

IN-BETWEEN PRODUCTION

In terms of the mode of production, popular modernism falls between the old studio-based production with regular employees and a Hollywood-like division of labour, and the emerging independent/package production system, where each production was put together separately. Some of the filmmakers discussed here worked primarily for the old studios (Kassila and Tarkas), while others operated as independent producers (Donner and Pasanen). In none of the cases, however, was the line between studio and independent productions quite clear.

Kassila and Tarkas had already attempted independent production in the early 1950s, after the popular and critical success of the film noirish action comedy *The Radio Commits a Burglary* (*Radio tekee murron*, 1951), co-written by the two and directed by Kassila. Discontented with the working conditions at Suomen Filmiteollisuus,[5] Kassila, together with Tarkas and the cinematographer Osmo Harkimo, founded a new company, Junior-Filmi, and started working on a sequel to their previous success. *The Radio Goes Mad* (*Radio tulee hulluksi*, 1952) was finally completed with the aid of the independent filmmaker Teuvo Tulio. Never seeing eye to eye with Tulio on the sharing of the profits, Junior-Filmi made only two other feature films: *The White Reindeer* (*Valkoinen peura*, 1952), directed by Erk Blomberg and produced by Tarkas, a mystical art house horror film and the first Finnish film to make the official selection at the Cannes film festival; and the crime film *The Night Is Long* (*Yö on pitkä*, 1952), Tarkas' debut as a feature director. Kassila and Harkimo returned to Suomen Filmiteollisuus, and Tarkas became a prolific director at Fennada-Filmi.

In the late 1950s, influenced by European modernist movements, Kassila and Harkimo made a fresh, and arguably more remarkable, attempt to break free from the studio system. The independently produced *The Glass Heart* (*Lasisydän*, 1959) was a road movie about a glass artist who goes through a creative crisis—or a 'walking film', as Kassila classifies it with reference to European films featuring protagonists drifting aimlessly from one place to another. Along with Maunu Kurkvaara's early films like *The Queen of Spades* (*Patarouva*, 1959) and *Darling* (*Rakas*, 1961), *The Glass Heart* can be seen as an important precursor of the 1960s New Wave era. Shot on location with portable equipment, the film broke away from several studio practices, for instance by using only post-produced sound and introducing jazzy popular tunes instead of a classical soundtrack. Otherwise Kassila, as well as Tarkas, worked mainly for the major studios throughout the 1950s and 1960s, introducing modernist elements within studio productions, as we shall see.

Mikko Niskanen first entered filmmaking as an extra at Suomen Filmiteollisuus, and after studying at the Moscow Film School he got the chance to direct his three first features—the war trilogy partly influenced by Soviet modernist cinema, *The Boys* (*Pojat*, 1962); *The Partisans* (*Sissit*, 1963); and *Silver from Across the Border*—at Suomen Filmiteollisuus and Fennada-Filmi (Fig. 10.1). For the rest of his career he worked for the independent companies (including his own) or the Finnish Broadcasting Company.

Of all the Finnish filmmakers, Jörn Donner's early career is probably closest to the European New Wave prototype. He started as a critic, an author of fact and fiction and an activist in cine-club and film

Fig. 10.1 A striking composition in depth in *The Partisans* (1963)

archive movements, before directing his debut short film for Suomen Filmiteollisuus in 1954. In the early 1960s he broke into feature films in Sweden with *A Sunday in September* (*En söndag i September*, 1963). After three more films in Sweden, Donner returned to Finland first as a producer. Having established his own company, Jörn Donner Productions, he started to cooperate with another start-up company, FJ-Filmi, which had had an immediate success with Mikko Niskanen's *Skin Skin*. With the major production companies of the studio era under pressure—Suomen Filmiteollisuus was practically bankrupt, while Suomi-Filmi and Fennada-Filmi had run down the business—there was room for new players. The major companies were replaced by smaller independent companies that sometimes produced only one or two films. Donner sought a mode of production that would be halfway between studio filmmaking and independent production, relying partly on public funding. In subsequent years FJ-Filmi became the biggest production company in Finland, and in 1971 it was merged with Jörn Donner Productions.[6] Donner himself divided his time between directing and producing, among other activities.

Spede Pasanen first gained success as a live comedian, and in the early 1960s made it into radio and television. He had already, however, also become acquainted with filmmaking in the 1950s, working as an extra in, for example, several of Tarkas' films. Starting with *X-Baron*, his role as a filmmaker was sometimes that of a director, but more of a producer-screenwriter, with Ere Kokkonen or Jukka Virtanen directing. Also, as an actor he eventually stood down, giving way to Vesa-Matti Loiri as the lead comedian. Although the number of his films cannot be compared to those made during the studio years, his position as a populist-minded comedy mogul bore some resemblance to T.J. Särkkä at Suomen Filmiteollisuus towards the end of the studio era.

AUTHORSHIP

The attitude towards authorship is one of the dividing lines between studio production and modernist cinema, and popular modernism is once again somewhere in between. While all of the filmmakers discussed here were definitely modernist-era auteurs in the sense that they were both screenwriters and directors, and that they preferred to be in charge of the whole production process whenever possible, they were such to a varying degree. Mikko Niskanen is the only one whose mode of authorship is close to the romantic conception of an artist with ups and downs of career, problems relating to self and others, including creative crises and fights with producers. The critical biography of Niskanen by Sakari Toiviainen is named appropriately *Tuska ja hurmio* ('The Agony and the Ecstasy'), implicating the inner aspects of the creative process. The outer obstacles culminated in a conflict between Niskanen as the director and Donner as the producer of *The Asphalt Lambs* (*Asfalttilampaat*, 1968). To this story of young lovers in a repressive small town Donner added an admittedly sensationalist scene, in which he himself plays a doctor who forces himself on a young pregnant woman, and afterwards prescribes her painkillers (Fig. 10.2). In a memo Donner claimed that Niskanen's previous films, while generally successful, contained scenes that did not advance the narration. In order to attract audiences both in Finland and abroad, more 'forceful narration' was needed. According to Donner, the added scene was thus justified as a means to sell the film.[7] Niskanen, for his part, disclaimed the film, stating that each time he tried to watch it, he had to stop at the scene with Donner.[8]

Tarkas and Kassila had their share of fights with producers, but, as children of the studio system, their attitude towards filmmaking was more that of a professional employee. Tarkas' ambition was in screenwriting and brainstorming, and according to many of his colleagues he frequently lost interest in the projects once the actual shooting began and left the

Fig. 10.2 *The Asphalt Lambs* (1968): Jörn Donner in a scene disowned by the director Mikko Niskanen

technical crew responsible for the rest of the process, including editing.[9] In this sense, Kassila was the opposite of Tarkas, being equally enthusiastic about all aspects of filmmaking, from scriptwriting to lighting, designing the soundtrack and editing. A dedicated admirer of Ingmar Bergman, he shared the idea of the auteur being responsible for the whole creative process. In practice, however, throughout the 1950s and early 1960s Kassila regularly negotiated his terms with the major production companies, being able to realize one of his own ideas every now and then in exchange for projects given by the producers. Among the latter was *The Wild Generation* (*Kuriton sukupolvi*, 1957), a remake of a 1930s film based on Mika Waltari's play about an unruly if fundamentally benevolent youth, made in exchange for one of Kassila's own favourites, *Harvest Month* (*Elokuu*, 1956), an adaptation of a novel by F.E. Sillanpää. Using Kassila's own, highly self-reflexive voiceover narration, characteristic of many of his films, *Harvest Month* is a lyrical account of the last day in the life of a canal guard, an alcoholic wannabe writer, who reminisces about his life and unfulfilled love (Fig. 10.3). A critical success in Finland, *Harvest Month* was also the second Finnish film to be included in the official selection at the Cannes Film Festival.

Despite their differences as filmmakers, Donner and Pasanen share similar attitudes towards authorship, since they have both had the dual

Fig. 10.3 Director Matti Kassila's voiceover narration interrupts the action in *Harvest Month* (1956)

role of producer-director. Donner—like Kassila a loyal admirer of Ingmar Bergman and the author of *The Personal Vision of Ingmar Bergman* (1964)—was already, as a critic, clearly an advocate of modernist auteur cinema. As a producer, however, he sometimes used his power not unlike the film moguls of the studio era, as we have seen. As a director, he often took a stance of self-irony towards his own films, well expressed in passages like this from his memoirs, reflecting in the third person on his Swedish film *Adventure Starts Here* (*Här börjar äventyret*, 1965):

> J imagines, while making a film as seriously as he can, that somewhere there is a world waiting to see his films. If there is such a world, it is shrinking. He is dependent on having Harriet Andersson play the lead. He is dependent on the Swedish subsidy system that will later reward this film. He is dependent on a certain international audience that shows up at festivals, but nowhere else. A few times he has to watch his film at these screenings; he is ashamed of the naivety and non-professionalism apparent in some scenes, of some poor performances and dead dialogues that the foreign audiences will not understand because of the subtitling.[10]

Donner's self-ironical authorship is further mirrored in some of his films, especially in *Portraits of Women* (*Naisenkuvia*, 1970), in which he plays a director of pornographic films. Having made his career in America, he wants to reshape Finnish erotic cinema by shooting explicit love scenes, but he ends up being summoned to appear in court for obscenity, and escaping the country with the negatives of his films. The self-reflective and self-ironic dimension is quite obvious, especially since by the late 1960s Donner had become a public figure, often as an advocate of 'Scandinavian sexuality'.[11] Donner himself claims that it took him some time to realize that *Portraits of Women* reflected his own position as a filmmaker.[12]

As a producer, Pasanen shared Donner's practical–economical attitude towards filmmaking. He constantly claimed that his guiding principles were, first, that making a film should be as much fun as watching it and, second, that films should make a profit. His position on authorship was not solely based on his suspicion of modernist art cinema, but it also had a more positive nuance that reflected back to the more collective traditions of popular culture. In 1985 he expressed his playful idea of collective authorship in an interview: 'Nowadays "Spede" is no longer just my own name; Simo [Salminen] and Vesku [Vesa-Matti Loiri] are an essential part of it, since I would not be able to do the Spede job alone.'[13]

INTERMEDIALITY

In contrast to various historical conceptions of 'Pure Cinema'—in the sense that the essence of cinema is distinct from the other arts and media—the popular modernism of the 1950s and 1960s was strikingly intermedial by nature. Boundaries between different media were not respected any more than those between genres. The intermedial aspects of popular modernism are now discussed from four different perspectives: adaptation, voiceover narration, self-reflexive films about media, and the filmmakers' intermedial careers.

Adaptation

Even though modernist cinema favoured original scripts, Kassila in particular had an affection for adaptations. Moreover, his adaptations were often of an unusual kind, exceeding the typical forms of adaptation from novels, short stories or plays. Kassila's *Song of Warsaw* (*Varsovan laulu*, 1953) and Tarkas' *We're All Guilty* (*Olemme kaikki syyllisiä*, 1954), co-scripted by Kassila, are both crime films adapted—at least to a degree—from newspaper stories. Newspapers and news headlines provided not only narrative content, but also expressive inspiration. In film noir style, the films of Kassila and Tarkas often used news headlines in order to achieve a forceful and effective impression. Both directors also favoured the use of the montage sequence, which in itself is a prime example of a popular modernist device, being developed in Hollywood but heavily influenced by Soviet montage cinema of the 1920s. The montage sequences, usually accompanied by non-diegetic music, typically consist of varying kinds of shots:

> Extreme close-ups, canted angles, silhouettes, whip pans, and other obtrusive techniques differentiate this sort of segment from the orthodox scene. … Flagrant as the montage sequence is, its rarity, its narrative function, and its narrowly conventional format assure its status as classical narration's most acceptable rhetorical flourish.[14]

An effective example is at the beginning of Kassila's *Professor Masa* (*Professori Masa*, 1949). The film opens with a postman dropping a newspaper in a mailbox, and as the paper falls down a star-shaped optical cut reveals the headline 'Harbour workers threaten to strike'. A rolling optical cut leads to a political agitator giving a speech, then to a close-up of a hand crumpling the newspaper, yet another headline, people crowding round a newsstand, a bourgeois man trampling on the newspaper and so on. The last headline of the montage sequence reads: 'What is this strike all about?' It leads us with a clever gimmick to a newsroom, where journalists start to ponder the question.

Among other unusual adaptations by Kassila were *The Radio Commits a Burglary*, based on a broadcast of a live break-in by a well-known radio reporter, and *The Girl from Moon Bridge* (*Tyttö kuunsillalta*, 1953), adapted from a radio play by Hella Wuolijoki. The latter adaptation was especially challenging, since the play consists of telephone conversations between the two protagonists, a middle-aged man and a woman, who had a short romance in their youth and now get reacquainted over the phone. Obviously a 'non-cinematic' starting point by any standard, this challenge was taken up by Kassila and his cinematographer Kalle Peronkoski by 'reinventing' an old—and in the opinion of many contemporaries an out-of-date—cinematic device, the double exposure. What started as a problem soon became the main source of the dramatic strength of the film. The first conversation starts with standard cross-cutting between the two, but soon changes to double exposure to show them simultaneously. During the next conversations, double exposure is utilized right from the beginning. These double exposures construct a special space, occupied only by the two lovers. Once their relationship becomes more intimate, the camera moves closer to them, and the background of their offices is dissolved to black. When they start to quarrel, the background becomes visible again. With the creative use of such an old-fashioned device, *The Girl from Moon Bridge* blurs the boundaries between studio realism and cinematic modernism and, in a sense, opens a view on the whole history of cinema in its archaic, classical and modernist forms.

Voiceover Narration

As Sarah Kozloff notes, voiceover has often been considered a non-cinematic, non-visual, literary and redundant device.[15] Accordingly, critics frequently complained about the use of voiceover in the films of Tarkas, Pasanen and especially Kassila. Often it seems that the critics dissatisfied with voiceover were committed to the purist—narratively harmonious and balanced, respecting the boundaries between different media, keeping up a homogeneous and uninterrupted narrative world—standards of classical narration, while the use of voiceover did incorporate elements of complexity, self-reflexivity and transgression into popular modernist films. Typically, this involved intermingling comic elements with modernist aspirations.

An early example is Kassila's small-town comedy *Hilma's Name Day* (*Hilmanpäivät*, 1954), in which the voiceover narrator constantly and playfully manipulates the events, comments on the characters, anticipates forthcoming events and reacts to the atmosphere by, for example, whispering when two of the characters have an intimate moment. At a narrative turning point the narrator suddenly orders 'Stop!'—and as a result, the image turns into a series of freeze frames.

Crazy Finland (*Pähkähullu Suomi*, 1967), directed by Jukka Virtanen and produced by Spede Pasanen, introduces an equally heterogeneous use of voiceover narration. The film opens as a mock-documentary celebrating Finland's 50th year as an independent state. The narrator constantly loses the thread of his task, paying attention to absurd details, throwing verbal–visual puns and apologizing for blinking his eye, while the image turns black. At the end of the film, one of the characters turns to the camera and admits that he has not understood anything. The voiceover narrator suddenly addresses him—he turns his head up to the sky expecting the narrator to be there—and paraphrases the whole film, while the image track is filled with extracts from documentaries and old feature films that have nothing to do with the actual events (Fig. 10.4).

While *Crazy Finland* playfully gives up the narrative world for the sake of fun and becomes a series of self-reflexive gags, Kassila's police mystery *The Stars Will Tell, Inspector Palmu* (*Tähdet kertovat komisario Palmu,* 1962) plays with the conventions of voiceover narration as far as possible, still maintaining a plausible narrative world. At the beginning of the film, the narrator—this time a homodiegetic narrator, one of the policemen—constantly interrupts the flow of action at the crime scene with his comments, sometimes offscreen and sometimes straight to camera. The first time the voiceover narration is introduced he actually starts by saying, 'Excuse me, but I'll have to interrupt and explain how it all began.' Soon there is a cut from the action at the crime scene to the policeman addressing the camera, and while he goes on with his account of the events, the image track features various obtrusive devices like quick zoom-ins

Fig. 10.4 A character in *Crazy Finland* (1967) addressed by the voiceover narrator from above

or freeze frames, and the soundtrack is characterized by sound effect–like music. In this interaction, the sounds and the images lean towards a peculiar blending of comedy, action and self-reflexive modernism. Thus, just like many of the French early 1960s New Wave films, *The Stars Will Tell, Inspector Palmu*, as well as the other three films in the series, functions simultaneously as both a classic detective story and a self-conscious reworking of the genre.

Films About Media

The overarching intermediality of the popular modernist cinema is also manifested by the fact that the films quite frequently are about media itself. In addition to films about newspapers or radio that have already been touched on, there are, for example, parodies of popular literature (Tarkas' *Conscript Hero/Sankarialokas*, 1955), filmmaking (Donner's *Portraits of Women* and Pasanen's *Leftovers from the North/Pohjan tähteet*, directed by Ere Kokkonen, 1969) and especially television. In Kassila's *Vodka, Inspector Palmu* (*Vodkaa, komisario Palmu*, 1969) glimpses from an actual television station are mixed with the fictive detective story. The story evolves from the murder of a television journalist, and soon the fictive policemen visit the actual premises of the Finnish Broadcasting Company, meeting with real-life reporters and even the president of the company. Later, the film displays, for example, parodies of television ads in Soviet style.

Kassila's *Let Not One Devil Cross the Bridge* (*Äl' yli päästä perhanaa*, 1968) is a film about filmmaking—once again a film celebrating Finnish independence—that features an episode about a presidential election that takes place on live television in the future. After a debate between the candidates, the audience gets to vote for a candidate by pressing a button, while questions presented by the viewers are displayed on a television screen. An almost uncannily accurate prophecy of present-day reality television formats, the episode also satirizes the contemporary role of television as a political forum: during the 1960s television had become an integral arena for political debate. The ultimate satirical—and self-reflexive—twist is that the person who is elected as president is none of the candidates, but rather the host of the show, played by the real-life television celebrity Matti Kuusla.

Intermedial Work Environment

Finally, while all of the popular modernists were sworn filmmakers, none of them devoted his artistic career solely to cinema. On the contrary, all moved almost continually from one medium to another. Donner has—besides being a prolific writer—directed for television. Kassila started as a stage actor and later directed in the theatre and served as a theatre manager. In the 1960s he also directed for television, as did Tarkas and Niskanen, whose arguably most distinguished work is the made-for-television film *Eight Fatal Shots* (*Kahdeksan surmanluotia*, 1972).

Pasanen's career epitomizes the centrality of intermediality to popular modernism. His roles as a film comedian, radio personality and television comedy host were inseparable, and the fictive worlds of his films and television shows constantly blended together and backed each other up. Many of the characters in his films, including the most popular one, Uuno Turhapuro, who featured in 19 films between 1973 and 2004, were first tested out in Pasanen's television show. The example of Pasanen shows that for popular modernists, other media were primarily not a problem, but rather an opportunity.

Notes

1. Mikkola 1968: 20.
2. Comolli and Narboni 1976: 26.
3. Hillier 1972: 42.
4. Pantti 1998.
5. Kassila 2004: 121.
6. Uusitalo 1998a: 367–68.
7. Toiviainen 1999: 128–32.
8. Niskanen 1971: 90.
9. Uusitalo 2006: 234–46.
10. Donner 2013: 396.
11. See Koivunen 2015: 93–108.
12. Donner 1970: 8.
13. Interview of Spede Pasanen, *Katso* 9/1985.
14. Bordwell et al. 1985: 29.
15. Kozloff 1988: 8–22.

The Age of Internationalization: Finnish Cinema Since 1980

PART IV

The Age of Internationalism:
Finnish Cinema Since 1980

CHAPTER 11

An Increasingly European Nation

Henry Bacon

The Cold War is generally considered to have ended with the dramatic fall of European socialism in the autumn of 1989, leading within a year to the reunification of Germany and within two years to the dissolution of the Soviet Union (USSR). Finland found itself completely free to deepen its economic relations with the West and immediately applied for membership of the European Union (EU). It joined the Union in 1995, and together with most other EU countries adopted the euro as its official currency.

However, bilateral trade with the Soviet Union had already diminished because of the problems the Soviet economy was facing, and now the highly profitable trade came to an end. This coincided with a major banking crisis that derived from overheating of the economy during the 1980s boom and problems in the handling of domestic and foreign debts, which had accumulated rapidly after restrictions on lending had been lifted in 1986. In 1991 the Finnish mark was tied to the European Currency Unit (ECU) at a very high rate, which actually hindered exports and increased unemployment. These developments led to one of the severest recessions Finland has ever experienced. Some filmmakers were acutely aware of its effects on the man in the street. Aki Kaurismäki for one had already

H. Bacon (✉)
Film and Television Studies, University of Helsinki,
Helsinki, Finland
e-mail: henry.bacon@helsinki.fi

© The Editor(s) (if applicable) and The Author(s) 2016
H. Bacon (ed.), *Finnish Cinema*, Palgrave European Film
and Media Studies, DOI 10.1057/978-1-137-57651-4_11

established in his 1980s films his highly idiosyncratic cinematic poetics through depicting the existential conditions of ordinary people who found themselves pushed to the margins of society. Suddenly his approach seemed almost prophetic and his *Drifting Clouds* of 1996, even as it evaded precise temporal coordinates, was like a melancholy statement about what was happening to people at a grass-roots level.

The late 1990s were characterized by political consensus, with Paavo Lipponen's 'Rainbow Government' having the support of all major parliamentary parties, with the sole exception of the Centre Party. Lipponen was a stern supporter of the EU and actively sought to strengthen Finland's position in its governing bodies. As the European economy was once again booming and as after initial difficulties the euro was beginning to gain strength, being a member of the Union seemed like a way of gaining access to operating freely and profitably not only on a European but also on a global level. The Finnish economy recovered dramatically towards the end of the millennium in the wake of the staggering success of Nokia. This allowed for a major increase in financing of cultural life. The film industry was at this point in top form and able to make the most out of the opportunities offered.

Already by the 1980s it had become clear that the system of state subsidies for the film industry had to be renovated in order to create a sound basis for the domestic cinema. The industry would have to be accountable for taxpayers' investment by providing films that audiences of reasonable numbers—on average at least—would be willing to see. New policymakers at the Finnish Film Foundation (FFF) began to put forward the idea of film as both art and industry, and did their best to convince politicians as well of the dual nature of national cinema as a commercial enterprise that, given the size of the population, could not be expected to cover its costs and had to be supported simply because of its national importance. Now the principal aim was not so much creating works of artistic value, but rather ensuring that there would be a national film industry that a major part of the population would recognize as its own. This entailed introducing a more market-oriented approach to film-subsidizing policy. It was not enough for Finnish films to be successful at foreign film festivals if this did not translate into an increase in box-office receipts. Films would have to be advertised and made attractive for their target domestic audiences. Thus, a significant part of the state subsidy was tied to success at the box office. Distribution was further guaranteed by a contract with Yleisradio, the national radio broadcasting company, in 1984, and with the commercial television broadcasting company MTV3 in the early 1990s. While possibly slightly reducing cinema attendance, this form of presales guaranteed a much wider audience than purely cinematic distribution could ever have hoped to achieve.

Towards the end of the 1990s the new strategies started to bear fruit. In 1999, with attendance figures amounting to 1.8 million, domestic productions took 25% of total box-office receipts. Since then the attendance figures have for the most part been close to and even exceeding 2 million spectators annually. In some ways, what certain Finnish producers in the 1990s referred to as the 'return to genres' has been one of the defining factors of this success. Both the style and content of the films, although indicative of great proficiency and aesthetic sensibility, remain for the most part within the conventions of the mainstream. Part of their success is due to the increased professionalism of production and marketing, as well as good working relationships between the public and private sectors in organizing funding. This has been made possible to a significant degree by the networks developed by the FFF. The major transnational operator is the Nordic Film & TV Fund, a collaborative effort by the Nordic national film institutions. However, there are also a host of other connections, both under the auspices of the FFF and with producers independently creating patterns of collaboration on a wider European as well as a global level.

Another important development in FFF's policy was that it started allocating subsidies to all the major stages of film production, from script-writing to marketing and distribution. This went hand in hand with creating international connections at all levels of filmmaking. These measures have led to a relative stabilization of film production, although the volume has remained fairly small and many production companies continue to operate on a weak financial basis. The distribution has shifted to foreign hands, which has had the benefit of ensuring that Finnish films are well advertised in the form of trailers shown before screenings of popular foreign films.

These institutional changes have ensured that productions meet the highest of technical standards as well as gaining reasonably high visibility on the international festival circuit. They have also allowed for something that may be broadly defined as art cinema to flourish, albeit in an ideologically less controversial form than when the New Waves hit the Finnish coasts. There is at least a handful of filmmakers with an individual style and a genuine wish to explore human concerns beyond providing spectators with the immediate pleasures of the mainstream. The relatively good commercial success of a number of Danish and Swedish films has encouraged Finnish filmmakers once again to try to find foreign commercial distribution after receiving attention and even winning prizes at international festivals.

Aki Kaurismäki, an independent producer as well as a celebrated director, has paved the way: after his *The Man without a Past* won the Grand Prix at the Cannes Film Festival, the film was seen by some 2 million people around the world. His brother Mika has also been eminently successful in creating international production cooperation for his films set in different parts of the world. Furthermore, the content of their films has often had a salient transnational quality, for example Aki's Finnish-French *Le Havre* (2011) and Mika's Finnish-German-Latvian-Russian production *Honey Baby* (2008). Aki in particular has no doubt been genuinely critical of the social developments linked to EU membership, and in *Le Havre* he depicts another kind of Europeanness, one characterized by the solidarity of ordinary people over national and ethnic boundaries.

Many other directors have engaged in rewarding transnational productions. Klaus Härö directed his first three films in Sweden, two of them with themes related to the attempts of Finns to find a place in Swedish society. Antti-Jussi Annila reached much further. In his *Jade Warrior* (2006), he combined elements from the Finnish national epic *Kalevala* with ancient Chinese stories in a Finnish-Chinese-German-Dutch-Estonian production. Perhaps the whimsiest transnational effort was the comic science fiction film *Iron Sky* (2012), a Finnish-Austrian-German production partly funded by crowdsourcing. The producers invited everyone interested to contribute ideas and resources to the project through the internet. Nevertheless, a significant amount of public funding was needed actually to realize these ideas.

Today the Finnish film industry continues for the most part to operate on the basis of a sound and wide domestic audience. Yet that does not provide anywhere near enough revenue to maintain the kind of film production that would meet contemporary professional standards. Subsidies are needed, but the global financial crisis that began in 2008 has led to cuts from most sources. At the time of writing, Finland finds itself in an awkward situation in respect to its eastern neighbor, complying with EU sanctions against Russia, imposed because of the political crisis in Ukraine, yet concerned about its ability to continue lucrative trade relationships. Nevertheless, for the time being domestic cinema flourishes: in 2014 attendance figures again reached almost 2 million spectators and the Finnish-French co-production animation *Moomins in the Riviera*, based on the comic strips of the Finland-Swedish Tove Jansson, has been sold to 40 countries.

CHAPTER 12

International Networks of Production and Distribution

Henry Bacon

FINNISH CINEMA IN THE NEW EUROPE

In the 1980s the Finnish Film Foundation fundamentally renewed its working practices. The people in charge succeeded in convincing the national government not only of the importance, but also of the popular appeal of a national film culture. The amount of state subsidy increased from 10 million marks in 1980 to 40 million in 1990, but this mainly served to compensate for inflation. The development suffered a severe setback in the 1990s when Finland entered one of the worst recessions of its economic history, leading to a substantial reduction in both subsidies and cinema attendance.[1] Eventually the economy recovered and developed impressively, until the effects of the international banking crises of 2008 also hit Finland. After all these vicissitudes, by 2013 the amount of state subsidy had increased to €28,034,000 (according to the Finnish Central Office of Statistics conversion table, 40 million marks in 1990 was the equivalent of €10,296,000 in 2014).

The changes that took place in the Finnish Film Foundation's policies since the 1980s were seen by some as a move from a welfare state style

H. Bacon (✉)
Film and Television Studies, University of Helsinki,
Helsinki, Finland
e-mail: henry.bacon@heslinki.fi

© The Editor(s) (if applicable) and The Author(s) 2016   191
H. Bacon (ed.), *Finnish Cinema*, Palgrave European Film
and Media Studies, DOI 10.1057/978-1-137-57651-4_12

of regulation and attempts to dictate criteria of quality from above to a more European style of operation. This entailed combining public and private funding and financing more films on the basis of their prospective commercial success, rather than concentrating subsidies on films that were expected to have specifically artistic merits. Now one major form of funding is the 50–50 subsidy, which can be awarded to productions that have secured half their funding from private sources.

These changes can also be seen as a response to the fact that since the 1970s Hollywood has achieved an ever firmer grip, particularly of the large young audiences in Europe. A survey conducted by Philippe Meers among young Flemish filmgoers was not encouraging for domestic film-makers: 'Flemish films were considered "low" quality while Hollywood meant "high" quality.'[2] One youth actually stated he preferred American films because they were not in Flemish, which for him made a film appear amateurish.[3] Meers summarizes the results of his survey: 'The perception of Hollywood as the norm for international cinema is reflected in the ways in which Flemish young people receive cinema.'[4]

This appears to be the state of affairs in Finland too. According to an audience survey compiled in 2008, 62 % of the 35–44 age group and 59 % of the 15–24 age group found domestic films to be gloomy (the opinion on this point of the 25–34 age group is for some reason omitted). Of both age groups, 69 % thought that domestic films were less likely to be interesting than foreign films. They were less likely than older people to attach positive attributes to Finnish films. In the qualitative part of the survey, members of the younger group tended to express a lack of enthusiasm for Finnish films, mentioning as faults poor scriptwriting and the frequent reoccurrence of familiar actors. Members of the slightly older group were more inclined to say that at least domestic films have improved. Yet even a person who admitted as much proceeded to state that they are not as high quality as Hollywood films and that 'one usually wants to see a good film and chooses a foreign one'. Members of the 45–59 age group are generally more positive about Finnish cinema, as are those over the age of 60, although they tend to prefer earlier films, mainly of the studio era.[5] According to a similar study conducted five years later and focusing specifically on new domestic films, those in the youngest age group were slightly more positive, although they thought that the topics of the films were not of interest to them. Those in the oldest age group were more negative and thought that new films were targeted at younger people.[6]

According to statistics available in 2011, the most successful Finnish film at the box office, the action film *Vares—Pahan suudelma*, ranked fifth on the list of most popular films (203,695 viewers; the top-ranking *Harry Potter and the Deathly Hallows: Part 2* had 386,520 viewers). The next film on the list directed by a Finn was Aki Kaurismäki's *Le Havre*, a Finnish-French-German co-production. Among the 20 most successful films were also another Vares film and a historical film about Hella Wuolijoki, a controversial wartime political figure. In that year the market share of American films was 64.13%, while Finnish films reached the figure of 17.22%. Other European films combined attained a slightly greater share of 17.67%, and the rest of the world only 0.98%.[7] Some years Finnish films achieve the commendable market share of some 25% while the share of American films remains fairly constant, amounting to a dominant market position. The balance is, according to European Audiovisual Observatory statistics, about the same as in the rest of Western Europe in general. The crucial point is that even in the most successful years, the box-office figures of domestic films are not sufficiently high to support a national film industry. Not only is the population of Finland only 5 million, the frequency of cinema attendance is estimated to be relatively low. This is a standard structural problem of small nation film industries, and in Europe various transnational funding schemes have been developed to alleviate this problem.

EUROPEAN PRODUCTION AND DISTRIBUTION COLLABORATION

In an effort to reach beyond any single national audience and to summon sufficient funding to attain the kind of production values that a large part of the cinema-going population has learned to expect, there has been an effort to transform 'the more than 300 million potential spectators spread across Europe's regions into a more coherent viewing public'.[8] Such efforts resurface the crucial question that has pestered European national cinemas since the 1920s: can Hollywood's dominance be countered in any other way than replicating it? If not, what point is there in maintaining a national or even some kind of European production? Thomas Elsaesser suggests that although 'each national cinema is both national and international', they are so 'in different areas of the cultural sphere'. What this means is that while art cinema participates nationally in the sphere of popular or literary culture, internationally or transnationally these films have, or at least used to have, inverse functions in respect of Hollywood genre films, in that they set fundamentally different horizons of audience expectations. The way this was achieved was part of the brand of a national cinema.[9] In both cases, the branding was in effect targeted only at a select sophisticated audience. Now the question is, even if Hollywood does give the majority of people what they want, might there still be a justification for securing the production of films that expand the scope of cinema by responding to other needs and concerns than the thirst for immediate pleasures offered by glitzy genre films—even if these would only attract audiences too small to make the production self-sustaining?

A full-scale free trade approach calls for abolishing subsidies altogether and letting the markets decide what kind of films are produced. This demand has been circumvented by the argument that national cultures represent values that are more significant than free trade. One seemingly legitimate demand is that people should be able to have access to audiovisual art and entertainment in their own language—even if, as Meers' study suggests, at least a part of the audience might find films in their native tongue amateurish. In many countries this is taken care of by dubbing at least the most popular foreign films, but in countries such as Finland films are for the most part distributed in their original languages and made approachable by subtitling. In such a context national and transnational aspects coincide in the all-important notion that for films to reach across borders, the characters and the way they live their lives or get into adventures have to appear recognizably authentic and lifelike in terms of a given ethnic and social context, as opposed to merely relying on the repetition of standard narrative formulas and worn-out stereotypes. In the words of Stephen Crofts, it is a question of endowing 'cultural universals ... with specific local inflections'.[10] Establishing identity is always a dialectical issue, the articulation of the particular in terms of the various more general factors that together articulate individual phenomena.

At least in a country where subtitling rather than dubbing of foreign films is the practice, the expectation is to hear the language of the people that the film is supposed to depict—however much we are, in practice, fooled in this respect. Yet even more fundamental notions about authenticity are involved. Dudley Andrew has explained how international festival circuits emerged to cater for such interests on the premise that '[e]very country—the mature ones at least—was thought to have its distinct industry, style, and thematic concerns'.[11] The critical question that soon emerged was: does participation at international festivals neverthe-less entail a degree of compromise in the face of foreign expectations? Elsaesser has pointed out that on the international festival circuit the notion of 'world cinema' has come to function as a quality label that steers the profile of film production: national cinemas strive to attain the standing of world cinema. Festivals function as clearing houses for those exhibition outlets that reserve screens for minority-interest films.[12] Elsaesser refers to Anne Jäckel and others who have examined 'how many of Europe's formerly national film industries now consist of a myriad of small production houses, often regionally based, financing one-off projects by deal-making, ad-hoc co-production arrangements, accumulating different types of state-subsidy, public and private financing, or entering into arrangements with national or transnational television industries'.[13] Since these operations increasingly take place on a transnational level, the director tends to become 'the sole vehicle for connoting pan-European identity'.[14]

Elsaesser's point can be seen in the way the Polish Krzystof Kieślowski, the Austrian Michael Haneke or the Finnish Aki Kaurismäki have made films in French in France. These films are generally classified as French, but the nationality of their directors gives them a pan-European transnational quality. Thus these films could be seen as instances of what Elsaesser has elsewhere referred to as *double occupancy*. Just as 'our identities are multiply defined, multiply experienced, and can be multiply assigned to us',[15] European films can often be multiply defined in terms of their national provenance. However, even then, films as well as people may be perceived as having some predominant qualities that are likely to make people who engage with them inclined to think of them in terms of one nation rather than another. This may apply equally to genre films. As Andrew points out in discussing the emergence of the festival circuit: 'Even small national cinemas could modify Hollywood's universally popular genres to deal with local themes and topics. Most important, they could display on screen, as on a mirror, the physical and verbal gestures that comprise the hum of life within the national community.'[16] From the point of view of maintaining national cinema with at least a degree of popular appeal, it is not necessary to try to do something distinctly different than genre films relying to a degree on stock characters, as even such fictional creatures can and should be made to have some kind of national or regional flavour. Nevertheless, to be competitive in this sphere calls for a substantial amount of funding.

Producers as well as policymakers in institutions in charge of funding film production on European, regional and national levels have made considerable efforts to respond to the free trade argument by creating schemes in which subsidies are tied to box-office appeal. The assumption behind these efforts is that productions would benefit from private funding and developing transnational networks of exchange of expertise. These have become an integral part of European film production as a whole. In Randall Halle's view, this new transformation 'represents a significant shift in the nature and qualities of national film production across Europe: film as national high cultural product in a rich subsidy system has given way to film as popular entertainment circulating in a for-profit transnational network'.[17] This ethos can be seen in the MEDIA programme launched by the European Union in an effort to promote European film and audiovisual industries by supporting the development, promotion and distribution of European audiovisual works within Europe and beyond. Viviane Reding, the European Commissioner in charge of the 2001–2006 MEDIA PLUS programme, stated that the scheme would ensure the emergence of a 'European audiovisual production which no longer relies on its inventiveness and originality, reflecting our cultural diversity, but sets out resolutely to win over European audiences and the rest of the world'.[18]

One relevant point of reference for these efforts are the 1970s multinational co-productions, which Halle argues were a way of circumventing 'the ideological control of the subsidy system'. By comparison, the MEDIA programme and Eurimages inverted this pattern for the good of the ideological purposes of promoting 'Europeanist transnationalism—to the telling of European stories, as it were'.[19] This was to take place through promoting the production and distribution of European films and developing cooperation between people working within the industry. Thus, the Council of Europe started the Eurimages fund in 1988 for the purpose of subsidizing European cinema and its distribution, as well as promoting collaboration between producers in different European countries. The stated aim is to promote projects that reflect the diversity of European culture as well as the shared features that emerge from the common interlaced history of European nations. Only producers who join forces from at least two European countries are funded. Since 2000 Eurimages has allocated funds on the basis of two factors: circulation potential assessed on the basis of pre-sales and sales estimates; and the plausibility of marketing and distribution schemes. The previous achievements of the director are also taken into account, and films can still be financed—even if less often—on the basis of their expected innovation and artistic quality.[20]

A major aspect of both the MEDIA programme and the Eurimage scheme has been the recognition that genuinely European could only mean something made to appear authentically local in some way or other. To make this possible in the prevailing commercial environment and in order to meet the expectations of high technical standards, channels have been created for a transnational flow of expertise to be available for national and even local film production. Nevertheless, the dream of many filmmakers and their financiers no doubt remains to gain world-wide release by a US distributor. This is needed to cover as many of the costs as possible soon after release, although a great part of the revenue actually comes from other sales than theatrical distribution: DVD, Blu-ray, television and, increasingly, streaming over the internet. Still, there are fundamental economic and structural differences that cannot easily be circumvented. As Gerben Bakker puts it:

> By 1997, ten years after the start of the [European Union large-scale sub-sidy] programme, a film made in the European Union cost 500,000 euros on average, was 70 to 80 per cent state-financed, and grossed 800,000 euros world-wide, reaching an audience of 150,000 persons. In contrast, the aver-age American film cost 15 million euros, was nearly 100 per cent privately financed, grossed 58 million euros, and reached 10.5 million persons. This seventy-fold difference in performance is remarkable.[21]

Another part of the equation is, as Thomas Elsaesser points out, that although US cinema is often felt to be a threat both culturally and eco-nomically, in effect '[e]conomically European films are so weak that they could not be shown on the big screen if the machinery of the blockbuster did not keep the physical infrastructure of cinema-going and public film culture going'. Elsaesser ends up with the seemingly paradoxical conclu-sion that 'Hollywood cinema's strong global market position is in fact the necessary condition for local or national diversity'.[22] Exhibitors every-where in Europe have been very much aware of this state of affairs since the 1920s. As we have seen in Chapters 2, 3 and 4, the Finns were already then engaged with their neighbouring regional film culture in seeking to find lucrative modes of operation. Over the studio era even small nation cinemas reached a degree of self-sufficiency, and after its collapse there was a clear need for a system of subsidies. All through these different phases in the varying political contexts, there have also been attempts to create a more or less comprehensive European system of production, in one form or another. As we have seen, over the past few decades a firm institutional basis has been created to consolidate such connections. This has not been easy, as an equally difficult problem is the fact that '[i]nternally, Europe has mostly been an archipelago of mutually exclusive cultural-linguistic spheres, where films from neighbouring countries rarely if ever succeed in finding a hospitable reception'.[23] Although Finnish filmmakers have right from the beginning been careful to take selective advantage of what other European and particularly their Scandinavian colleagues have to offer, the traffic has not flowed easily in the opposite direction. However, more recently Finland has become an equal partner in the new Nordic funding system.

NORDIC PRODUCTION COLLABORATION

Among the Nordic countries, the success of the contemporary Danish cinema and television industry has been seen as a model in seeking to globalize a small nation cinema. As Mette Hjort notes, this breakthrough has taken place largely because of the 'performative media circus that the enfant terrible of Danish film, Lars von Trier, generates'.[24] Nevertheless, the phenomenon has more profound transnational aspects:

> Danish films are now seen by viewers around the globe, and these viewers increasingly approach these films as part of a larger phenomenon—that of the New Danish Cinema—rather than as discrete texts by established auteurs or lesser-known directors with funny names that might be Danish but could just as well be Belgian, Swiss, or Dutch.[25]

Danish filmmakers appear to have succeeded in creating a brand, one perhaps not quite as distinct from Hollywood cinema as European cinemas in the heyday of modernism, but nevertheless one with a recognizable national quality. One point of resistance is commitment to a small nation language, which can take on a 'structural character'.[26] This goes together with the realization that setting the action of a film in recognizably local conditions need not impede global appeal. Correspondingly, transnational film production is increasingly focused on joint efforts at cooperation and circulation rather than pursuing a joint cultural heritage.[27] This is national cinema without any taint of nationalism. This pattern has been followed, if not with quite as impressive success, by many other small nation cinemas, particularly in northern Europe. One aspect of this development has been a new kind of international networking, which would allow for making films with a distinct national flavour but with at least the potential for global reach. Thus national cinemas could appear more transnational than ever.

Hjort ends up with a positive conclusion of sorts: 'And if hybrid works involving elements of the local and the global can infuse new life into quasi-moribund cinematic cultures defined primarily along national lines, then it is indeed appropriate to consider the idea that globalization might be an engine of positive change under certain circumstances.'[28] In other words, whether operating or observing on the national, regional or European level, in the film world today the primary task is not to express pre-conceived identity but rather to explore and enhance patterns of cultural negotiation, allowing for the emergence of a genuinely transnational film culture that models the relationships of individuals and interactions between different social configurations in the contemporary ethnically heterogeneous, culturally multilayered and transnational social context. For all practices and purposes, nations remain the key structural component simply because they are still the key level of social and political organization, even in the age of globalization.

Something of this simultaneous appeal to the national and the transnational has been built into the way Nordic film funding organizations have institutionalized their collaboration. One important factor in creating the enabling conditions for inter-Nordic film production has been a range of institutions that seek to promote Nordic cooperation and exchange. Nordic festival collaboration began as early as 1978. Nordic Film & TV Fund was established in 1992, the year of 'Nordic Cooperation and Distribution'. The aim was to produce five feature films, each of which was to be distributed simultaneously in all the Nordic countries and jointly presented at the Cannes film festival under the title *Focus on Nordic Film*. Collaboration was also developed between Nordic and German producers. According to the final report of the project supervisor Per Dogger, although the production side was successful, the distribution failed.[29]

Over the years these institutional frameworks have developed further and have helped in creating a broader basis for film production and even increased production budgets. The fund has become a major agent in the funding of Nordic film production. It receives one-third of its resources from the Nordic Ministers Council, another third from national funding institutions such as the Finnish Film Foundation, and the last third from television channels. A major part of the collaboration and coordination takes place through the national institutions in charge of distributing state subsidies in these countries. All in all, the collaboration has quite a broad base, involving both political and commercial commitment to Nordic film cultural collaboration, made possible by the considerable similarities of the social structures in these countries. According to Petri Kemppinen, former Head of the Production Department at the Finnish Film Foundation and at the time of writing Chief Executive Officer of the Nordisk Film & TV Fond, this has become increasingly strong over the past few years. However, this does not make the region into a unified market area for film distribution. What it does mean is that the infrastructure exists for the free movement of creative and technological talent. This takes place at ease between

Scandinavian countries that share mutually comprehensible languages, but Finns too, due to the considerable similarities of Finnish society with its Scandinavian counterparts, can fairly easily participate in this exchange— Swedish speakers obviously having a slight advantage. Some Finnish film-makers such as Klaus Härö have sought not only to exploit this as a funding opportunity, but also to use it as way of participating in the long and continuous tradition of professional filmmaking in Sweden and Denmark.

One part of Nordic collaboration in the field of film culture has been the attempts at increasing the distribution of Nordic films in other Nordic countries. This has been facilitated by the fact that many of the big distribution companies operating in this region—Nordisk, SF, Scanbox, and Sandrew while still in operation—have been under Nordic ownership and have been active in distributing Nordic films in the Nordic region, albeit mainly big films with significant market potential. This has been a part of a concentrated effort to maintain a regional alternative to Hollywood cinema. Kemppinen thinks that Finnish audiences are relatively receptive to films from other Nordic countries—more so than audiences in Sweden or Denmark.[30] However, Nordic countries have eventually preferred to profile themselves separately at international festivals. It might well be that international audiences favour cultural distinctions even at this level, as opposed to blendings that all too likely will appear bland. On the other hand, there is the danger that a single prominent figure might guide expectations of national quality to a detrimental extent. Producer Markus Selin stated in an interview:

> The Aki Kaurismäki problem—from the point of view of other Finns—is that he makes films that are so idiosyncratic. All the rest of us suffer from this abroad: when we offer a Finnish project which is not Aki narration people are disappointed. In terms of structure and technical accomplishment, Finnish films look just the same as other Nordic films, but because of Aki people think of us Finns as freaks. He has created such a fine brand for himself, that the rest of us have been somewhat trodden under it. We have not a made a single equally luminous film which would allow us to cope. Such a film would have to be distinguished from Kaurismäki narration, which is not easy, and on top of that it should be interesting and plausible.[31]

Aki Kaurismäki has not created around him the kind of 'performative media circus' that von Trier has. The interviews he has given are performances of a more subdued if no less surreal sort, and his quirky and subversive behaviour on festival occasions seems more like a manifestation of his anti-establishment sentiment than an attempt to promote a wider scheme of film production. Yet as the case of Klaus Härö—to be explored in Chapter 14—indicates, there are other Finnish directors who have developed modes of transnational operation that can be more easily emulated.

NOTES

1. Pantti 2005: 167.
2. Meers 2004: 160.
3. Ibid.: 168.
4. Ibid.: 172.
5. Finnish Film Foundation, *Audiences of domestic films 2008*: 16–18.
6. Finnish Film Foundation, *Audiences of domestic films 2013:* 20–21. The results of these studies are somewhat difficult to assess, as the informants have been asked to make categorical judgements about a highly diverse phenomenon.
7. Finnish Film Foundation: *Facts and Figures 2011*: 14, 24.
8. Halle 2010: 303.
9. Elsaesser 2005: 467.
10. Crofts 2006: 53.
11. Andrew 2010: 65.
12. Ibid.: 504.
13. Elsaesser 2005: 505.
14. Ibid.: 506.
15. Ibid.: 109.
16. Andrew 2010: 66.
17. Halle 2010a, b: 304.
18. Miller et al. 2001: 164. The Reding quotation originally appeared in 'Circulation', 1999.
19. Halle 2010a, b: 305.
20. Miller et al. 2001: 91.
21. Bakker 2008: 409.
22. Elsaesser 2005: 17.
23. Ibid.: 493.
24. Hjort 2005b: 33.
25. Ibid.: 2.
26. Ibid.: 30.
27. Ibid.: 161.
28. Ibid.: 235.
29. Jensen 2014: 36.
30. Interview with Petri Kemppinen, Head of Production Department at Finnish Film Foundation 24/2/2012.
31. Seppä 2009: 32. Translated by the author.

CHAPTER 13

Producer-led Mode of Film Production

Pietari Kääpä

The film industry receives substantial public support. Because of this, enterprises which have received support can be considered to have a moral and material obligation to the tax payers—their customers.[1]

That statement, included as part of the Finnish Film Foundation's (Suomen Elokuvasäätiö) funding application documentation for taxation, is indicative of the ongoing debate over film policy in this small nation film culture. As film production in Finland continues to be heavily subsidized, debates over the role of institutional influence over cultural production continue in a very similar vein to those of previous decades. Yet the emphasis on business language—enterprise, the customer—indicates a sense of readjustment in policy debates from those of previous decades.

By 1994, the Finnish film industry had fallen to a deep low, comparable to 1974 when only two domestic films were released, and evidently a change in strategy was required. The 1980s had seen clear policy revisions aimed at reorganizing the cultural mandate of domestic film production, with Spede Pasanen's popular comedy *Double Uuno* (*Tupla Uuno*, 1987) famously receiving previously elusive state support. However, while the gates had now been opened, the state of the industry had deteriorated even further. Occasional domestic blockbusters such as the war epic *The*

P. Kääpä (✉)
University of Stirling, Stirling, Scotland

© The Editor(s) (if applicable) and The Author(s) 2016
H. Bacon (ed.), *Finnish Cinema*, Palgrave European Film
and Media Studies, DOI 10.1057/978-1-137-57651-4_13

Winter War (*Talvisota*, 1989) had managed to lure domestic audiences in considerable numbers, but the majority of domestic films continued to struggle at the box office. The reasons for this lack of engagement can be attributed to many factors, ranging from a lack of infrastructural support for competitive commercial productions to the absence of independent private investment in domestic production. The latter is particularly indicative of the insecurity felt concerning the financial feasibility of domestic cinema. Two of the most consistently successful producers of Finnish cinema in the twenty-first century, Markus Selin and Marko Röhr, argue that film production can only provide, at its very best, a sustainable level of income for a limited number of professionals in Finland. To provide a truly healthy cinema industry capable of competition, financial incentives are needed at a more substantial level than is currently available.[2]

Yet even as state support structures continue to characterize this small nation film culture, producer-led incentives and private sources of investment have played an increasing role in developing Finnish cinema. The introduction of the 50–50 scheme in 2011 was one way of channelling private capital into film production. Such schemes have their roots in policy changes and individual producer-led initiatives developed in the 1990s and early 2000s. The dynamics between art and commerce, between national relevance and market-led competition, are revealing in what they tell us about the realities of small nation film culture. To explore these dynamics, this chapter chronicles some of these key changes from the perspective of Marko Röhr, a central force in realizing some of the transformations of the period. Röhr provides an intriguing case study, as his role in the negotiations between commercial and artistic interests reflects many of the key debates of the era.

MARKO RÖHR: A COMMERCIAL FORM OF NATIONAL CINEMA

Marko Röhr's role in the film industry spans decades, starting in the 1980s as a director of productions at National Filmi, one of the premier production companies in Finland at the time. Röhr studied at the Helsinki School of Economics and wrote a thesis on the state of financing in the film industry. Titled 'The development of the international film industry in recent times, and the competitive factors influencing it, as well as the competitive settings of Finnish cinemas',[3] the thesis sets out to investigate how the international film industry (here meaning predominantly the large

Hollywood companies) has negotiated the challenges of technological innovation such as home video and television. Röhr argues that the most successful industries are those that work on a multinational basis in terms of vertical integration and conglomeration. This factor was largely missing in Finland in the late 1980s, as the organization of the industry was still based on small independent companies focused on either production or distribution, not on full integration of these aspects of cinema.

Much of Röhr's thesis is centred on the ways in which the Finnkino corporation has consolidated its status as a leader in production and distribution in the Finnish film industry. The head of Finnkino (the parent company of National Filmi), Jukka Mäkelä, was sufficiently impressed to employ Röhr as lead producer in charge of product development. For Röhr it was clear that the then-current practice of producing art cinema relying almost completely on state subsidies was not audience friendly and was thus not sustainable. He argued for a new approach to producing films in Finland:

Currently, cinema is considered a cultural activity and not a business one. We must try to produce films that will gradually change this approach to business thinking. And for that we need professionals. The economic and business side of a corporation can only be run by those who are educated and have experience in the field.[4]

Röhr's comments reflect a wider neoliberal trend in domestic culture, which advocates the need to increase competitiveness and economic thinking, as opposed to the bureaucratic managerialism that used to dominate the system: 'The 1980s model never functioned as one had to contend with production boards, production management, and the government. If you were good at lobbying for your production, you got it accepted.'[5] Suggesting that directionless policies and bureaucratic organization led to mismanagement of the public accountability of the Finnish Film Foundation (FFF), Röhr called the era 'year zero' in contemporary Finnish film culture. This echoes the well-known article 'Finnish Cinema in Year Zero' by Jörn Donner, published in 1959, in which the author suggested that the then-contemporary Finnish film industry had reached an artistic and cultural nadir. In the 1960s, director- and producer-led initiatives slowly replaced the decaying studio system, resulting in the New Wave. The situation was similar in the 1990s as producers such as Markus Selin, Tero Kaukomaa, Klaus Heydemann and Röhr consolidated their professional status. The producers often discuss a 'generational' shift in

Finnish film culture, reflecting similar perceptions of transformation in the 1960s and 1980s. Instead of sharing artistic or political principles, the generation in question was now united on the basis of an economic approach to film production. Kaukomaa outlines this well in stating:

> We have a new generation of directors willing to produce features that authentically cater for audiences. Simultaneously we have a new generation of producers that have professionalized film production. When I initially decided to go into cinema production, domestic film held a 4% market share. But in a few years there was a radical shift in perceptions as domestic film increased its market share.[6]

Many of the producers of this generation credit the educational initiatives of the Helsinki School of Economics as paving the way for more professionalism in the industry. Institutional, state-supported education truly started having a clear impact in the late 1990s, one major step being the launching of a MBA programme in film production. The consolidation or establishment of independent production companies such as Selin's Solar Films, Kaukomaa's Blind Spot, Heydemann's part in Villealfa Productions, Timo Koivusalo's Artista Filmi and Röhr's MRP were crucial in restructuring the organization of film production in Finland.

A NEW MODE OF PRODUCTION

The emergence of what Röhr and Kaukomaa call a new 'production philosophy'[7] changed some of the basics of production, which until then had revolved around artist-directors and their ability to meet the paradigmatic principles of the FFF funding committees. In contrast, the new producers would initiate projects and choose directors to suit the material. The pay-off came in 1999, when Solar Films' *The Tough Ones* (*Häjyt*), Artista's *The Wanderer and the Swan* (*Kulkuri ja joutsen*), *Tommy and the Wildcat* (*Poika ja ilves*, produced 1999 as an international co-production under the Wildcat Productions banner) and MRP's *Ambush* (*Rukajärven tie*) each attracted an audience of over 400,000 spectators, resulting in the 'boom years' of Finnish cinema.[8] The success of these films was a victory for the producers, as they had considerable personal investment in each production, not only in terms of capital but also in the sustainability of their production company. These successes demonstrated that it was possible to produce financially viable films within the Finnish confines. The ability to connect with the audience with a range of films 'brought the producers a lot of self-confidence and showed what types of films should be produced. All of us vocalized in concert that the production system has to be producer led as we take all the risks. This is a business enterprise, and it is we who have the real vision and if we fail we exit from the scene as in any other type of business.'[9]

Röhr was recognized as the producer of the year by the Finnish Film Producers Guild (Suomen elokuvatuottajien keskusliitto) in 2000. The Guild's statement read: 'Röhr's activities have from the beginning been characterized by a sure touch of a professionalism, with which he has been able to secure international funding for domestic productions. MRP's contribution strengthens faith in the continued success of domestic cinema.' The statement is intriguing for both what it contains and what is absent. Financial concerns override cultural concerns, especially as the comments emphasize the professionalism and continuity of MRP's activities. The latter is especially significant, since Röhr has argued that short-term project funding is one of the fundamental problems of the Finnish film industry. According to him, this does not allow for the long-term development of production portfolios or infrastructure that could be utilized to foster international connections. For Röhr, the ideal model would be based on funding from large state-supported entities like the national broadcasting company YLE or the commercial television channel MTV3 for small production companies. The funding would be assigned not only on the basis of projects, but also in the form of specific types of company support. Based on the so-called Ireland model, this would allow production houses to engage in long-term planning and activity and, crucially, avoid the type of uncertainty that proved to be fatal for many small companies throughout the 1970s–1980s. However, such development has not taken place and FFF funding remains focused on individual projects.

INTERNATIONAL CONNECTIONS

For Röhr, any robust funding model has to be premised on access to European funding sources, which is something he has fostered since the financial success of the co-production *Jerusalem* (1995). Röhr has been especially careful about unwarranted expansion into international markets, because he was heavily involved in the attempt to secure an Oscar nomination for National Filmi's epic *The Winter War* (*Talvisota*, 1989). This failed to amass the level of critical success necessary for the nomination at its sponsored screenings and led to substantial financial and reputational losses for the company. MRP has continued to act as a minority partner in neighbouring markets, including Russia (*The Ninth Company*) and Estonia

(*The Names in Marble*). *Mother of Mine*, on the other hand, is an example of a YLE-facilitated co-production that enabled MRP to consolidate its links with a range of Swedish production companies such as Film i väst.

These examples bring into perspective not only the complexities involved in small nation films seeking to make a breakthrough in the competitive international environment, but also the problems independent production companies face in seeking to maintain continuity of their output. Röhr argues that the most substantial development in domestic cinema recently has been the kind of international networking that has been a key factor in sustaining MRP as a production company. In the 2000s, regional distribution companies such as Egmont and Bonnier have actively engaged with Finnish production houses. Röhr emphasizes the importance of these Nordic companies taking a risk with Finnish productions and making solid profits with this activity.[10] He sees this type of collaboration with the largest distribution company in the Nordic countries as an essential factor for establishing financial stability for Finnish producers.

NATIONAL CINEMA

While Röhr is a staunch supporter of internationalization and economic thinking, he is also a firm proponent of the notion of national cinema—as a commercial tactic. For him, the rhetoric of national cinema sells tickets domestically. This is especially the case if the products are marketed clearly as part of the general parameters of established conventions in each respective national film culture. Röhr's comments touch on a frequent catch-22 of commercial forms of national cinema rhetoric: national films are not supposed to be merely commercial ventures, but are rather intended to reflect the general values of a nation—thus justifying state subsidies. Yet they are also intended to cater for the national population—implying that they are conceptualized as popular culture for domestic audiences and thus should be self-supporting.

For Röhr, a change of perspective is required, where Finnish elements are not in opposition to commercial interests, but instead these elements provide the commercial appeal. Supporting this assertion are multiple examples that have shown that audiences do support domestic productions with populist appeal, such as the comedies of Spede Pasanen or the folk comedy *Backwoods Philosopher* (*Havukka-ahon ajattelija*, 2010), which 'was not even conceptualized as something for foreign audiences'.[11] Without such a connection with domestic culture, 'films will get lost as the resources for competing with imports are not adequate and profits are limited'.[12] Importantly, securing distribution in foreign markets is not a way to compensate for the limitations of the domestic market:

> Even if a film sells extremely well abroad, it brings in less box-office takings than a domestic production that is able to attract a domestic audience of 200,000. The problem is that Finnish producers gain little profit from the overseas distribution of even big hits such as *Rare Exports* (2011). The costs of distributing abroad and the complexity of co-funding schemes reduce any proceeds that may come back to the producers and complicate their distribution. We do not have the financial or operational means to aim at distributing a film directly in 100 markets.[13]

Thus it seems that international competition only becomes practical in cases where a sufficient claim to domestic relevance can be made, a notion that is often supported by examples that clearly correlate with established ways of representing the nation. Röhr credits heritage productions such as *Call of the Plains* (*Lakeuden kutsu*, 2000) and *Backwoods Philosopher* as some of MRP's biggest successes, as opposed to genre fare such as the detective thriller *The Priest of Evil* (*Harjunpää ja pahan pappi*, 2011) and the horror film *Body of Water* (*Syvälle salattu*, 2011), both of which reached only just over 50,000 viewers. Röhr suggests that this is not so much to do with any perceived failures in domestic approaches to genre, but points to more systemic patterns in audience taste. Even imported productions in the detective genre can only be expected to reach 80,000 viewers, with horror films occupying an even smaller niche at generally 20,000–50,000 viewers. While there will be anomalies and break-out hits, the general indications of box-office statistics suggest that genre does not fare well in comparison to heritage products such as *Princess* (*Prinsessa*, 2009; an audience of over 250,000) and *Backwoods Philosopher* (again, an audience of over 250,000).

Röhr's comments are intriguing, as the emphasis on the commercial potential of heritage cinema goes against some of the basic marketing philosophies espoused by the Hollywood studios as well as their global affiliates, where a clear genre identity (in comparison to a more general thematic framework) provides films with their marketing hook. In the somewhat limited confines of small nation cinema, at least in Röhr's view, national specificity (or 'heritage') is the ingredient that enables films to succeed, an observation that reflects the fact that the idea of 'commercialism' has different implications in markets of different sizes.

NOTES

1. Remes 2007: 5.
2. Interview with Marko Röhr, 4/9/2011.
3. Röhr 1987.
4. Taina West: "Markkinoille mahtuu kymmenisen kotimaista elokuvaa vuosittain," *Kansan Uutiset*, 22/7/1987.
5. Interview with Marko Röhr, 4/9/2011.
6. Interview with Tero Kaukomaa, 10/10/2011.
7. Antti Arve: "Elokuvatuottajien tusina," *Iltalehti*, 20/1/2001.
8. See Ahonen et al. 2003.
9. Interview with Marko Röhr, 4/9/2011.
10. Ibid.
11. Ibid.
12. Ibid.
13. Ibid.

CHAPTER 14

Two Modes of Transnational Filmmaking

Henry Bacon and Jaakko Seppälä

As previous chapters have demonstrated, a fairly wide range of transnational modes of operation is now available for Finnish filmmakers. In this chapter two particularly interesting directors who have found their aesthetic inspiration in certain other film cultures as well as creatively absorbed carefully chosen Hollywood modes have been selected for case study: Klaus Härö and Aki Kaurismäki. Härö is a Finland-Swedish film director who made his first three feature films—*Elina: As If I Wasn't There* (*Näkymätön Elina*, 2002), *Mother of Mine* (*Äideistä parhain*, 2005) and *The New Man* (*Uusi ihminen*, 2007)—in Sweden. He offers a particularly interesting example of studying transnationalism in practice as well as in terms of content, as his first films explore the relationships between Finland and Sweden on a profoundly human level. The films were given a distinctly Nordic stylistic quality by the cinematographer Jarkko T. Laine, whose love of Swedish cinema made him eager to learn how to exploit the possibilities offered by the gradual changes of Nordic light, so splendidly captured in many classical Swedish films.

Kaurismäki in turn, as Finland's all-time most internationally celebrated filmmaker, exemplifies how a director can develop a highly individual style that transcends national limits and captures the attention of audiences

H. Bacon (✉) • J. Seppälä
Film and Television Studies, University of Helsinki, Helsinki, Finland
e-mail: henry.bacon@helsinki.fi; jaakkoseppala@gmail.com

© The Editor(s) (if applicable) and The Author(s) 2016
H. Bacon (ed.), *Finnish Cinema*, Palgrave European Film
and Media Studies, DOI 10.1057/978-1-137-57651-4_14

worldwide. Stylistically, there is little that is 'Finnish' in Aki Kaurismäki's cinema. No Finnish film tradition would help one to appreciate his systematic and significant use of cinematic devices. Kaurismäki draws influences from world film, literary and art histories, as a result of which his cinema is inherently transnational.

KLAUS HÄRÖ: BETWEEN TWO SMALL NATION FILM CULTURES

Klaus Härö has sometimes mentioned Jan Troell and Bille August as directors who have moulded his own cinematic ideals, offering a model of how to treat universal concerns in terms of a specific historical context and communal experience. In some ways the Swedish filmmaking context appeared very inviting for Härö. Films like Bille August's *Pelle the Conqueror* (*Pelle erobreren*, 1987) and Lasse Hällström's *My Life as a Dog* (*Mitt liv som hund*, 1985) made him wonder how they could be so familiar, come so close to him, yet be somehow universal—while nothing similar seemed to be available in contemporary Finnish cinema. Härö gained a better idea of how this could be achieved while working as a runner on August's production of *Jerusalem* (1996).[1]

In the first phase of his career as a director, Härö had as his chief cinematographer Jarkko T. Laine, one of whose idols was Sven Nykvist. Through studying Nykvist's art Laine gained not only the initial impetus to his career, but also the aesthetic goal of taking full advantage of the expressive potential of Nordic light, the fine, gradual changes of shades and angles of light through the year and the day that give his art an almost painterly quality. Of slightly earlier masters, Gunnar Fischer provided another inspiring model.[2]

Yet attempting to follow in the footsteps of these great models was not simple. In Sweden there are severe production-related constraints to shooting at the hours when Nordic light is at its most evocative: early morning or late evening. Working hours are quite strictly stipulated, and a director needs many administrative skills and a considerable talent for persuasion to bend these rules. Eventually production timetables and logistics set the limits to what can be achieved, even if the cast and crew are willing to try to achieve something truly memorable.[3] According to Laine, if the director and cinematographer happen to find a superb location that is far away from the base the crew is using, they might just succeed in persuading the producer to allow them to shoot there, but the timetable will be extremely tight and then, of course, at the end of the day the weather conditions might not be conducive to the aesthetic aims.[4] It is a continual balancing act between not only art and economy, but also nature and pragmatic considerations. All this might make it difficult to exploit that magical quality of northern light, but when a specific effect really is needed for the film, some kind of deal can usually be negotiated between the creative and the technical staff, with the producer acting as an intermediary. The young Finns working in Sweden had to adapt to a rather different way of organizing shooting schedules than they were used to through their Finnish experience. Obviously, it was not wise to challenge practices such as adherence to working hours, even for such a perfect cinematic excuse as wishing to exploit optimal lighting conditions.

These experiences crystallized in an aesthetic ideal: how to dare to be very personal and local, yet tell a story in a way that would communicate with people anywhere. This, of course, is an age-old challenge, and models are to be found from the entire history of storytelling. Recent discussion on the transnational features of contemporary film production in the Nordic area has centred on how the aspiration to succeed in the global market has led, first of all, to a pooling of resources across borders. Nordic Film & TV Fund and other funding institutions enable filmmaking on a much bigger scale than would be possibly with Finnish funding alone, but they also create the temptation to produce the kind of films that can be expected to appeal to audiences on a global level by choosing topics, treatments and approaches alienated from their original cultural context, on the assumption that their appeal will thus transcend national boundaries. Mette Hjort has referred to this phenomenon as misguided transnationalism, in which a surface appeal to national heritage is actually diluted by denationalizing and deauthenticating elements so as to ensure international success.[5] Hjort sets such a practice against appealing to a sense of cultural ownership, which may even take the form of what may be referred to as *natural co-production*: the story told refers to two or more national contexts and interactions that have historically taken place, *Pelle the Conqueror* serving as a good example. Such films serve the purpose of 'be[ing] able to move Nordic audiences by making salient forms of deep cultural content that are "multiply claimed" inasmuch as they sustain national imaginings in more than one Nordic nation'. This relies on 'the existence of multiple perspectives (arising from various national identities) on key cultural events or achievements that animate the nations in question'.[6] An even more fundamental basis for this kind of transnationalism is captured in the notion of homophily, 'the idea being that intercultural relationships depend on concepts of similarity and difference'.[7]

For Härö this kind feeling of familiarity emerged from the milieus and the different ways the characters related to them in the films of Jan Troell. What touched him was the strong presence of nature, the way changes of seasons affect people, as well as the way interiors, with their exquisite dim lighting, provide safe havens for the characters. Härö admired particularly *The Emigrants* (*Utvandrardna*, 1971) which he thought had an almost documentary touch, free from gimmicks and theatricality. Troell also has an eye for small, telling gestures through which his sensitivity for human concerns finds its expression. Yet Härö would also find something to appreciate in the not so highly critically appreciated folk comedies of Colin Nutley. The setting is based on British models and stereotypes, which Nutley found easy enough to transplant to Swedish soil. Härö did not think of them as particularly great films, but he could sense a certain atmosphere and human warmth in them, gently captured by cinematic means and conveyed to an appreciative audience.[8]

Still another source of inspiration for him came from much further away, the 1970s works of American directors such as Arthur Penn, Sydney Lumet, Sydney Pollack and George Roy Hill. They had the studio-era knowhow at their disposal, but, often in collaboration with cinematographers from Eastern Europe, they were able to develop a new, fresh naturalistic approach. Härö saw in this an inspiring synthesis of European finesse and American clarity of storytelling. Also in later US 'indie' films he found a certain lightness of touch: the characters could be complex and awkward, but there was a kind of narrative simplicity, to the point that one could momentarily forget about the story altogether.

Härö and Laine's first film together—*Elina: As If I Wasn't There*, the story of a little Finnish-speaking girl's attempts to cope with the loss of her father in a Swedish-language environment—connected well with certain long lines of Swedish cinema: Bibi Andersson as the stern school matron won the Swedish Guldbagge Award for best female supporting role. There were also a number of other members of the cast and crew who helped to give the aspiring Finnish filmmakers the sense of joining a tradition. This impression was sealed when the film was awarded the 2003 Ingmar Bergman prize, the winner of which was chosen by Bergman himself. In his personal message to his young colleague, the old master acknowledged that with his movie Härö had managed to touch cinemagoers' hearts.[9] Ironically, when the Finnish equivalent of the Academy Awards, the Jussi Statues, were awarded, *Elina* did not qualify as a Finnish film. The Bergman Award changed this, and later on *Elina* was Finland's candidate for Best

Foreign Film Academy Award. This serves as a fine example of the recognition of the merits of transnationalism as a mode of practice; yet even more important was the genuinely transnational aesthetic inspiration that had occurred. Whatever the problems with working hours, timetables and logistics, the scenes that take place in a bog, Elina's haven, have a similar enchantingly luminous quality to what Jörgen Persson achieved in similarly located scenes in Bille August's *Jerusalem*, admirably expressing the feelings of the lonely little girl trying to flee from social conflicts she is unable to handle. Also, the light on the faces of Elina, Mrs. Holm and Elina's mother is often every bit as expressive and conducive to revealing the inner life of the characters as Nykvist could offer Bergman in some of their most soul-searching collaborations. Laine's cinematography captures admirably these lonely figures within landscapes tenderly embraced by the most refined gradations of Nordic light (Fig. 14.1).

The Laine–Härö collaboration was facilitated by their mutual love of Scandinavian cinema, both in terms of cinematic style and the way that could be employed to tell deeply human stories. Their participation in the great Nordic cinematic tradition was enabled by long-term Nordic production collaboration and the opportunity offered to Finns to develop their technical expertise by working and learning in Sweden—for example, Esa Vuorinen, Laine's teacher at the School of Industrial Arts Film School,

Fig. 14.1 Bergman–Nyqvist type of lighting effect in *Elina: As If I Wasn't There* (2002)

did his apprenticeship in Sweden in the 1970s. Today, Finns are in a much better position to act as equal partners in Nordic as well as all other kinds of international co-productions.

From a transnational point of view, Härö's Swedish films contrast in an interesting way with Swedish films that have been located outside Sweden. Anders Marklund has observed that as a rule, they 'have not attempted to reach a high level of realism; they are not documentaries depicting Swedes' contacts with foreign peoples, countries and communities'.[10] In *Elina* as well as his second film, *Mother of Mine*, Härö treats the experience of Finns (or Finnish speakers) in Sweden in a way that relates to distinct historical situations and social experiences, and seeks to give psychological depth as well as more general human resonance to these experiences. Neither of these films is set in a country commonly associated with social instability, such as those in Eastern Europe or the Middle East, which has been the trend in Swedish films in the 2000s, but in a country the social stability of which has grown to almost mythical proportions. However, there are also a number of Swedish films in which journeys to a neighbouring country with relatively familiar foreign settings 'suggest a possible change in a person's life in a way that appears fairly realistic'.[11] Härö's first two films have a similarly calibrated foreign–familiar structure. They are fine examples of natural co-productions and of homophily, relating as they do to realistically depicted transnational historical experiences, showing how vulnerable little people try to relate their individuality to strange environments or circumstances, torn between a painful sense of alienation and a deep craving for belonging.

Aki Kaurismäki's Transnational Aesthetics of Contradiction

Aki Kaurismäki has also found aesthetic influences from a great variety of sources. He once stated: 'I am an eclectic person so everything influences everything. Robert Bresson has influenced me directly and permanently. But maybe most of all I have been influenced by the narration of the classical Hollywood B film.'[12] Because he draws influences from both modernist and classical cinemas, critics are having a hard time classifying his works.

Andrew Nestingen recognizes post-modern elements in Kaurismäki's oeuvre, but feels that 'the films might be more richly situated in a modernist framework'.[13] Jarmo Valkola, another critic who has recently written a book on the director, concurs.[14] Modernism is often seen as a historical movement in cinema that came to an end in the late 1970s.[15] In spite of this, it can be productive to discuss films that contain modernist elements in terms of modernism, no matter when the films were made. Classicism, modernism and post-modernism serve here as frameworks that permit one to understand and discuss the aesthetics of Kaurismäki's films and their relation to film history and the cultures of their times. Viewed like this, the concepts need not be incompatible. Although every Kaurismäki film can be experienced and discussed on all three levels, each film 'likewise signals that level on which its most significant work will occur',[16] to use the words of Dudley Andrew. Therefore, without overlooking issues like seriousness and moral purpose, building on the work of Roger Connah it can be persuasively argued that the style of Kaurismäki's films is best understood as post-modern.[17] Linda Hutcheon defines post-modern as

a fundamentally contradictory enterprise: its art forms (and its theory) at once use and abuse, install and then destabilize convention in parodic ways, self-consciously pointing both to their own inherent paradoxes and provisionality and, of course, to their critical or ironic re-reading of the art of the past.[18]

This description is spot on when it comes to Kaurismäki's cinema, where things are often said and shown as if in inverted commas. Kaurismäki's films seem to be very Finnish and yet they are not; they feel melancholic and yet they can make the audience laugh; their tone is nostalgic, but one is not sure what they are nostalgic for. Contrary to Nestingen's argument, Kaurismäki does not 'seek a new and challenging formal expression'[19] of intellectual convictions, the truth is quite the opposite. As András Bálint Kovács points out, '[i]n this era one cannot speak of auteurism in the sense that someone invents an original stylistic or narrative solution that will become the mark of his/her authorship.'[20] Kaurismäki exemplifies this in that he relies on conventions of the past out of which he creates new peculiar combinations, rather than inventing new cinematic devices.

Göran Hermerén argues that the concept of influence includes a wide range of possibilities, from copy to allusion.[21] To employ his categories, Kaurismäki's films can be discussed as paraphrases: Kaurismäki uses old canonical films as points of departure for his work and creates something reminiscent of them in his own personal style. Old styles are often present in his films as evident imitations and ironic reworkings[22]; that is, his films can be seen as containing elements of pastiche and parody. According to Hutcheon, parody can be understood as the ultimate post-modern form of expression: 'repetition with ironic critical distance'.[23] Pastiche, on the other hand, can be used to mean a form that is closer to imitation, as it is analogous to its referent.[24] Consequently, while it is true that Kaurismäki uses classical and modernist conventions, it is illuminating to interpret his take on them as post-modern.

Kaurismäki's most obvious intertextual link to the modernist cinemas is minimalism, 'a systematic reduction of expressive elements in a given form'.[25] Minimalism is the overriding stylistic feature in all his 16 feature-length fictional films. The main aspects of Bresson's style are extensive use of offscreen space, elliptical narration and radically dispassionate acting style.[26] In his films Kaurismäki imitates and ironically reworks these self-imposed restrictions. His films resemble those of Bresson and yet they are far from the latter's seriousness.[27] Kaurismäki mixes Bressonian devices with visual comedy (reminiscent of Jacques Tati) and surrealism (reminiscent of Luis Buñuel). Tati's films contain moments when he does not foreground his comic gags but leaves them for the spectator to find, and at times he hints at humorous situations, but leaves them undeveloped.[28] Kaurismäki's deadpan comedy relies on similar parameters. While Buñuel and other surrealist filmmakers 'sought to tap the unconscious mind' with 'startling juxtapositions' and stories that 'follow the inexplicable logic of a dream',[29] Kaurismäki's surrealism is better described as surrealism of everyday life. It is a very mild form of surrealism that manifests itself in peculiar elements of the mise-en-scène that lack a narrative motivation and therefore feel strange. These elements are often so down-to-earth that they might even go unnoticed.

A good example of minimalism mixed with visual comedy and surrealism of everyday life is found in *The Match Factory Girl* (*Tulitikkutehtaan tyttö*, 1989). The protagonist, Iris, receives a letter from her lover in which he tells her to get an abortion. She then walks dispassionately under a moving car, but the accident takes place offscreen. Kaurismäki's narration is elliptical: instead of showing the moment when Iris makes her decision, he cuts to her act of walking. Iris survives the crash and is hospitalized, but when her stepfather comes to visit her the austere film becomes more tragicomic. Against expectations the audience could derive from the real world, the stepfather bluntly informs Iris that she is not welcome in their home and gives her an orange. This is a moment of visual comedy. The absurd combination of cruelty and kindness can make one smile and chuckle. The fruit is an everyday item, but in this sequence it seems to emanate a strange atmosphere from deep inside. Kaurismäki shoots the orange for 48 seconds altogether. The warm colour of the fruit is in sharp contrast to the whites and blues of the room, as a result of which it looks out of place and humorous. In short, cinematic devices are used to heighten the presence of the orange, even though its narrative function is non-existent.

The strong influence of classical cinema is evident in Kaurismäki's reliance on genre conventions and, above all, the classical style. Many of his films could be classified as melodramas, even though one can detect in them the influence of old slapstick comedies, road movies and crime films. When it comes to his style, Kaurismäki said after making his first feature *Crime and Punishment* (*Rikos ja rangaistus*, 1983) that he 'strived for rather classical or should I say Hawksian narration in which the spectator should not notice the movements of the camera or cuts, except on those rare occasions when it serves a purpose'.[30] This is in accord with the principles of the classical style.[31] He has later given similar statements about his relation to classicism.[32] The influence of American B films—low-budget films of the studio era in general—is more difficult to pinpoint, because their style has not been systematically studied. What is known is that these films were made quickly and cheaply, as a result of which their narration is often economical and laconic. Manny Farber argues that B film producer Val Lewton's 'stock in trade became the imparting of much of the story through such low-cost suggestions as frightening shadows', which made 'the audience think much more about his material than it warranted'.[33] The directors of B films had an unusual amount of creative freedom and hence their films could contain a dose of strangeness. The influence of this tradition is not only related to the minimalism and strangeness of Kaurismäki's films, but also to their carelessness, which results from his small budgets, fast shooting schedules and him simply not wanting his films to appear too polished. He insists on using the first take: 'I take a shot in rehearsal and that's what I use.'[34]

Besides the classical Hollywood cinema, Kaurismäki has been deeply influenced by the French poetic realist cinema. This 'describes a genre of urban drama, often set among the Paris proletariat or lower middle classes, with romantic/criminal narratives emphasising doom and despair'.[35] To make this description fit Kaurismäki's cinema, one only needs to replace Paris with Helsinki. The mise-en-scène of his films is atmospheric in the tradition of these French films and American film noir, which rely on similar conventions and devices. A stylistic feature that is found in all three is a sharp contrast of lighting that is used to make nighttime city streets and shabby interiors atmospheric, with peculiar patterns and strange highlights. A good example is found in Kaurismäki's *Drifting Clouds* (*Kauas pilvet karkaavat,* 1996). Ilona has lost her job as a head waiter and happens to meet the unemployed Melartin, a former porter. The sequence is set in front of a bar where Melartin has drank more than he could afford. Light falls on the street from a high angle. Ilona and the open door of the bar cast long, dark and oblique shadows (Fig. 14.2). The sequence could appear dark or gloomy, as it probably would in the French and American cinemas, but it does not. Kaurismäki plays George Frideric Handel's tender 'Con rauco mormoria' from *Rodelinda* in the background, thus emphasizing the warmth that is present in the colouring (Ilona's red coat, the yellow wall of the bar) and themes (meeting an old friend, helping one in need) of the sequence. The atmosphere is better described as loving. To answer Melartin's question of whether Ilona could help him with his bill, Kaurismäki, following the classical conventions, cuts to a shot of them in the bar. He then adds tragicomedy to the sequence. 'They don't need porters any more,' Melartin explains, 'people can come and go like in a railway station.' Looking at the serious faces of the characters, they do not see any humour in this comment. They decide

Fig. 14.2 Some lighting patterns in *Drifting Clouds* (1996) are reminiscent of French poetic realist films and American film noir

to order 'the whole bottle', after which a new scene sets an ironic contrast to the whole sequence: Ilona, assisted by her loving husband, vomits in their well-lit bathroom. These examples from Kaurismäki's films are not instances of modernist innovation, neither are they a nostalgic return to the old genres and styles. Instead, they exemplify the post-modern nature of Kaurismäki's cinema, his method of mixing and ironically reworking old conventions.

NOTES

1. Interview with Klaus Härö, 20/5/2013.
2. Interview with Jarkko T. Laine, 18/2/2013.
3. Interview with Klaus Härö, 20/5/2013.
4. Interview with Jarkko T. Laine, 18/2/2013.
5. Hjort 2005a: 208.
6. Hjort 2005a, b: 198.
7. Hjort 2005a, b: 210.
8. Interview with Klaus Härö, 20/5/2013.
9. "Director Klaus Härö receives the 2003 Ingmar Bergman Award," *Helsingin Sanomat International Edition*, 28/1/2004.
10. Marklund 2010: 100–101.
11. Marklund 2010: 99.
12. Martti Puukko: "Keskustelu Aki Kaurismäen kanssa", Parnasso 4/2000, Folder Aki Kaurismäki, Clipping collection, NAI.
13. Nestingen 2013: 21.
14. Valkola 2012: 108.
15. Kovács 2007: 303.
16. Andrew 1995: 236.
17. Connah 1991: passim.
18. Hutcheon 1988: 23.
19. Nestingen 2013: 21.
20. Kovács 2013: 3.
21. Hermerén 1975: passim.
22. Nestingen 2013: 44.
23. Hutcheon 2000: xii.
24. Dyer 2007: 47 & passim.
25. Kovács 2007: 140.
26. Kovács 2007: 141.
27. Nestingen 2013: 44.
28. Thompson 1988: 252, 257.
29. Thompson and Bordwell 2010: 163.

30. Mikko Piela: "En ole löytänyt vielä omaa tyyliäni," Kansan Uutiset, 24/12/1983, Folder Aki Kaurismäki, Clipping collection, NAI.
31. Bordwell 2002: 1–84.
32. Martti Puukko: "Keskustelu Aki Kaurismäen kanssa", Parnasso 4/2000, Folder Aki Kaurismäki, Clipping collection, NAI.
33. Farber 2009: 351–352.
34. Ali 2012.
35. Vincendeau 1992: 52.

CHAPTER 15

Finnish Films and International Festivals

Anneli Lehtisalo

International film festivals have been—and still are—one of the main channels for the foreign distribution of Finnish films. Since the 1950s in particular, international film festivals have offered visibility to 'the cinemas of small nations',[1] and now serve as an alternative distribution network for them.[2]

Finnish films have been screened at the major European festivals, such as Venice, Cannes and Berlin, almost since their inception in the middle of the twentieth century. The Finnish film industry's interest in film festivals increased during the 1950s, when the success of a few films raised expectations regarding international recognition for Finnish cinema. Finnish film managers realized that festivals offered opportunities to expand the markets for their products. For instance, it was typical that a film presented at the Berlinale continued its circulation in what was then West Germany.[3] The new business prospects were particularly important during a period of decreasing profitability in Finnish markets.

At the beginning of the 1960s, the film production system changed radically, and a new generation of filmmakers emerged. However, participation in international film festivals continued. Both the old and new

A. Lehtisalo (✉)
e-mail: anneli.lehtisalo@kotiportti.fi

© The Editor(s) (if applicable) and The Author(s) 2016
H. Bacon (ed.), *Finnish Cinema*, Palgrave European Film
and Media Studies, DOI 10.1057/978-1-137-57651-4_15

generations had learned that international festivals were important venues for professional contacts and business opportunities. The Finnish Film Foundation (FFF), founded in 1969, subsidized festival participation from the outset.[4] Ever since, it has granted Finnish production companies and filmmakers subsidies for the production of exhibition copies for international festivals or for travel expenses. Grants related to international festivals have constituted a notable part of 'cultural export support' (or 'support for international activities'). Over the years the forms of cultural export support have changed and diversified, but copying and travel grants for participating in international film festivals have remained a staple within the basic support model. It is notable, however, that cultural export support has constituted only a fraction, approximately 2–3%, of the total subsidy.[5]

The terms 'cultural export' or 'international activities' illustrate the mindset behind Finland's official film policies. Although the FFF has also aimed to support commercial exports, for a long time its rhetoric has emphasized cultural values. In 1988 its annual report explained:

> A film is a useful and marketable vehicle for cultural export. It provides an effective means of reaching a wide audience and its international transportation is cheap. It reaches its audiences quickly, efficiently and inexpensively. As a synthesis of different art forms a film is well suited to presenting its home country in diverse ways.[6]

During the 1990s, however, commercial exports and international markets—particularly within the European Union—gained ground in the strategic thinking of the FFF. In its 1994 annual report, it stated that 'the aim of cultural export is to show Finnish films at as many important international film festivals and similar settings as possible, and thus promote Finland, domestic film art, Finnish culture and for its part enhance overseas film sales'.[7] The changes in rhetoric reflect the overall transformation in film politics in Europe and in Finland. As Mervi Pantti has noted, in the 1990s there was a clear shift from cultural values to economic thinking.[8] In the course of the 2000s, commercial international distribution has become a part of the FFF's mission.[9]

International film festivals have been at the heart of this film policy. Not only has the production of festival copies and travel costs been continuously subsidized, but since the 1990s the FFF's strategic thinking has gradually begun to emphasize the importance of international film festivals—one obvious reason for this is the emerging success of a number of Finnish filmmakers at film festivals.[10] International film festivals have been well suited to the 'dual aims' of the FFF, as they offer a forum both for film art and cultural encounters, and for commercial promotion. During the 2000s, the FFF focused increasingly on how exposure at international film festivals might facilitate commercial distribution and the financial opportunities of filmmakers.[11] It was recognized that mere presence at the festivals and cultural diplomacy were no longer sufficient.

This strategy is understandable considering that both the number of international film festivals and Finnish films participating in them have increased exponentially over the past three decades. As feature film production has expanded, so has the number of films that circulate at festivals. On the other hand, by the 1980s quite a number of Finnish fiction films were already participating in one film festival or another.[12] The real challenge was to get Finnish films into the A status festivals accredited by the International Federation of Film Producers Associations (FIAPF). In the studio era, Finnish films had actively taken part in festivals in Berlin, Karlovy Vary and Moscow,[13] and they continued to be exhibited at these festivals in the 1980s and 1990s, but the films did not necessarily participate in official competitions.[14] Since then the situation has changed little, although some Finnish films have had success at major festivals.[15] The main focus of the FFF is nevertheless on the major festivals; according to the Finnish Cinema Export Strategy launched by the Ministry of Education and Culture, the presence of Finnish films at the major film festivals—that is, Cannes, Berlin, Venice and Toronto—is a starting point for their cultural and commercial export, even if they do not participate in competition series.[16]

All in all, Finnish films circulate actively within the film festival circuit, which nowadays may spread over several years. In contrast to earlier years when circulation meant only festival distribution, nowadays success at a festival may also open the doors to commercial distribution, as happened for example in the case of *Rare Exports: A Christmas Tale* (Jalmari Helander, 2010).[17] On the other hand, persevering with festival touring has borne fruit, for example for the Kaurismäki brothers, who have participated in festivals continuously from the 1980s to the present and who have at times been successful in turning festival fame into commercial success. Finnish children's films and documentaries have also participated in film festivals, occasionally with considerable success. In the 2000s festival films have no longer been confined to so-called art house films, and the repertoire now includes different genres ranging from comedies to horror films. The general changes in Finnish subsidy policy are in full accord with this development.[18]

In the FFF's *Target Programme for Finnish Film 2011–2015* it was stated that 'international film festivals will retain their importance for launching, promoting and exporting films'.[19] There is no doubt that the international film festival circuit continues to be important for the smaller film producing countries such as Finland. However, in the *Target Programme* the FFF is already looking ahead, anticipating the impact of new distribution technologies. These may offer fresh ways of reaching international audiences and should thus enhance global distribution. How this will affect the support system and festival practices remains to be seen.

NOTES

1. Hjort and Petrie 2007b.
2. E.g. de Valck 2007.
3. Lehtisalo 2014.
4. Annual report 1970, FFF, NAIL.
5. E.g. Finnish Film Foundation, *Annual Report 2011*.
6. Annual Report 1988: 9, FFF, NAIL.
7. Annual Report 1994: 15, FFF, NAIL.
8. Pantti 2005: 182–186; see also Kääpä in this volume.
9. E.g. Finnish Film Foundation, *Annual Report* 2008, 2009: 5; *Annual Report* 2013, 2014: 7.
10. See Annual Report 1990: 8; Annual Report 1995: 3, FFF, NAIL.
11. Annual Report 2006: 11, FFF, NAIL.
12. Finnish National Filmography 9: passim.
13. Lehtisalo 2014.
14. Finnish National Filmography 10–12: passim.
15. E.g. *Mies vailla menneisyyttä/The Man without a Past* in Cannes (Aki Kaurismäki, 2002), *Elina—Som jag inte fanns/Elina: As if I Wasn't There* in Berlin (Klaus Härö, 2003).
16. Ministry of Education, *Proposal for Finnish Cultural Exports Promotion Programme 2007–2011*: 25.
17. Finnish Film Foundation, *Annual Report* 2010, 2011a: 20–21.
18. See Kääpä in this volume.
19. Finnish Film Foundation, *Target Programme for Finnish Film 2011–2015*, 2011b: 19.

CHAPTER 16

Conclusion: The Transnational Persistence of National Cinemas

Henry Bacon in collaboration with Outi Hupaniittu and Jaakko Seppälä

COLLECTING AND INTERPRETING FILM HISTORICAL DATA

The study of the transnational aspects of a small nation cinema throughout its history entails first of all systematically collecting data in a variety of ways, ranging from thorough exploration of relevant archives to developing methods for comparative stylistics. The data then has to be interpreted in the light of our increasing understanding of why certain decisions were made in the context in which people operated, taking into account the practical, economic and technical constraints, focusing especially on how their horizons of expectation were formed between the desire to create and maintain a genuinely national film culture on the one hand, and to relate to a variety of developments abroad on the other. All this makes sense only in relation to how such developments were conditioned by the vicissitudes of social, political and ideological changes that have connected the nation with the rest of the world.

H. Bacon (✉)
Film and Television Studies, University of Helsinki, Helsinki, Finland
e-mail: henry.bacon@helsinki.fi

O. Hupaniittu
Finnish Literature Society, Helsinki, Finland

J. Seppälä
Film and Television Studies, University of Helsinki, Helsinki, Finland

© The Editor(s) (if applicable) and The Author(s) 2016   227
H. Bacon (ed.), *Finnish Cinema*, Palgrave European Film
and Media Studies, DOI 10.1057/978-1-137-57651-4_16

At times interpretation has to be somewhat speculative due to the unavailability of materials: certain statistics have been systematically collected only after a certain point in time, both films and archival materials have disappeared or are for compelling—and sometimes quite obscure—reasons not available (see the Appendix for statistics compiled by Outi Hupaniittu and her account of the availability, or lack, of relevant data). Nevertheless, reasonably reliable estimates can be made on the basis of surviving public statements, company records and reminiscences by business professionals, cultural critics and commentators as well as members of the audience. Through such records we can form a focused idea of what different people thought about their national cinema in respect of transnational developments that were taking place.

As regards stylistic analysis, the opposite problem might also arise: if the corpus of films is large, on what basis can legitimate generalizations be made? This is a core question in exploring how stylistic influences have penetrated a film culture. In recent years tools and methodologies have been developed that have made stylistic analysis significantly more rigorous than before. This has helped in overcoming certain misconceptions that have occurred from traditional impressionistic writing, but it has not freed us from the task of interpretation, seeking to understand what certain measurable changes and variations actually imply, what they can tell us about how filmmakers and spectators have appreciated domestic cinema vis-à-vis Hollywood and other national cinemas. Here again, we have to return to statements that have been preserved and made available in archives to complement the critical readings and statistical interpretations that are inevitably part of any retrospective analysis of authorial intentions or positioning of artistic strategies in specific cultural historical mo(ve)ments. They allow us to create a coherent image of how stylistic innovations and thematic developments positioned Finnish cinema as part of a reciprocal transnational matrix.

In the contemporary world, the transnational study of both film production and style has to be related to the persistent centrality of nations—despite globalizing tendencies on the one hand, and increasing internal heterogeneity on the other. These dual developments can clearly be seen in the cultural policies of small nations. They have recognized the need to protect their film industries by subsidizing domestic activities, not so much with the aim of maintaining a sense of national identity but with the need to provide their people with art and entertainment in their own languages, set in environments that look familiar in terms of their own immediate experience. Another reason might simply be the need to increase employment and expand export markets in this field, as well as seeking cultural prestige by demonstrating the nation's commitment to supporting arts by not leaving its film culture completely at the mercy of Hollywood cinema.

The struggle began already in the interwar period, when for example Britain tried to protect its domestic film industry by means of quotas. At that time the purpose was, according to Andrew Higson, to 'offer coherent images of the nation, sustaining the nation at an ideological level, exploring and celebrating what [was] understood to be the indigenous culture'. By the time of the various New Waves things started to look quite different, as a new generation of filmmakers emerged intent on exploring both the possibilities of film as a medium and its potential for challenging prevailing notions about society and life in general. Higson categorizes this kind of cinema, 'characterized by questioning and inquiry', as implicitly left-wing critical cinema. He is no doubt correct in suggesting that such critical cinema 'need not be nationally based in its funding, its textual concerns or its reception'. It is also true that such cinema does not form the full range of nationally produced films.[1] And as Higson himself points out, he is discussing mainly British cinema. The situation looks quite different in countries in which even quite popular domestic films, let alone the critical ones, could not be made without public support. Often the critical cinema has been thought to address major national concerns, whereas attempts to domesticate genres such as action films has frequently been seen as selling out. Yet it has been acknowledged that these too, simply by virtue of being made in the native tongue of the small nation, have an implicit national quality. This may be even more important than an explicit preoccupation with national identity.

While Higson is no doubt right in stating that 'the contingent communities that cinema imagines are much more likely to be either local or transnational than national',[2] it must also be recognized that these categories are nested rather than mutually exclusive. Local scenes take place within given nations, and people generally have their roots in national contexts as well as various other social configurations—and if they do not, they are likely to have problems worthy of cinematic treatment. Equally importantly, the notion of transnational only makes sense in terms of nations, and vice versa. Even if we make a distinction between nation as a community and state as a legal and political set of institutions, we have to acknowledge that in many respects states can only function effectively because of the symbolic value conveyed to them by notions of nation, whether that is conceived as being homogeneous or heterogeneous. Britain with its tortuous relationship with the European Union is a good example of how ardently the sense of the nation is kept up and its interest guarded, even at a time when multiethnicity and the presence of various diasporic minorities are acknowledged as major facts of the cultural and social life of the nation. A national cinema is likely to reflect this state of affairs. There is a paradox here, captured perceptively by Susan Hayward:

within a limited sphere of cultural expression at least, identity co-existing with difference(s) has become a reality—the very thing that nationalism seeks to deny. The paradox of national cinema becomes clear in that henceforth it will always—in its forming—go against the underlying principles of nationalism and be at cross-purposes with the originating idea of the nation as a unified identity.[3]

One source of confusion might be the false expectation that a national cinema is supposed to address above all concerns thought to be topical within the nation. As Mette Hjort has pointed out, filmmakers at least today see themselves as addressing primarily perennial concerns rather than 'topical themes of nation'.[4] Yet even perennial themes must have a distinct setting and be articulated in some culturally specific way. They can be convincingly depicted only with such a degree of specificity as to create the effect of genuine lived experience. Making such attempts financially viable—not to say profitable—at the level of the production values the audience has learned to expect has always been an arduous effort for a small nation cinema.

VICISSITUDES OF FINNISH FILM FUNDING

As the preceding chapters have amply demonstrated, throughout its history, even at its most nationalistic, Finnish cinema has always found the necessary technology and knowhow, as well as the necessary models and vital inspiration from other national film cultures. As regards both economy and aesthetics, it has for all practices and purposes been dependent on the integration of domestic pursuits and transnational networks. This is how it got started, how it has survived and maintained its relevance, and this remains a key factor of its present moderate success.

While there has been continual development throughout Finnish film history, certain limiting parameters related to being a small nation film industry have remained the same. Production has, on the whole, been economically self-sustaining only during the heyday of the studio system. Domestic films have constituted only a minority of all the films screened at Finnish cinemas. Since the turn of the 1920s, there have been releases of domestic feature films every year, but the number has fluctuated from 2 to the record figure of 29 in 1954 and 1955. Meanwhile, since the beginning of the sound era the number of all premieres within a year has ranged from the low point of 127 in 1940 to the record of 428 in 1956 and 1957. Since 1929, after which data on first nights is available, only 6% of screened features have been domestic productions. The number of earlier premieres is not known, but according to Hupaniittu's calculations the share of Finnish films was even lower before 1929.[5] All in all, the economic viability of Finnish film culture has always depended on imports, distribution and exhibition rather than the production of original domestic films. This is a rather one-sided form of transnationalism, as only a precious few Finnish films have been so successfully exported that they would have brought any significant amount of revenue.

In the early years of Finnish cinema, domestic production was possible only through being financed privately in conjunction with the exhibition sector. The exhibition side in turn has only been profitable because of the attraction of foreign films. At least by the mid-1920s, possibly from as early as 1916 at least as regards the number of films imported, Hollywood assumed a leading position that it has retained ever since. It may well be assumed that through the studio era, possibly already from 1935, many domestically produced films have been more popular than imported ones, but not enough statistical evidence is available to reach firm conclusions. We do know for certain that ever since the beginning of the 1970s, after which audience statistics are available, with the exception of the years 1993–1997, the annual share of tickets sold for Finnish films has always been higher than the share of premieres. In recent years (2011–2014) the share of audience has been around 25%, while the share of premieres has only been around 13%.[6]

Finnish films were at their most popular between 1935 and 1941, attracting much bigger audiences than nowadays.[7] Even after that, for about 15 more years, audience attendance was high enough for the system of production and exhibition to remain profitable. However, before and after that period production has not been self-sustaining. When the domestic audience is small and exports do not play a significant role in financing operations, even considerable popularity does not automatically bring significant revenues to producers. The box-office income is shared between the producer, distributor and exhibitor, and thus only part of the income reaches the filmmaker. As Hupaniittu demonstrates in Chapter 3, in the early phases of Finnish film production gaining revenues was far from certain, and even the large producers were only able to break even or make diminutive profits with filmmaking. Meanwhile the smaller companies were continually struggling to survive. At the early stage of consolidation of the film industry, this meant that Suomi-Filmi as the first-mover was the only significant producer to reach the sound era. During the studio era just three companies, Suomi-Filmi (est. 1919, about 120 features), Suomen Filmiteollisuus (1933–1965, 238 features) and Fennada-Filmi (1950–1983, 62 features) produced the majority of the films and took practically all the revenue.

Before the mid-1930s and after the mid-1950s, the finances of even the biggest companies were in dire straits. The most efficient producers were able to break even with filmmaking, but for the most part production had to be supported by other branches of operations, such as film distribution, exhibition, advertising and commercial short film production. Later on, television productions helped to balance the economics. Nevertheless, all these factors would not have sufficed to save Finnish cinema after the fall of the studio system. Both overall attendance figures and the proportion of tickets sold for Finnish films fell sharply, necessitating the creation of a form of state subsidy. After furious cultural political debates, this was organized through the establishment of the Finnish Film Foundation (FFF) in 1969. This fundamentally altered the basis of financing feature production, enabling film production to divest itself from the exigencies of the market, a seemingly noble but eventually unsustainable idea, as through the 1970s the attendance figures for Finnish films continued to decline. Popular comedy, which for quite some time was not subsidized, alleviated the problem, but only the thorough revision of the FFF's funding policy made it possible for the Finnish film industry to acquire a decent share of the cinemagoing audience. In the early years, the subsidies channelled through the FFF were nominal, but they have risen significantly and have become a major source of funding. According to the statistics for 2013, the FFF supported features with an average of 47% of the median budget.

After the passing of the studio system, only a handful of companies have been able to sustain their operations and maintain at least some degree of continuity. In terms of production numbers the most important producer has been Pertti 'Spede' Pasanen, who made some 45 popular features and numerous television series from the mid-1960s to the turn of the millennium. He was also an exceptional producer, who only received state subsidies at a fairly late stage because his comic films were not regarded as of a sufficient artistic standard to merit public funding. He was able to continue film production because his films were genuinely popular and because his company also made profits with its television production. Three other companies, Filminor (1962–1997), Jörn Donner Productions (est. 1966) and Solar Films (est. 1995), have produced about 30 features each.

The difficulties the Finnish film industry has faced through most of its history derive to a significant extent from just how small the national film audience to which it primarily caters really is. In terms of population there might be a critical mass that just about allows for a national film industry to be self-sustaining, or even only to get properly started, as Hupaniittu points out in her analysis of the advantage gained by first-movers. In the 1920s the population of Finland was over 3 million; today it is 5.5 million. Sweden offers an illuminating contrast. Its population was well over 5 million already at the beginning of the 1920s, and is now approaching 10 million. Sweden made an early start at film production, succeeded in remaining non-belligerent in both world wars and, despite losing much of the foreign audience it had in the silent era, has always been able to maintain a healthy foundation in terms of domestic audience interest and gaining significant revenue from abroad too. Whereas in Finland there was a major break in tradition when the studio system collapsed, in Sweden the tradition of filmmaking has continued uninterrupted all the way from the silent era until today. The studio system was even able to absorb and gain strength from the New Waves, and the impact of modernism was not conceived as a major break with tradition. It must have helped that one of the figureheads of European cinematic modernism, Ingmar Bergman, had from fairly early on been in full command of the resources of the great Swedish studios. He had established himself as a major figure in the Swedish studio system, and never severed these ties. In Finland only Matti Kassila had even a roughly similar role, but he never took his modernism particularly far. Another similar figure is Mikko Niskanen, although he merely got started within the studio system and then, as Pietari Kääpä has analysed in Chapter 9, adapted New Wave influences to create some of the most notable films of the early post–studio era Finnish cinema.

This difference in continuity between Finnish and Swedish filmmaking eventually meant that Finns once again had much to learn from their Swedish colleagues, as the working careers of the cinematographers Esa Vuorinen in the 1970s and his student Jarkko T. Laine in the 2000s testify. As examined by Henry Bacon in his analysis of the transnational features of Klaus Härö's first films in Chapter 14, this entailed learning about the kind of working practices as well as aesthetics that operating within a national film industry with a more steady flow of production—made possible by a steadier and larger cash flow—enabled. Since then, as already examined, Nordic funding collaboration and other transnational networks have slightly levelled these differences. Nevertheless, it is obvious that differences of a few million in the size of the domestic audience still influence the prospects of a national film industry.

THE TRANSNATIONAL NATURE OF A NATIONAL STYLE

As Jaakko Seppälä meticulously demonstrates in Chapter 4, the tools available today for statistical analysis of film style offer an illuminating method for the study of transnational influences on filmic narration. While we do not see the classical Hollywood style as the universal measure of cinematic excellence, it seems fair to assume that in its early phases it spearheaded the sophistication of cinematic narration. There were dissenting voices, but generally it was identified as such by contemporaries, and gradually domestic as well as foreign films were to a degree assessed according to whether they were following this development or not.

However, the prominent use of large shot scales that characterized the Finnish group style of the 1920s indicates that many filmmakers adhered for quite a long time to the model provided by the stage theatre and the earlier European tableau-style of filmmaking. Eventually, despite a certain cultural prejudice towards American culture, in comparison with Hollywood products films adhering to the tableau style began to appear increasingly old-fashioned. In the last years of the silent era, Finnish cinema evolved stylistically from the tableau style towards the classical style. This development constantly lagged behind the major filmmaking nations, which suggests that conventions of the classical style were gradually adapted from imported films rather than discovered through experimentation. The parameters of this style, with its emphasis on the centrality of individual characters and on narrative clarity, had been developed in the USA, but they were not American as such. Rather, they served as a model for employing cinematic means to tell a story in an interesting and involving way. The transformation of Finnish film style was not a straightforward process of Americanization, even though it was greatly advanced by Hollywood films. Even in the late 1920s most Finnish films were not fully fledged representatives of the classical style, as they contain stylistic elements that are not used according to the principles of classical storytelling. These films are characterized by a heavy reliance on intertitles, large shot scales, the insert style of editing and nationally charged mise-en-scène. The ways these conventions evolved in Finland was to a significant degree influenced also by European cinema. Furthermore, the way they were actually employed derived at least partly from Finnish literature, theatre and painting, thus giving these transnational features a distinctly national quality.

Stylistic development could only take place in step with getting hold of new technology and knowhow. Since the beginning of the sound era there were two film studios, Suomi-Filmi and Suomen Filmiteollisuus, in full operation, enabling sufficiently fluent and continuous production processes to ensure a steady output. By then the basic norms of the classical style had been more or less adopted. It was as if the studios were now following the advice given by Robert Florey in the mid-1920s to French film producers wanting to compete with the Americans. In his view, all cinematic means should 'contribute[ ] to producing a normal film – so normal, that one would forget its nationality. Because of this, it becomes international. It can show on all the screens of the world, so that all audiences can understand it as they understand simple, normal American films ....'[8]

Florey clearly assumes what we now call the classical style to be *the* 'normal' way of making films. Apparently, by the 1930s, most Finnish filmmakers had more or less internalized this line of thinking, even if these influences were to a significant degree adopted through European models, rather than via Hollywood cinema directly. In this they were at times helped by foreign technical talent employed by producers seeking to ensure that the output of their studios could be advertised as being on the level of contemporary developments abroad. Thus, in their advertising they could appeal either to the genuinely Finnish quality of their products or, say, to the exquisitely French style of the cinematography. This was to be achieved by importing French talent. Such technical transnationalism sometimes gave rise to controversy concerning the nationalist vocation to which many people thought the cinema of the young nation was bound.

Some foreigners had already found their way into Finnish film production during the era of silent film. Most commentators of the 1910s and early 1920s sought technical expertise from abroad. The inadequacy of technological competence was considered to be the most acute problem, while the ability of Finnish directors was questioned only by some film production insiders. It was often stated that employing a foreign director or screenwriter should not be considered as they would not be able to illustrate the true essence of Finnishness.[9] In the background there was also the fact that assigning an internationally renowned screenwriter or director would have been much more expensive and difficult than using their Finnish counterparts. The need for an experienced cinematographer was a more urgent issue, because at the time the role of cinematographer was recognized as being more crucial from the point of view of the quality of the product. The Finnish film entrepreneurs turned their eyes to Germany, partly due to political allegiance, German troops having taken part in the civil war and aided the Whites to victory, but also because

German film production was considered to be highly advanced and exceptionally financially lucrative.[10] Above all, the country was relatively close and because of the financial situation after the First World War, purchases from there were not that expensive.

Suomen Filmikuvaamo (established in 1919, name changed to Suomi-Filmi in 1921) made a large number of acquisitions from Germany. A camera, lighting equipment, a printing machine and film stock were ordered, despite the many difficulties in getting the purchases from the war-ridden country transported to Finland.[11] In the following years, these connections were maintained in an effort to keep up with technological developments. Most importantly, on a visit to Germany in 1921 the company employed the cinematographer Kurt Jäger. His appointment was reported as a great achievement. In fact he was not at all that well known in his home country, but his alleged professional background gave credibility to the company and attested to the expertise it would hold with his contribution. As it turned out, his significance to Finnish film production was extensive, as besides his achievements in filming many of the feature films of the 1920s, he was responsible for setting up a new laboratory for Suomi-Filmi.[12] His significance and involvement in the improvement of filmmaking in Finland continued until the mid-1940s. He even developed a sound recording system that was essential during the transition to sound, as well as the first applicable technique used for subtitling imported sound films.[13]

Suomi-Filmi did not limit its contacts to Germany and in late 1923 the French cinematographer Raoul Reynols was recruited as the technical director of the company. He was advertised as a highly skilled professional with 20 years of experience in filmmaking, first in France (Pathé, Gaumont, Films d'Art), then in Russia and after the revolution in Nordic countries.[14] On this occasion the cooperation with an imported technical director was not fruitful, as Reynols filmed only one feature and left the country soon afterwards. The next foreign professionals were not recruited until the 1930s.

The employment of foreign talent in the service of a cinematic enterprise was at times criticized in nationalistic terms, giving rise to debate and some flamboyant gestures. In 1927 one of the early Finnish film directors, Teuvo Puro, left Komedia Filmi and gave as the reason his dislike of working in a company that was in the hands of foreigners. Later on a founder of one of the major studios, Erkki Karu, fulminated against the influx 'of all sorts of foreigners', which he claimed would certainly have many sad consequences. Such statements were somewhat hypocritical, as clearly the real issue was the ongoing battle for market share. It also appeared that Karu had conveniently forgotten that six years earlier, when employing foreigners was considered to be a marketable aspect of film production, he himself had invited Jäger to come and work in Finland. And soon it could not be denied that filmmakers with a touch of foreign ancestry were making a significant contribution to the effort of establishing a genuinely national cinema. Once Valentin Ivanoff, of Russian extraction, and Theodor Tugai, whose parents came from Latvia, established themselves in the business of filmmaking, they soon emerged as two of the most notably Finnish film directors. By that time they had changed their names to Valentin Vaala and Teuvo Tulio, respectively.[15] Some enterprising young Finns, on the other hand, travelled abroad to expand their notions about what film could be. One of the first was Nyrki Tapiovaara, who went to study in Paris, Stockholm and Moscow, and became a great admirer of French poetic realism as well as the German expressionist style.[16] Influences from these cinematic styles can be clearly seen in his *Stolen Death* (*Varastettu kuolema*, 1938).

Some Finnish directors as well as a number of craftsmen seeking to reach the cutting edge of their profession were to follow in Tapiovaara's footsteps abroad, but the importation of craftsmen from abroad probably had a more far-reaching influence as regards film style. This connected with the need both to keep up with international technical standards and to follow the newest stylistic trends. Even when studios sought to develop a distinctly Finnish house style, they looked for inspiration in other national film cultures—'French poesy and stylishness, German seriousness and grandeur, American speed and efficiency'—although only within limits, so that the sense of one's own national character would not be compromised.[17]

One of the strengths of the classical style is its ability to absorb influences and to line them up with the basic parameters of storytelling. Within these parameters a fair amount of variation can take place, with directors and other filmmakers developing more or less clearly established personal styles. As the output of the studios of even a small film culture is usually quite large, stylistic analysis has to take place in terms of samples and relevant reference groups that allow for legitimate generalization. Determining samples and reference groups might not always be easy in the analysis of corpuses as large as the output of the studio era, but the problems should not be exaggerated. Standard knowledge of the films made in this context suggests that the studio styles were uniform enough for legitimate generalizations to be made. For example, in the late 1930s French cinema is likely to be an interesting reference point as regards cinematography in order to assess the impact of the two Frenchmen Marius Raichi and Charlie Bauer, employed in 1937 by the Suomi-Filmi studio. A practical problem emerges: how is one to gain sufficient knowledge of these other national cultures to be able to make comparisons? It is not likely to be possible to explore those others as meticulously as one is expected to treat one's actual object of study. In practice it is necessary to rely on the hopefully solid work of foreign colleagues and then to study a more limited number of films that are recognized as being representative in some relevant respect.

The problems of analysing style are again different after the studio era. The end of this phase led to a fairly substantial break in the tradition of Finnish filmmaking. There were a variety of reasons for this, ranging from the ideological through the economic to the aesthetic. The major aesthetic factor was the influence of modernism, which in one form or another seeped into almost all major categories of filmmaking, even into what in many ways could be described as a continuation of the studio tradition. This phase entailed an increased and perhaps also more self-conscious transnationalism, entering into dialogue with modernistic trends in European film cultures in an attempt to create a new mode of filmmaking that could respond to the political and social developments moulding the nation on the one hand, and international and national aesthetic and cultural developments on the other. As Pietari Kääpä demonstrates in Chapter 9, attention to such developments guided Finnish filmmakers in taking possession of New Wave influences, thus ensuring that the process of adaptation was not just fashion-conscious imitation, but rather one of finding means in cinematic modernism that could be employed to articulate the current concerns intensively felt by a generation who found that their thinking and the lifestyle to which they aspired differed significantly from those of their parents.

However, while the treatment of certain social issues can be traced back to the role cinema was perceived to have in the new political and production context, the analysis of stylistic influences becomes difficult because of modernism's refusal to adhere to any single aesthetics. This was part of the cult of the auteur, which became a defining feature of art house cinema. Thus, while the various stylistic features to which modernism gave rise may readily be spotted, they do not yield easily to comparative analysis. A more sophisticated content-related approach is needed, taking into account, for example, the number of close-ups of hands in a Bresson film and analysing to what extent this feature makes the film different from either a standard mainstream product or an art house film by another modernist director such as Bergman or Antonioni. For the most part we have to be content with analysing a number of prominent films as instances of the creative domestication of what the New Waves had to offer. In Finland these features produced some quite refreshingly personal films, and as Kimmo Laine demonstrates in Chapter 10, the creative freedom was not only put to good use in art films sponsored by the newly founded FFF, it also invigorated genres such as popular film comedies. Whereas the studio style across genres had for the most part adhered to the classi-cal style and the realism effect it produces, the New Waves inspired film-makers to take a distance from it and assume a more playful attitude. In the films that for the most part still adhered to the studio style, digres-sions from studio realism together with a more fractured depiction of the diegetic universe would often be motivated by an undetermined degree of character subjectivity.

The output of this period of Finnish film production could be divided into four roughly established, inevitably overlapping categories: continuation of studio aesthetics, popular comedies, moderate New Wave and radical New Wave. The next step would be the selection of representative or salient films from each category, with the purpose of both exploring how modernism took root in Finnish filmmaking and assessing how broad and varied this influence was. The films selected are then subjected to a thorough exami-nation of both style and content. This entails charting instances of salient or striking use of techniques and exploring their functions, whether they be narrative, thematic, expressive or instances of stylistic flourishes. This analysis is followed by a comparison of the pertinent modernist features of the films studied with similar instances in other relevant contexts, such as the various European New Waves. This will serve as a basis for assess-ing whether there may be a basis for making generalizations about style. At this stage we may also explore whether analogies thus discovered are instances of the domestication of foreign influences, or whether it could be said that there have been more specifically Finnish or some idiosyncratic brands of modernism that have shaped the Finnish cinema of this period. These findings will be compared with contemporary statements about film aesthetics and policy. It should be appreciated that the comparative stylistic analysis of this phase is still very much a work in progress, hopefully to be pursued in a future research project.

Modernism in European cinema as a whole can be seen as lasting only for about three decades—András Kovács in his excellent study dates it to between 1950 and 1980.[18] In Finland modernist influences had already waned for the most part in the 1970s and even the art cinema of the 1980s is not markedly innovative. In the 1980s, Aki Kaurismäki emerged as a director with a distinctive style based on employing a carefully chosen set of conventional cinematic methods in an idiosyncratic way. Seppälä has already demonstrated the applicability of Cinemetrics to the study of what actually are the parameters that create a distinct impression of a personal style of an auteur such as Kaurismäki, and how much variation might actually take place within those parameters.[19]

In many ways, what certain Finnish producers in the 1990s referred to as the 'return to genres' has been one of the defining factors of the success of Finnish cinema at the domestic box office. This new phase is again quite open to formal analysis. Both the stylistics and the content of the films, although indicative of great proficiency and aesthetic sensibility, contain a few surprises. Part of their overall success is due to the increased professionalism of production and marketing, as well as good working relationships between the public and the private sectors in organizing funding. Meanwhile, something that may well be defined as art cinema continues to flourish, albeit free from ideologies that would be contoversial enough to cause much of a stir—in this day and age the mildly subversive attitudes displayed by a filmmaker of Aki Kaurismäki's calibre are rendered harmless by his status as an art house filmmaker. Yet at least in him we have a filmmaker with a genuine wish to explore human concerns by cinematic means.

THE IMPACT OF FINNISH FILMS ABROAD

As Anneli Lehtisalo has demonstrated in Chapter 7, despite the marginality and scarce resources of the Finnish film industry, distributing films abroad was considered desirable and even important. Finnish film companies and filmmakers actively used their foreign contacts in order to export their products. Over the decades, they enhanced their international marketing, for example by reorganizing the company or by participating in international film festivals. Filmmakers could also produce films specifically targeted for the Nordic markets. All in all, foreign distribution was one dynamic activity of the Finnish film industry. Although the number of exported films was not significant, there was a constant flow of films from Finland to international film markets, in particular to Sweden and the niche markets in North America. Although it is generally thought that films produced within a small national film culture seldom travel across borders, the case of Finland demonstrates that these kinds of marginal flows have existed, and foreign distribution was part of standard film business activities, at least in the major film production companies. Occasionally an independent producer such as Teuvo Tulio would also make the effort to reach foreign markets.

Small nation cinemas have always been conceptualized in terms of certain geopolitical constellations.[20] In Finland, the most significant and long-lived of these was the concept of the national, which long dominated public discourses. The idea that there actually existed a cinema that expressed and promoted national indigenousness, 'Finnishness', can be understood as a fundamental rationale for the export business, the reason it was considered culturally important. In practice, this supposed Finnishness and the Finnish language did appeal to the niche markets of Finnish films, Finnish-Americans and audiences in northern Sweden. Together with a national Finnish cinema, the idea of a shared Nordic film culture continued to play a key role. Although not as dominant as the concept of a national cinema, the idea of a Nordic cinema guided the plans of some Finnish filmmakers.

The most short-lived geopolitical constellation in which some Finnish filmmakers sought to take part was the notion of a European cinema as promoted by Nazi Germany during the Second World War. The major Finnish film companies wanted to benefit from the export opportunities it offered, but the end of the war also meant the end of the German-led European cinema. After the war, political and cultural relations with the Soviet Union and other socialist countries occasionally opened up export channels. Other routes were also available, sometimes through the notion of a Nordic cinema. It turned out to be a suitable vehicle for promoting certain Finnish films in international markets in the 1950s and 1960s, often by using the, however brief, appearance of the leading lady naked amidst summery nature. Later, new patterns of organization emerged on national, Nordic, as well as European levels, which continued to affect and guide the export trends of Finnish films.

Ideally, in order to understand the dynamics between Finnish and foreign film cultures, we should explore the reception of foreign films in Finland as well as the reception of Finnish films both at home and abroad. The former is an important part of examining the reception of stylistic features and notions about what can be achieved in films; the latter is obviously interesting from the point of view of assessing the global impact of this small nation culture. Addressing these large questions has to be left for a future project.

PROSPECTS FOR A TRANSNATIONAL FUTURE

Cinema is an art form that acts as the collective memory of our nation. In the contemporary situation, the content of the films diminishes in importance as producers are only required to focus on ensuring commercial profit.[21]

Member of Parliament Kirsi Ojansuu's statement in a debate on national film policy in 2007 exemplifies a very conservative view of the role of national cinema. It continues the opposition of cultural relevance and commercial enterprise in the more or less similarly simplistic terms that had prevailed since the late 1950s. As we have seen throughout the last few chapters, such arguments have been increasingly challenged not only by film producers but also by the FFF, which previously championed this division. There is a genuine need to rethink how the implications of this traditional opposition still affect the strategies adopted by producers as well as public funding organizations, in order to ensure that their products are of sufficient quality to appeal to domestic audiences as well as to have a measure of impact in foreign markets.

The argument for national quality is as strong as ever. Productions that gain international success and producers who are well versed in a networked production environment are increasingly vital for improving Finnish cinema's position in European film culture. Most of the recent international successes of Finnish films rely on distinctly traditional forms of domestic culture and industrial organization. It is fairly obvious that film production and policy are increasingly connected to 'the logic of the market'. 'The new production philosophy' outlined by producers Marko Röhr and Tero Kaukomaa is now a central part of the policy and operations of the FFF as it seeks to fulfil its mandate. It now seems that many of the supposed threats posed by the increased level of collaboration and flow across borders, the 'transnationalization' or globalization of 'authentic' film cultures, actually strengthen the very features they are supposedly diluting.

In this day and age, national cinema is generally not expected to extol the nation or national virtues. In most of Europe even films that are quite far from flattering to the nation are, despite occasional controversy, subsidized by national institutions. This can function as proof of a liberal arts policy and be promoted abroad by state agencies such as the FFF. Yet then again, the purpose of such institutions today is usually not thought to be the promotion of ideas about the nation but rather, as stated on the homepage of the FFF, 'to support and develop Finnish film production, distribution and exhibition'. This entails having wide international contacts that allow for collaboration in most practical aspects of filmmaking: funding, production, technology and distribution. Nordic cooperation is particularly intensive in most of these fields. This can be seen as a reaction to the demands of the global cinema of our time. As Mette Hjort puts it from the perspective of organizing the funding of Danish cinema, it is an instance of 'reactive globalization, for the aim was to ensure that Nordic culture would continue to find cinematic expression in a global media culture dominated by Hollywood, that budgets for Nordic film projects would be such that the production values of Nordic film projects would meet audience expectations shaped largely by Hollywood products, both in the North and globally'.[22] On the other hand, as Hjort and Duncan Petrie also point out, 'small filmmaking nations clearly do tend to confront certain types of problems and to have recourse to certain types of solutions, depending on the particular form of small nationhood in question'.[23]

Nordic collaboration, as already discussed, can be seen as an instance of seeking to overcome centre–periphery patterns that tend to marginalize small nation cinemas—one of the major concerns of transnational efforts in the field of cinema. Several recent initiatives, such as the Nordic Genre Invasion promotional platform, act as forms of regional collaboration in ways that can if not challenge, at least provide an alternative means of revenue for these film industries.[24] Between the major film cultures with global reach, transnationalism has often been a symmetrical relationship, with as much give and take as the spirit of fair play and laws allow—and often far beyond that. The relationship of a small nation film culture to the big players in the world market is unavoidably structurally asymmetrical: it can only survive by accepting the fact that not only the world market but also the domestic market are heavily influenced and to a considerable extent dominated by global trendsetters—mainly Hollywood through most of film history—and that its own contribution beyond its national borders is likely to remain small. The balance may be partially offset by luminous individuals, such as the director Ingmar Bergman or the cinematographer Sven Nykvist, who have had a significant impact on world cinema even as they were faithful to their distinctly Swedish-born artistic identity. Their influence is for the most part restricted to art house cinema, but in that sphere it has been groundbreaking. A relative latecomer such as the Finnish Aki Kaurismäki appears more like the loner who is worthy of celebration in his own right and might be occasionally imitated, but who in the ever more heterogeneous world market appears as just another interesting voice among many. Diametrically opposed to this, genre film production has also emerged as a viable strategy, with ventures such as Timo Vuorensola's *Iron Sky* (2012) receiving global distribution especially through video-on-demand (VOD) platforms, and the exhibition and marketing of the film making ample use of its 'quirky' roots as a Finnish CGI (computer-generated imagery) blockbuster.[25]

Meanwhile, the industry continues for the most part to operate on the basis of a soundly broad domestic audience as regards justifying subsidies, even if that does not provide anywhere near enough revenue to maintain the kind of film production that would meet contemporary professional standards. Regrettably, the global financial crises that began in 2008 have led to cuts from most sources, the television companies as well as the FFF. European political conflicts have further worsened matters. At the time of writing, Finland finds itself in an awkward situation in respect of its eastern neighbour: complying with EU sanctions against Russia, imposed because of the political crisis in Ukraine, yet deeply concerned about its ability to maintain this major trade relationship. Nevertheless, despite these difficulties, domestic cinema flourishes: in 2014 attendance figures exceeded 2 million spectators, achieving a percentage of 28.1% of total attendance—a figure seconded in Europe only by France with its 44%.[26] Such figures fluctuate, but at least for the time being things look even better for the Finnish film industry. Finnkino, the major exhibitor, has been doing exceedingly well, with three of its all-time financially successful days having occurred within a month based on the strength of a fairly varied combination of American and Finnish films—and a conspicuously low presence of European cinema. The lack of European cinema from the commercial circuit is partly compensated for by a great variety of festivals, mainly in Helsinki but also in several provincial centres. Many festivals also offer notable programming from Asia, Africa and Latin America.

Several international achievements are indicative of the continuing success of Finnish cinema. The Finnish-French co-production *Moomins in the Riviera* (*Muumit Rivieralla*, 2014), an animation based on the comic strips of the Finland-Swedish Tove Jansson, has been sold to 40 countries. Jalmari Helander's adventure film *Big Game* (2015), starring Samuel L. Jackson, has received high-profile distribution in many countries, including a heavily advertised release in the UK. Several Finnish filmmakers are now also able to export their expertise at the highest level. In 2015 cinematographer Peter Flinckenberg received the Spotlight Award from the American Society of Cinematographers for his work on Pirjo Honkasalo's film *Concrete Night* (*Betoniyö*, 2013). He expressed great delight at the opportunities this gave him to create connections with major colleagues on an international level.[27] Tuomas Kantelinen, the composer of scores for several recent domestic hits, continues to receive commissions from film industries as widely dispersed as Hollywood, Russia, Macedonia and the USA, as well as garnering awards such as the Nordic Film Music Prize in 2013.

The prospects for the continuation of the system of national subsidies look good in that the government appears to be committed to continuing this practice. At the opening of the 2015 season of the Film Foundation, Pia Viitanen, the Minister for Culture and Housing, emphasized the importance of subsidies both from the point of view of cultural politics and given the need to maintain competitiveness and employment in the field of audiovisual production. And very wisely, she put a great deal of emphasis on social benefits that go beyond economic interests. It remains to be seen whether this positive development continues after a new conservative government with an economic programme characterized by severe cuts in almost all fields of administration assumed office in the spring of 2015.

NOTES

1. Higson 2000: 71.
2. Ibid.: 73.
3. Hayward 2000: 95.
4. Hjort 2000: 107.
5. Hupaniittu 2015. See also Appendix, Figs. A.1, A.2 and A.3.
6. Ibid.
7. Ibid.
8. Quoted in Thompson 2005: 109.
9. See for example Lilius 1958: 339–340. All Finnish silent features except one were directed by a Finn. *The Burglary* (*Murtovarkaus*, 1926) from Suomi-Filmi was directed by the Swedish actor and theatre director Hans Roeck Hansen. At the time he was the main director at the Swedish Theatre in Helsinki. Previously he had appeared in several Swedish films.
10. "Suomalainen filmiteollisuus," Helsingin Sanomat, 17/9/1921.

11. Annual report 1920; Board meeting 18/2, 17/3, 26/9 and 2/11/1920; Company meeting 8/1 and 21/1/1920, SuFiA, NAI.
12. Annual report 1921, SuFiA, NAI.
13. The sound recording system was called Jägerton. It seems to be the sole reason why Suomi-Filmi purchased Komedia-Filmi in 1932. Company Meeting, 15/4 and 20/5/1932, SuFiA, NAI. Suomi-Filmi was also very interested in the subtitling technique, which resulted in a bitter battle over the patent that lasted for a decade from the mid-1930s onwards. See for example file Subtitling case; Board meeting, 5/4/1933, SuFiA, NAI.
14. The filmographies list only a couple of Scandinavian films in which he had participated, but this does not imply that the information about his career would be false, as early credit lists are often far from complete.
15. Uusitalo 1972: 123–125.
16. Ibid.: 121–122.
17. Laine 1999: 213.
18. Kovács 2007.
19. Seppälä 2015: 20–39.
20. See Ďurovičová and Newman 2010; Andrew 2010.
21. Representative Kirsi Ojansuu, Plenary 19/9/2007, Minutes 50/2007, Parliament Proceedings Database.
22. Hjort 2005b: 162.
23. Hjort and Petrie 2007a, b: 3.
24. See Kääpä 2015.
25. Ibid.
26. European Audiovisual Observatory 2015.
27. Harri Römpötti: "Suomalainen kuvaaja herättää kiinnostusta Hollywoodissa: 'Meno kävi ihan villiksi'", *Helsigin Sanomat*, 27/2/2015.

Appendix

Outi Hupaniittu

Figure A.1 shows the number of Finnish feature and long documentary films released annually between 1907 and 2015. Only films that have received commercial theatrical distribution are included in order to chart the magnitude of the mainstream film industry. The sources of the chart are somewhat ambiguous and open to debate, as the definitions of both the feature film and long documentary have varied through film history. Also, the available statistics are not entirely compatible. Especially in the numbers of long documentaries, there is considerable ambiguity as the sources do not always indicate clearly whether all the films included actually received commercial theatrical distribution or not. Furthermore, as regards the early years, the numbers refer to films that received the status of main film of the programme and were considered 'long' according to contemporary standards.

Despite problems in defining exact figures, the chart does indicate that there have been two periods of particularly extensive domestic production: during the so-called studio era or golden years of Finnish film, when film production was (at least partly) financially lucrative, and during the later era of the Finnish Film Foundation, when public subsidy has been an essential part of film funding. The first period of extensive production extends from the mid-1930s to the early 1960s, with the peak years the mid-1950s, and the second from the mid-1980s onwards, with the peak at the beginning of the 2010s.

© The Editor(s) (if applicable) and The Author(s) 2016
H. Bacon (ed.), *Finnish Cinema*, Palgrave European Film
and Media Studies, DOI 10.1057/978-1-137-57651-4

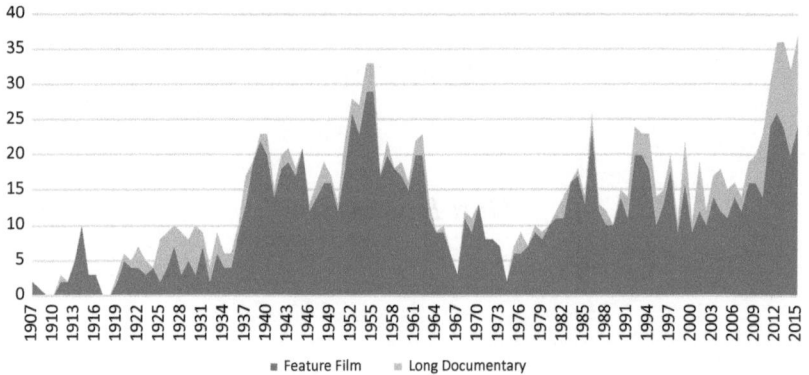

Fig. A.1   Number of domestic first releases, 1907–2015 (Originally published in Hupaniittu 2015b, 15. Sources: Uusitalo 1972, 162; Uusitalo 1975, 165; Uusitalo 1977, 201; Uusitalo 1978, 297; Uusitalo 1981, 345; Uusitalo 1984, 281; Silius 1980, 146; Silius 1984, 149; Annual Report 1990: 37, 1995: 10 and 1998: 34, FFF, NAIL; Finnish Film Foundation: *Annual Statistics 2004–2013*; Finnish Film Foundation 1972–2014; Elonet Database)

Figure A.2 shows the market share of Finnish films in commercial distribution in the years 1929–2014. Admission statistics—or any comparable information on audience numbers—are available only since 1972. From previous decades there is information only on the share of first releases. There is no information on first releases from 1964–1965 to 1996–1997. There is variation in the collation of these statistics caused by the inclusion of long documentaries, as their definition has changed over the years and this cannot be tracked on the basis of the source material. Also, in the early years some variation in the statistics occurs, because in 1929–1934 the information was gathered on the basis of the screening season (September–May), not annually. From the period before 1929 information is available only on the films that were inspected for public screening, which is not the same as the number of films that were actually released through commercial distribution.

Variations in the sources notwithstanding, the chart highlights the importance of domestic production. The number of Finnish releases has always been small when compared with imported films, but on average they have gathered larger audiences. The statistics reveal this to be the case ever since the early 1970s—with the sole exception of the mid-1990s.

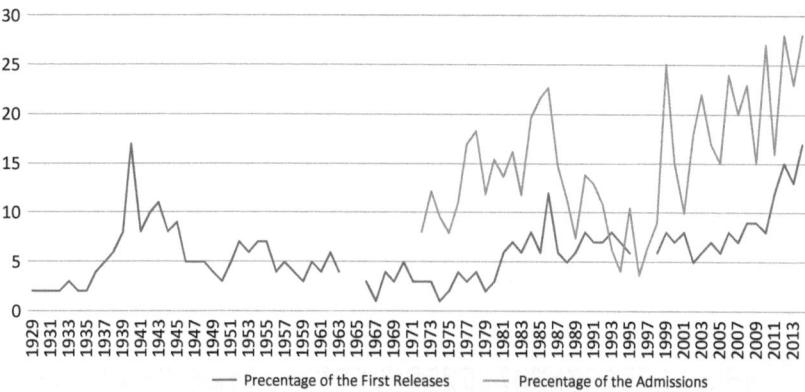

— Precentage of the First Releases   — Precentage of the Admissions

Fig. A.2 Market share of domestic releases, 1929–2014 (Originally published in Hupaniittu 2015b, 18. Sources: *Cinema Owner's Calendars* 1936–1937; 1941; 1951, 228–229; 1963, 228–229; 1976, 97; 1984, 120; 1989, 45–47; 1993, 42–43; 1997, 43–44; Finnish Film Foundation: *Annual Statistics 2009 and 2013*; 'Suomen Elokuvateatterinomistajien Liitto ry:n kertomus toimintavuodelta 1962,' *Kinolehti – Elokuvateatteri*, 2/1963:2, 25; 'Suomen Filmikamarin kertomus toimintavuodelta 1963–1964,' *Kinolehti – Elokuvateatteri* 3/1964, 15; 'Suomen Filmikamari (toimintakertomus 1966),' *Kinolehti—Elokuvateatteri* 3/1967, 16; 'Otteita Suomen Filmikamarin ja sen jäsenjärjestöjen toimintakertomuksista.' *Kinolehti—Elokuvateatteri* 4–5/1968, 20; Finnish Film Foundation, 2015)

The peak of 1940 in share of releases tells more about the problems in importing films caused by the Winter War (1939–1940) than about Finnish production, although this was also a peak time as regards the number of releases.

Figure A.3 shows where the films in commercial distribution between 1929 and 2014 originated. Again, there is some variation in the basis of these figures caused by the problematic inclusion of long documentaries, as well as changes in the period through which the statistics have been gathered; there is no information from the years 1964–1965 and 1996–1997. The films have been divided into only three categories (Finland, USA and other countries), as available data and variation in categorization do not allow for more precise division.

The chart throws light on the significance of US production for Finnish distribution, while highlighting the fact that Hollywood has not always

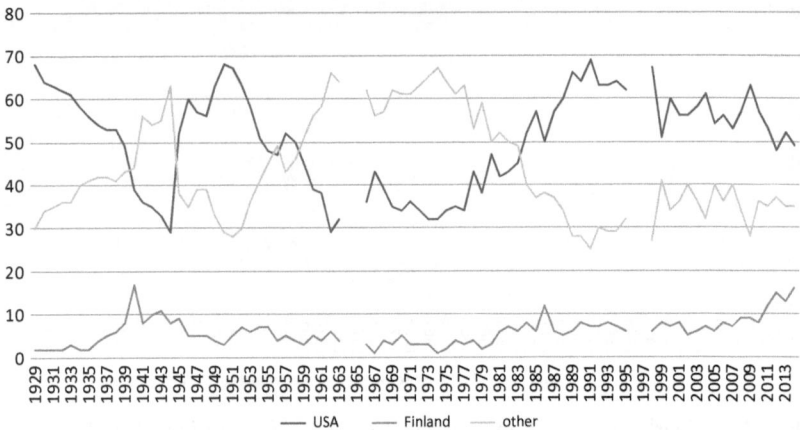

Fig. A.3 Percentage of first releases by country of origin, 1929–2014 (Sources: *Cinema Owner's Calendars* 1936–1937; 1941; 1951, 228–229; 1963, 228–229; 1976, 97; 1984, 120; 1989, 45–47; 1993, 42–43; 1997, 43–44; Finnish Film Foundation: *Annual Statistics 2009 and 2013*; 'Suomen Elokuvateatterinomistajien Liitto ry:n kertomus toimintavuodelta 1962,' *Kinolehti—Elokuvateatteri*, 2/1963:2, 25; 'Suomen Filmikamarin kertomus toimintavuodelta 1963–1964,' *Kinolehti—Elokuvateatteri* 3/1964, 15; 'Suomen Filmikamari (toimintakertomus 1966),' *Kinolehti—Elokuvateatteri* 3/1967, 16; 'Otteita Suomen Filmikamarin ja sen jäsenjärjestöjen toimintakertomuksista.' *Kinolehti—Elokuvateatteri* 4–5/1968, 20)

dominated the number of releases. During the Second World War, pro-German politics significantly decreased the number of films imported from the USA. From the late 1950s to the early 1980s, the origin of films varied significantly and the number of new Hollywood releases was relatively small.

REFERENCES

ARCHIVES

(Located in Helsinki, Finland, except when otherwise noted)
Central Archive for Finnish Business Records (FBR), Mikkeli, Finland
Licence Committee Archive (LCA)
Labour Movement Archives and Library in Sweden (ARBARK), Huddinge,
   Sweden
Nordisk Tonefilm Archive (NTA)
Ministry for Foreign Affairs
Ministry for Foreign Affairs Archive (FMA)
National Archive of Finland (NAF)
Board of Film Classification Archive (BFCA)
Helsinki Police Department Office Archive (HPDOA)
Trade register
National Audiovisual Institute (NAI)
Komedia Filmi Archive
Suomi-Filmi Archive (SuFiA)
Suomen Filmiteollisuus Archive (SFA)
Unidentified scrapbook, 1923–1930
Clipping collection
Library of National Audiovisual Institute (NAIL)
Finnish Film Foundation (FFF), collection of annual reports
National Theatre
National Theatre Archive
Society of Swedish Literature in Finland
Swedish Theatre Archive

© The Editor(s) (if applicable) and The Author(s) 2016   251
H. Bacon (ed.), *Finnish Cinema*, Palgrave European Film
and Media Studies, DOI 10.1057/978-1-137-57651-4

Swedish Film Institute (SFI), Stockholm, Sweden
Svensk Filmindustri Collection (SFC)
Wive-film Collections (WFC)

NEWSPAPERS

(Published in Finland, except when otherwise noted)
Aamulehti 1942, 1944, 1966
Accion (Uruguay) 1954
Dagens Press 1921
Helsingin Sanomat 1919, 1921, 1934, 1937, 1954–1955, 1960, 2015
Helsingin Sanomat International Edition. (2004). Online newspaper. http://
   www2.hs.fi/english/archive/archive.asp. Accessed 10 June 2015.
Hufvudstadsbladet 1934, 1938, 1962, 1998
Hämeen Sanomat 1939
Iltalehti (I) 1922
Iltalehti (II) 2001
Ilta-Sanomat 1947
Jyväskylän Sanomat 1955
Kaleva 1955
Kansan Uutiset 1959, 1965, 1983, 1987
Los Angeles Times (USA) 1958
New Yorkin Sanomat (USA) 1954
New Yorkin Uutiset (USA) 1942–1944, 1946
Päivälehti (USA) 1938, 1940
Raivaaja (USA) 1945
Satakunnan Kansa 1963
Suomen Sosialidemokraatti 1942, 1955, 1962
Turun Sanomat 1991
Uudenmaan Sanomat 1963
Uusi Aika 1938
Uusi Päivä 1958
Uusi Suomi 1919–1921, 1936, 1942, 1953, 1955
Vapaa Sana 1956

PERIODICALS

(Published in Finland, except when otherwise noted)
Aikamme 1956
Biograafilehti, 1915
Biografbladet (Sweden) 1943
Elokuva 1928–1929.

Elokuva-aitta 1939, 1955, 1958
Elokuvateatteri—Suomen Kinolehti 1947, 1950
Elokuvateatteri 1942–1943
Fama 1936
Filmiaitta, 1922, 1925
Jaana 1974
Katso 1967, 1973, 1985
Kinematograph Weekly (UK) 1955
Kinolehti 1955–1956, 1959–1960, 1962–1964, 1967–1968
Kuva 1942
Parnasso 2000
Seura 1942
SF-Uutiset 1937, 1939–1940
Studio 6 (1961)
Suomen Kinolehti 1936, 1937–1938
Suomi-Filmi Uutisaitta 1937–1940, 1944
Valvoja-Aika 11 (1933)

INSTITUTIONAL REPORTS, SURVEYS, PUBLISHED
PROCEEDINGS, ETC

Cinema Owners' Calendar 1936–1937. (1935). *Elokuvamiehen kalenteri 1936–1937.* Helsinki: Weilin + Göös.
Cinema Owners' Calendar 1941. (1940). *Elokuvamiehen kalenteri 1941.* Helsinki: Weilin + Göös.
Cinema Owners' Calendar 1951. (1950). *Elokuvamiehen kalenteri 1951.* Helsinki: Weilin + Göös.
Cinema Owners' Calendar 1963. (1962). *Elokuvamiehen kalenteri 1963.* Helsinki: Weilin + Göös.
Cinema Owners' Calendar 1976. (1975). *Elokuvakalenteri 1976.* Espoo: Weilin + Göös.
Cinema Owners' Calendar 1984. (1983). *Elokuvakalenteri 1984.* Espoo: Weilin + Göös.
Cinema Owners' Calendar 1989. (1988). *SEOL:n yrittäjäkalenteri 1984.* Kuopio: Savon yrittäjät.
Cinema Owners' Calendar 1993. (1992). *Elokuvateatterikalenteri 1993.* Helsinki: Weilin + Göös & Suomen elokuvateatteriliitto.
Cinema Owners' Calendar 1997. (1996). *Elokuvateatterikalenteri 1997.* Helsinki: Weilin + Göös & Suomen elokuvateatteriliitto.
European Audiovisual Observatory. (2015). Box office up in the European Union in 2014 as European films break market share record. Press release 05/05/2015.

Available online: http://www.obs.coe.int/en/-/pr-cannes-2015-film-market-trends-2014. Accessed 17 June 2015.

Finnish Film Foundation. (2004). *Annual statistics in Finnish and English.* Tilastoja 2004 Facts and Figures. Available online: http://ses.fi/fileadmin/dokumentit/Tilastot2004.pdf. Accessed 31 Jan 2016.

Finnish Film Foundation. (2005). *Annual statistics in Finnish and English.* Tilastoja 2005 Facts and Figures. Available online: http://ses.fi/fileadmin/dokumentit/FactsAndFigures2005.pdf. Accessed 31 Jan 2016.

Finnish Film Foundation. (2006). *Annual statistics in Finnish and English.* Tilastoja 2006 Facts and Figures. Available online: http://ses.fi/fileadmin/dokumentit/Tilastoja_2006.pdf. Accessed 31 Jan 2016.

Finnish Film Foundation. (2007). *Annual statistics in Finnish and English.* Tilastoja 2007 facts and figures. Available online: http://ses.fi/fileadmin/dokumentit/Tilastot2007.pdf. Accessed 31 Jan 2016.

Finnish Film Foundation. (2008a). *Audiences of domestic films 2008.* Kotimaisen elokuvan yleisöt -tutkimus. Survey in Finnish, executed by Parametra, January 2008. Available online: http://ses.fi/fileadmin/dokumentit/Kotimaisen_elokuvan_yleisot_tutkimus.pdf. Accessed 11 June 2015.

Finnish Film Foundation. (2008b). *Annual statistics in Finnish and English.* Elokuvavuosi 2008 facts and figures. Available online: http://ses.fi/fileadmin/dokumentit/Elokuvavuosi_2008.pdf. Accessed 31 Jan 2016.

Finnish Film Foundation. (2009a). *Annual report 2008.* Toimintakertomus 2008. Available online: http://ses.fi/julkaisut/arkisto/. Accessed 6 June 2015.

Finnish Film Foundation. (2009b). *Annual statistics in Finnish and English.* Elokuvavuosi 2009 facts and figures. Available online: http://ses.fi/fileadmin/dokumentit/Elokuvavuosi_2009.pdf. Accessed 31 Jan 2016.

Finnish Film Foundation. (2010a). *Annual report 2010.* Toimintakertomus 2010. Available online: http://ses.fi/julkaisut/arkisto/. Accessed 6 June 2015.

Finnish Film Foundation. (2010b). *Annual statistics in Finnish and English.* Elokuvavuosi 2010 facts and figures. Available online: http://ses.fi/fileadmin/dokumentit/Elokuvavuosi_2010_Facts___Figures.pdf. Accessed 31 Jan 2016.

Finnish Film Foundation. (2011a). *Target programme for Finnish Film 2011–2015.* Suomalaisen elokuvan tavoiteohjelma 2011–2015. Avalable online: http://ses.fi/julkaisut/uusimmat-julkaisut/. Accessed 6 June 2015.

Finnish Film Foundation. (2011b). *Annual statistics in Finnish and English.* Elokuvavuosi 2011 facts and figures. Available online: http://ses.fi/fileadmin/dokumentit/Elokuvavuosi_2011_Facts___Figures.pdf. Accessed 11 June 2015.

Finnish Film Foundation. (2012a) *Annual report 2011.* Toimintakertomus 2011. Available online: http://ses.fi/julkaisut/arkisto/. Accessed 6 June 2015.

Finnish Film Foundation. (2012b). *Annual statistics in Finnish and English.* Elokuvavuosi 2012 facts and figures. Available online: http://ses.fi/fileadmin/dokumentit/Elokuvavuosi_2012_Facts___Figures.pdf. Accessed 31 Jan 2016.

Finnish Film Foundation. (2013a). *Audiences of domestic films 2013.* Kotimaisen elokuvan yleisöt –tutkimus. Survey in Finnish, executed by Parametra, March 2013. Available online: http://ses.fi/fileadmin/dokumentit/Kotimaisen_ elokuvan_yleisoet_2013.pdf. Accessed 11 June 2015.

Finnish Film Foundation. (2013b). *Annual statistics in Finnish and English.* Elokuvavuosi 2013 facts and figures. Available online: http://ses.fi/fileadmin/ dokumentit/Elokuvavuosi_2013.pdf. Accessed 31 Jan 2016.

Finnish Film Foundation. (2014a). *Annual report 2013.* Toimintakertomus 2013. Available online: http://ses.fi/julkaisut/arkisto/. Accessed 6 June 2015.

Finnish Film Foundation. (2014b). *Annual statistics in Finnish and English.* Elokuvavuosi 2014 facts and figures. Available online: http://ses.fi/fileadmin/ dokumentit/Elokuvavuosi_2014_Facts__Figures.pdf. Accessed 31 Jan 2016.

Finnish Film Foundation. (2015). *Suomalaisen elokuvan katsojaluvut 2015,* Admission Data for the domestic films. Available online: http://ses.fi/tilastot-ja-tutkimukset/vuositilastot/kotimaiset-katsojaluvut-2015/. linkki tarkistettu 31 Jan 2016.

Finnish Parliament. (1923). *Minutes 1, Parliament Proceedings 1922.* Pöytäkirjat I, Valtiopäiväasiakirjat 1922. Helsinki: Valtioneuvoston kirjapaino.

Finnish Parliament Proceedings Database. Valtiopäiväasioiden ja -asiakirjojen haku. Available online: https://www.eduskunta.fi/FI/search/Sivut/vaskire-sults.aspx. Accessed 17 June 2015.

Ministry of Education. (2007). *Do Finnish cultural exports have saying power? YES! Proposal for Finnish cultural exports promotion programme.* Onko kulttuu-rilla vientiä? ON! Esitys Suomen kulttuuriviennin kehittämisohjelmaksi 2007–2011. Publications of the Ministry of Education 2007:9. Helsinki: Helsinki University Press.

FILMOGRAPHIES AND FILM DATABASE

Barry Salt's Database. Camera movement, shot scale, average shot length database on cinemetrics portal. http://www.cinemetrics.lv/satltdb.php. Accessed 25 Aug 2014.

Elonet. Film database by the National Audiovisual Institute. http://www.elonet. fi/. Accessed 5 June 2015.

Feature films in Sweden 1930–1939. Information about the 3 465 feature films approved or banned for exhibition in Sweden. Wredlund, B., & Lindfors, R. (1983). Lång film i Sverige 1930–1939. Fakta om 3.465 långfilmer godkända för visning eller censurförbjudna i Sverige 1930–1939. Stockholm: Proprius.

Feature films in Sweden 1940–1949. Information about the 3 243 feature films approved or banned for exhibition in Sweden. Wredlund, B., & Lindfors, R. (1981). Lång film i Sverige 1940–1949. Fakta om 3.243 långfilmer godkända för visning eller censurförbjudna i Sverige 1940–1949. Stockholm: Proprius.

Feature films in Sweden 1950–1959. Information about the 3 966 feature films approved or banned for exhibition in Sweden. Wredlund, B., & Lindfors, R. (1979), *Långfilm i Sverige 1950–1959. Fakta om 3.996 långfilmer godkända för visning eller censurförbjudna i Sverige 1950–1959.* Stockholm: Proprius, Svenska Filminstitutet.

Filmografia Fennica 1904–1930. In K. Uusitalo (1972). *Eläviksi syntyneet kuvat. Suomalaisen elokuvan mykät vuodet 1896–1930* (pp. 171–206). Helsinki: Otava.

Finnish National Filmography 1. In K. Uusitalo et al. (Eds.). (1996). *Suomen kansallisfilmografia 1. Vuosien 1907–1935 suomalaiset kokoillan elokuvat.* Helsinki: Suomen elokuva-arkisto & Edita.

Finnish National Filmography 9. In K. Uusitalo et al. (Eds.). (2000). *Suomen kansallisfilmografia 9: Vuosien 1981–1985 suomalaiset kokoillan elokuvat.* Helsinki: Edita.

Finnish National Filmography 10. In S. Toiviainen et al. (Eds.). (2002). *Suomen kansallisfilmografia 10: Vuosien 1986–1990 suomalaiset kokoillan elokuvat.* Helsinki: Edita.

Finnish National Filmography 11. In S. Toiviainen et al. (Eds.). (2004). *Suomen kansallisfilmografia 11: Vuosien 1991–1995 suomalaiset kokoillan elokuvat.* Helsinki: Edita.

Finnish National Filmography 12. In S. Toiviainen et al. (Eds.). (2005). *Suomen kansallisfilmografia 12: Vuosien 1996–2000 suomalaiset kokoillan elokuvat.* Helsinki: Edita.

INTERVIEWS

All interview notes are held by the interviewers.

Jarkko T. Laine (cinematographer), interview by Henry Bacon and Jaakko Seppälä, 18/2/2013.

Klaus Härö (film director), interview by Henry Bacon 20/5/2013.

Marko Röhr (film producer), interview by Pietari Kääpä, 4/9/2011.

Maunu Kurkvaara (film director), by Anneli Lehtisalo, Pietari Kääpä, Jaakko Seppälä and Henry Bacon, 19/3/2013.

Petri Kemppinen (head of production department at Finnish Film Foundation), interview by Henry Bacon, 24/2/2012.

Tero Kaukomaa (film producer), interview by Pietari Kääpä 10/10/2011.

BIBLIOGRAPHY

Ahonen, K., Rosenqvist, J., & Valotie, P. (Eds.). (2003). *Taju kankaalle: uutta suomalaista elokuvaa paikantamassa.* Turku: Kirja-Aurora.

Alanen, A. (1999). Born under the sign of the scarlet flower: Pantheism in Finnish silent cinema. In J. Fullerton & J. Olsson (Eds.), *Nordic explorations: Film before 1930* (pp. 77–85). Sydney: John Libbey.

Ali, O. (2012). Aki Kaurismäki, Little white lies online magazine, originally published 05/04/2012. http://www.littlewhitelies.co.uk/features/articles/aki-kaurismaki-18011. Accessed 14 Apr 2015.

Altman, R. (1999). *Film/Genre*. London: BFI Publishing.

Anderson, B. (2002/1991/1983). *Imagined communities—Reflections on the origin and spread of nationalism*. London/New York: Verso.

Andersson, P., & Kangassalo, R. (2003). Suomi ja meänkieli Ruotsissa. In H. Jönsson-Korhola & A.-R. Lindgren (Eds.), *Monena suomi maailmalla: Suomalaisperäisiä kielivähemmistöjä* (pp. 30–163). Helsinki: SKS.

Andrew, D. (1995). *Mists of regret: Culture and sensibility in classic French film*. Princeton: Princeton University Press.

Andrew, D. (2010). Time zones and jetlag: The flows and phases of world cinema. In N. Durovicová & K. Newman (Eds.), *World cinemas, transnational perspectives* (pp. 59–89). London/New York: Routledge.

Aumont, J. (2006). Griffith: The frame, the figure. In T. Elsaesser (Ed.), *Early cinema: Space, frame, narrative* (pp. 348–359). London: British Film Institute.

Bakker, G. (2008). *Entertainment industrialised—The emegence of the international film industry, 1890–1940*. Cambridge/New York: Cambridge University Press.

Balio, T. (1993). *Grand design: Hollywood as a modern business enterprise, 1930–1939*. Berkeley/Los Angeles/London: University of California Press.

Bordwell, D. (1985). The introduction of sound. In D. Bordwell, J. Staiger, & K. Thompson (Eds.), *The classical Hollywood cinema: Film style and mode of production to 1960* (pp. 298–308). London: Routledge.

Bordwell, D. (1997). *On the history of film style*. Cambridge/London: Harvard University Press.

Bordwell, D. (2002/1985). The classical Hollywood style, 1917–60. In D. Bordwell, J. Staiger, & K. Thompson (Eds.), *The classical Hollywood cinema: Film style and mode of production to 1960* (pp. 1–84). London: Routledge.

Bordwell, D. (2005). *Figures traced in light: On cinematic staging*. Berkeley/Los Angeles/London: University of California Press.

Bordwell, D., Staiger, J., & Thompson, K. (1985). *The classical Hollywood cinema. Film style & mode of production to 1960*. London/Melbourne/Henley: Routledge and Kegan Paul.

Bowser, E. (1994/1990). *The transformation of cinema: 1907–1915*. Berkeley/Los Angeles/London: University of California Press.

Bozak, N. (2010). *The cinematic environment: Lights, camera, environment*. Newark: Rutgers University Press.

Brewster, B. (2006). Deep staging in French films 1900–1914. In T. Elsaesser (Ed.), *Early cinema: space, frame, narrative* (pp. 45–55). London: British Film Institute.

Broe, D. (2014). *Class, Crime and International Film Noir: Globalizing America's Dark Art*. New York: Palgrave Macmillan.

Brouwers, A. (2010). The name behind the titles: Establishing authorship through inter-titles. In S. Bull & A. Söderbergh Widding (Eds.), *Not so silent: Women in cinema before sound* (pp. 103–114). Stockholm: Acta Universitatits Stockholmiens.

Brunetta, G. P. (1994). The long march of American cinema in Italy from Fascism to the Cold War. In D. W. Ellwood & R. Kroes (Eds.), *Hollywood in Europe— Experiences of a cultural hegemony* (pp. 139–154). Amsterdam: VU University Press.

Carrol, N. (2008). *The philosophy of motion pictures*. Malden/Oxford/Carlton: Blackwell Publishing.

Chandler, A. D. (2004). *Scale and scope: The dynamics of industrial capitalism*. Harvard: Harvard University Press.

Comolli, J-L., & Narboni, J. (1976/1969). Cinema/ideology/criticism. In B. Nichols (Ed.), *Movies and methods: An anthology* (pp. 22–30). Berkeley/Los Angeles/London: University of California Press.

Connah, R. (1991). *K/K: A couple of Finns and some Donald Ducks*. Helsinki: VAPK.

Crofts, S. (2006). Reconceptualising national cinema/s. In V. Vitali & P. Willemen (Eds.), *Theorising national cinema* (pp. 44–58). London: BFI Publishing.

Danan, M. (1999). Hollywood's hegemonic strategies. Overcoming French nationalism with the advent of sound. In A. Higson & R. Maltby (Eds.), *'Film Europe' and 'Film America'. Cinema, commerce and cultural exchange 1920–1939* (pp. 225–248). Exeter: University of Exeter Press.

de Grazia, V. (1998). European cinema and the idea of Europe 1925–1995. In G. Nowell-Smith & S. Ricci (Eds.), *Hollywood and Europe: Economics, culture, national identity: 1945–95* (pp. 19–33). London: British Film Institute.

De Valck, M. (2007). *Film festivals from European geopolitics to global cinephilia*. Amsterdam: Amsterdam University Press.

Deleuze, G. (2005). *Cinema 2*. New York: Continuum.

Donner, J. (1970). *Tapaus Naisenkuvia*. Helsinki: Otava.

Donner, J. (2013). *Mammutti*. Helsinki: Otava.

Ďurovičová, N., & Newman, K. (Eds.). (2010). *World cinemas, transnational perspectives*. London/New York: Routledge.

Dyer, R. (2007). *Pastiche*. London/New York: Routledge.

Ellwood, D. (2012). *The shock of America—Europe and the challenge of the century*. Oxford: Oxford University Press.

Elsaesser, T. (2005). *European cinema—Face to face with Hollywood*. Amsterdam: Amsterdam University Press.

Farahmand, A. (2010). Disentangling the international festival circuit: Genre and Iranian cinema. In R. Galt & K. Schooner (Eds.), *Global art cinema—New theories and histories* (pp. 263–281). Oxford: Oxford University Press.

Farber, M. (2009). Val Lewton. In R. Polito (Ed.), *Farber on film: The complete writings of Manny Farber* (pp. 51–354). New York: The Library of America.

Frisvold Hanssen, E., & Rossholm, A. S. (2012). The paradoxes of textual fidelity: Translation and intertitles in Victor Sjöström's silent film adaptation of Henrik Ibsen's *Terje Vigen*. In L. Raw (Ed.), *Translation, adaptation and transformation* (pp. 145–161). London/New York: Continuum International.

Furhammar, L. (1991). *Filmen i Sverige: en historia i tio kapitel.* Höganäs: Wiken.

Furhammar, L. (2010). Selma Lagerlöf and literary adaptations. In M. Larsson & A. Marklund (Eds.), *Swedish film: An introduction and reader* (pp. 86–91). Lund: Nordic Adacemic Press.

Garncarz, J. (1999). Made in Germany. Multiple-language versions and the early German sound cinema. In A. Higson & R. Maltby (Eds.), *'Film Europe' and 'Film America': Cinema, commerce and cultural exchange 1920–1939* (pp. 249–273). Exeter: University of Exeter Press.

Gaudreault, A. (2009). *From Plato to Lumière. Narration and monstration in literature and cinema.* Toronto/Buffalo/London: University of Toronto Press.

Green, N. (2007). *French new wave: A new look.* London: BFI.

Guback, T. H. (1969). *The international film industry: Western Europe and America since 1945.* Bloomington: Indiana University Press.

Gunning, T. (2006). Modernity and cinema. A culture of shocks and flows. In M. Pomerance (Ed.), *Cinema and modernity* (pp. 297–315). New Brunswick/New Jersey/London: Rutgers University Press.

Hake, S. (2002). *German national cinema.* London/New York: Routledge.

Halle, R. (2010a). Offering tales they want to hear: Transnational European film funding as neo-orientalism. In R. Galt & K. Schoonover (Eds.), *Global art cinema—New theories and histories* (pp. 303–319). Oxford: Oxford University Press.

Halle, R. (2010b). Offering tales they want to hear: Transnational European film funding as neo-orientalism. In R. Galt & K. Schooner (Eds.), *Global art cinema—New theories and histories* (pp. 303–319). Oxford: Oxford University Press.

Hayward, S. (2000). Sociological scope of national cinema. In M. Hjort & S. Mackenzie (Eds.), *Cinema & nation* (pp. 19–31). London/New York: Routledge.

Hermerén, G. (1975). *Influence in art and literature.* Princeton: Princeton University Press.

Higson, A. (1989). The concept of national cinema. *Screen, 30*(4), 36–46.

Higson, A. (2000). Limiting imagination of national cinema. In M. Hjort & S. Mackenzie (Eds.), *Cinema & nation* (pp. 15–25). London/New York: Routledge.

Higson, A., & Malby, R. (1999). 'Film Europe' and 'Film America': An introduction. In A. Higson & R. Maltby (Eds.), *'Film Europe' and 'Film America': Cinema, commerce and cultural exchange 1920–1939* (pp. 1–31). Exeter: University of Exeter Press.

Hillier, J. (Ed.). (1972). *New cinema in Finland.* Helsinki: The Finnish Film Archive.

Hjort, M. (2000). Themes of nation. In M. Hjort & S. Mackenzie (Eds.), *Cinema & nation* (pp. 103–117). London/New York: Routledge.

Hjort, M. (2005a). From epiphanic culture to circulation: The dynamic of globalization in Nordic cinema. In A. Nestingen & T. G. Elkington (Eds.), *Transnational cinema in a global North.* Detroit: Wayne State University Press.

Hjort, M. (2005b). *Small nation, global cinema—The new Danish cinema.* Minneapolis/London: Minnesota University Press.

Hjort, M., & Petrie, D. (2007a). Introduction. In M. Hjort & D. Petrie (Eds.), *The cinema of small nations* (pp. 1–19). Edinburgh: Edinburgh University Press.

Hjort, M., & Petrie, D. (Eds.). (2007b). *The cinema of small nations.* Edinburgh: Edinburgh University Press.

Hobsbawm, E. J. (1990). *Nations and nationalism since 1780—Programme, myth, reality.* Cambridge: Cambridge University Press.

Honka-Hallila, A. (1994). Laulavan jääkärin mykkä morsian: Teknologia ja elokuvan historia. In R. Kinisjärvi, T. Malmberg, & J. Sihvonen (Eds.), *Elokuva ja analyysi: Katsauksia elävän kuvan erittelyyn ja tulkintaan* (pp. 11–29). Helsinki: Painatuskeskus and Suomen elokuva-arkisto.

Honka-Hallila, A. (1995a). Elokuvakulttuuria luomassa. In A. Honka-Hallila, K. Laine, & M. Pantti (Eds.), *Markan tähden: Yli sata vuotta suomalaista elokuvahistoriaa* (pp. 11–68). Turku: Turun yliopiston täydennyskoulutuskeskus.

Honka-Hallila, A. (1995b). *Kolme Eskoa: Nummisuutarit ja sen kolmen filmatisoinnin kerronta.* Helsinki: Suomalaisen Kirjallisuuden Seura.

Honka-Hallila, A. (1996). Äänielokuva tulee Suomeen. In K. Uusitalo et al. (Eds.), *Suomen kansallisfilmografia 1* (pp. 463–469). Helsinki: Edita and Suomen elokuva-arkisto.

Honka-Hallila, A., et al. (1995). *Markan tähden: yli sata vuotta suomalaista elokuvahistoriaa.* Turku: Turun Yliopisto.

Hupaniittu, O. (2011). Leskirouva Larissan avioliitto eli kuinka Gustaf Molinin elämäntyö katosi. In S. Laine, M. Leskelä-Kärki, K. Kallioniemi, H. Kiiskinen, P. Paju, & H. Rantala (Eds.), *Historian aikakoneessa: Onnittelukirja Hannu Salmelle* (pp. 211–221). Turku: k&h-kustannus.

Hupaniittu, O. (2013). *Biografiliiketoiminnan valtakausi. Toimijuus ja kilpailu suomalaisella elokuva-alalla 1900–1920-luvuilla.* Turku: Annales Universitatis Turkuensis.

Hupaniittu, O. (2015a). Suomalaisen elokuvan pientuottajat 1920–1930-luvuilla. In *Elonet—Kansallisfilmografia.* Helsinki: Kansallinen audiovisuaalinen instituutti. Electronic publication, first published 18/2/2015. http://www.elonet.fi/fi/kansallisfilmografia/suomalaisen-elokuvan-vuosikymmenet/1919-1929/suomalaisen-elokuvan-pientuottajat-1920-1930-luvuilla. Accessed 28 May 2015.

Hupaniittu, O. (2015b). Elokuva, teatteri ja tilasto—Suomalainen elokuvateatteri-toiminta määrällisessä analyysissä. *Lähikuva, 29*, 6–26.

Hupaniittu, O. (2015c). Gustaf Molin—suomalaisen elokuva-alan unohdettu suu-ruus. In *Elonet—Kansallisfilmografia.* Helsinki: Kansallinen audiovisuaalinen instituutti. Electronic publication, forthcoming. http://www.elonet.fi/fi/kan-sallisfilmografia/suomalaisen-elokuvan-vuosikymmenet/1919-1929/gustaf-molin-suomalaisen-elokuva-alan-unohdettu-suuruus

Hutcheon, L. (1988). *A poetics of postmodernism: History, theory, fiction.* New York/London: Routledge.

Hutcheon, L. (2000/1985). *A theory of parody: The teachings of twentieth-century art forms.* Urbana/Chicago: University of Illinois Press.

Iordanova, D. (2010). Rise of the fringe. Global cinema's long tail. In D. Iordanova, D. Martin-Jones, & B. Vidal (Eds.), *Cinema at the periphery* (pp. 23–45). Detroit: Wayne State University Press.

Iordanova, D., Martin-Jones, D., & Vidal, B. (Eds.). (2010). *Cinema at the periphery.* Detroit: Wayne State University Press.

Iversen, G. (1998). Norway. In T. Soila, A. Söderbergh Widding, & G. Iversen (Eds.), *Nordic national cinemas* (pp. 102–141). London/New York: Routledge.

Jalonen, O. (1985). *Kansa kulttuurien virroissa: Tuontikulttuurin suuntia ja sisältöjä Suomessa itsenäisyyden aikana.* Helsinki: Otava.

Jarvie, I. (1994). The postwar economic foreign policy of the American film indus-try: Europe 1945–1950. In D. W. Ellwood & R. Kroes (Eds.), *Hollywood in Europe—Experiences of a cultural hegemony* (pp. 155–175). Amsterdam: VU University Press.

Jeancolas, J.-P. (1995). The inexportable: The case of French cinema and radio in the 1950s (trans: Graham, P.). In R. Dyer, & G. Vincendeau (Eds.), *Popular European cinema* (pp. 141–148). London: Routledge.

Jensen, M. (2014). Scandinavian films—"Nordic cooperation in a 20-year per-spective". In J. E. Holst (Ed.), *Stork flying over pinewood—Nordic Baltic film cooperation 1989–2014* (pp. 33–37). Oslo: KOM forl.

Jokisipilä, M., & Könönen, J. (2013). *Kolmannen valtakunnan vieraana: Suomi HItlerin Saksan vaikutuspiirissä 1933–1944.* Helsinki: Otava.

Kalha, H. (2009). The case of Theodor Tugai: The filmstar and the factitious body. In T. Soila (Ed.), *Stellar encounters: Stardom in popular European cinema* (pp. 132–142). New Barnet: John Libbey.

Kaplan, E. A. (2010). European art cinema, affect, and postcolonialism: Herzog, Denis and the Dardenne brothers. In R. Galt & K. Schooner (Eds.), *Global art cinema—New theories and histories* (pp. 285–302). Oxford: Oxford University Press.

Kassila, M. (2004). *Käsikirjoitus ja ohjaus: Matti Kassila.* Helsinki: WSOY.

Keil, C. (2001). *Early American cinema in transition: Story, style and filmmaking, 1907–1913.* Madison: The University of Wisconsin Press.

Kero, R. (1997). *Suomalaisena Pohjois-Amerikassa: Siirtolaiselämää Yhdysvalloissa ja Kanadassa.* Turku: Siitolaisinstituutti.

Keto, J. (1974). *Elokuvalippujen kysyntä ja siihen vaikuttaneet tekijät Suomessa 1915–1972.* Helsinki: The Helsinki School of Economics.

Kivimaa, A. (1937). *Teatterivaeltaja. Kirjoista, kirjailijoista ja näyttämön taiteesta.* Porvoo: WSOY.

Kivimies, Y. (Ed.). (1937). *Pidot Tornissa.* Jyväskylä: Gummerus.

Koivunen, A. (1995). *Isänmaan moninaiset äidinkasvot. Sotavuosien suomalainen naisten elokuva sukupuoliteknologiana.* Turku: Suomen elokuvatutkimuksen seura.

Koivunen, A. (2015). Authorial self-fashioning in Jörn Donner's *Portraits of Women. Journal of Scandinavian Cinema,* 5(2), 93–108.

Kovács, A. B. (2007). *Screening modernism: European art cinema, 1950–1980.* Chicago/London: University of Chicago Press.

Kovács, A. B. (2013). *The cinema of Bela Tarr: The circle closes.* London/New York: Wallflower Press.

Kozloff, S. (1988). *Invisible storytellers: Voice-over narration in American fiction film.* Berkeley/Los Angeles/London: University of California Press.

Kreimeier, K. (1996). *The Ufa story: A history of Germany's greatest film company 1918–1945.* New York: Hill and Wang.

Kroes, R. (1994). Between rejection and reception. In D. W. Ellwood & R. Kroes (Eds.), *Hollywood in Europe—Experiences of a cultural hegemony* (pp. 21–43). Amsterdam: VU University Press.

Krämer, P. (2011). Hollywood and its global audiences: A comparative study of the biggest box office hits in the United State an outside the United States in the 1970s. In R. Maltby, D. Biltereyst, & P. Meers (Eds.), *Explorations in new cinema history—Approaches and case studies* (pp. 171–184). Chichester: Wiley–Blackwell.

Kuusela, P. A. M. (1976). *Puoli vuosisataa filmiäänitekniikkaa Suomessa.* Helsinki: Suomen elokuvasäätiö.

Kääpä, P. (2010). *The national and beyond. The globalisation of Finnish cinema in the films of Aki and Mika Kaurismäki.* Oxford: Peter Lang.

Kääpä, P. (2015). A culture of reciprocity: The politics of cultural exchange in contemporary Nordic genre film. In T. Gustafsson & P. Kääpä (Eds.), *Nordic genre film: Small nation film cultures in the global marketplace* (pp. 242–261). Edinburgh: Edinburgh University Press.

Kärjä, A.-V. (2005). *'Varmuuden vuoksi omana sovituksena': kansallisen identiteetin rakentuminen 1950- ja 1960-luvun taiteen suomalaisten elokuvien populaarimusiikillisissa esityksissä.* Turku: University of Turku.

Laine, K. (1999). *'Pääosassa Suomen kansa': Suomi-Filmi ja Suomen Filmiteollisuus kansallisen elokuvan rakentajina 1933–1939.* Helsinki: Suomalaisen kirjallisuuden seura & Suomen elokuva-arkisto.

Laine, K. (2007). Seitsemän veljestä, kahdeksan käsikirjoitusta: kilpailu kansallisromaanin filmaamisesta. In H. Bacon, A. Lehtisalo, & P. Nyyssönen (Eds.),

Suomalaisuus valkokankaalla: kotimainen elokuva toisin katsoen (pp. 53–86). Helsinki: Like.

Laine, S. (2011). *Pilvenpiirtäjäkysymys, Urbaani mielikuvitus ja 1920-luvun Helsingin ääriviivat.* Turku: Turun yliopisto.

Lamberg, J.-A., Ojala, J., & Eloranta, J. (1997). Uusintitutionalismi ja taloushistoria: Kollektiivisen valinnan ja liiketoiminnan kustannusten problematiikka. In J.-A. Lamberg & J. Ojala (Eds.), *Uusi institutionaalinen taloushistoria: Johdanto tutkimukseen* (pp. 15–47). Jyväskylä: Atena Kustannus Oy.

Larsson, M. (2010). Art cinema, auteurs and the art cinema 'institution': Introduction. In M. Larsson & A. Marklund (Eds.), *Swedish film: An introduction and reader* (pp. 216–218). Lund: Nordic Academic Press.

Lehtisalo, A. (2013). Emerging Nordic film culture? The varied ways of cooperation between Swedish and Finnish film industries from the late 1930s to the 1950s. Presentation at the conference Kulturhistorisk medieforskning III— nordiska perpektiv. The University of Lund, Sweden, 23–24/4/2013.

Lehtisalo, A. (2014). From the periphery to the world: International film festivals and the internationalisation of Finnish cinema 1941–1965. A presentation held at the ECREA European Communication conference 13–15/11/2014, Film Studies Group, Lisbon, Portugal.

Lilius, A. (1958). *Nuori mies panee toimeksi.* Orig. *Ung man i farten* (trans: Vuoristo, A.). Porvoo: WSOY.

Maltby, R. (2011). New cinema histories. In R. Maltby, D. Biltereyst, & P. Meers (Eds.), *Explorations in new cinema history—Approaches and case studies* (pp. 3–40). Chichester: Wiley–Blackwell.

Marklund, A. (2010). Beyond Swedish borders: On foreign places in Swedish films 1980–2010. In E. Hedling, O. Hedling, & M. Jönsson (Eds.), *Regional aesthetics: Locating Swedish media* (p. 15). Stockholm: Media historiskt Arkiv.

McGrath, J. (2008). The new formalism: Mainland Chinese cinema at the turn of the century. In J. Lu (Ed.), *China's literary and cultural scenes at the turn of the twenty-first century* (pp. 207–221). London: Routledge.

Meers, P. (2004). "It's the language of film!": Young film audiences on Hollywood and Europe. In M. Stokes & R. Maltby (Eds.), *Hollywood abroad—Audiences and cultural exchange* (pp. 158–175). London: BFI Publishing.

Melgosa, A. P. (2010). *Cinema and inter American relations: Tracking transnational affect.* New York: Routledge.

Mikkola, M.-L. (1968). Ei roskaa Kansan silmille. Marja-Leena Mikkola haastattelee Spede Pasasta. *Filmihullu, 1*(1), 26.

Miller, T., Nitin, G., McMurria, J., & Maxwell, R. (2001). *Global Hollywood.* London: BFI Publishing.

Montebello, F. (1994). Hollywood films in a French working class milieu: Longwy 1945–1960. In D. W. Ellwood & R. Kroes (Eds.), *Hollywood in Europe— Experiences of a cultural hegemony* (pp. 213–246). Amsterdam: VU University Press.

Neale, S. (1985). *Cinema and technology. Image, sound, colour*. London: BFI and MacMillan.

Neale, S., & Krutnik, F. (1990). *Popular film and television comedy*. London/New York: Routledge.

Nestingen, A. (2013). *The cinema of Aki Kaurismäki: Contrarian stories*. London/ New York: Wallflower Press.

Neupert, R. (2007). *A history of the French new wave cinema*. Madison: University of Wisconsin Press.

Niskanen, M. (1971). *Vaikea rooli*. Helsinki: Kirjayhtymä.

Nowell-Smith, G. (1998). Introduction. In G. Nowell-Smith & S. Ricci (Eds.), *Hollywood and Europe. Economics, culture, national identity: 1945–95* (pp. 1–16). London: British Film Institute.

Nygård, M. (1997). *Sähkökuvia siirtolaisille: Elokuva kulttuurisen harrastetoiminnan muotona 1920- ja 1930-luvuilla*. Master's thesis in general history. University of Turku, Turku.

Pantti, M. (1998). *Kaikki muuttuu… elokuvakulttuurin jälleenrakentaminen Suomessa 1950-luvulta 1970-luvulle*. Jyväskylä: Suomen elokuvatutkimuksen seura.

Pantti, M. (2000). *'Kansallinen elokuva pelastettava': Elokuvapoliittinen keskustelu kotimaisen elokuvan tukemisesta itsenäisyyden ajalla*. Helsinki: Suomalaisen Kirjallisuuden Seura & Suomen elokuva-arkisto.

Pantti, M. (2005). Art or industry? Battles over Finnish cinema during the 1990s. In A. Nestingen & T. G. Elkington (Eds.), *Transnational cinema in a global north. Nordic cinema in transition* (pp. 165–190). Detroit: Wayne State University Press.

Perez, G. (2000/1998). *The material ghost: Films and their medium*. Baltimore/ London: The John Hopkins University Press.

Perkins, V. F. (2005). Where is the world? The horizon of events in movie fiction. In J. Gibbs & D. Pye (Eds.), *Style and meaning: Studies in the detailed analysis of film* (pp. 16–41). Manchester/New York: Manchester University Press.

Qvist, P. O. (2010). The 1930s' *Folklustspel* and film farce. In M. Larsson & A. Marklund (Eds.), *Swedish film. An introduction and reader* (pp. 119–133). Lund: Nordic Academic Press.

Rai, A. (2009). *Untimely Bollywood: New media and India's new media assemblage*. Durham: Duke University Press.

Raskin, R. (1998). Five explanations for the jump cuts in Godard's *Breathless*. *P.O.V*, 3:6. Available online: http://pov.imv.au.dk/Issue_06/section_1/ artc10.html. Accessed 15 Jan 2014.

Remes, K. (2007). *Verotuksen perusteet elokuva-alan yrittäjille*. Helsinki: Suomen elokuvasäätiö. Available online: http://ses.fi/fileadmin/dokumentit/Verotuksen_perusteet_elokuva-alan_yrittaejille.pdf

Röhr, M. (1987). *Kansainvälisen elokuvateollisuuden taloudellinen kehitys viime aikoina ja siihen vaikuttaneet kilpailutekijät sekä suomen elokuvateattereiden kilpailuasetelma.* MBA thesis, Helsinki School of Economics, Helsinki.

Salmi, H. (2002). *Kadonnut perintö. Näytelmäelokuvan synty Suomessa 1907–1916.* Helsinki: Suomen elokuva-arkisto and Suomalaisen Kirjallisuuden Seura.

Salt, B. (1992). *Film style & technology, history & analysis.* London: Starword.

Salt, B. (2006). *Moving into pictures: More on film history, style and analysis.* London: Starword.

Saunders, T. J. (1994). *Hollywood in Berlin. American cinema and Weimar Germany.* Berkeley/Los Angeles: University of California Press.

Sedergren, J. (1999). *Filmi poikki. Poliittinen elokuvasensuuri Suomessa 1939–1947* (Bibliotheca Historica, Vol. 39). Helsinki: Suomen Historiallinen Seura.

Seppä, S. (2009). *Kotimaisen elokuvan rahoittaminen—Mitä, mistä ja miten?* Tampereen ammattikorkeakoulu Viestinnän koulutusohjelman tutkintotyö. Mediatuotanto12/2009.

Seppälä, J. (2012). *Hollywood tulee Suomeen. Yhdysvaltalaisten elokuvien maahan-tuonti ja vastaanotto kaksikymmentäluvun Suomessa.* Helsinki: Helsingin yliopisto.

Seppälä, J. (2015). On the heterogeneity of cinematography in the films of Aki Kaurismäki. *Projections, 9*(2), 20–39.

Silius, R. (Ed.). (1980). *Studio 10: Elokuvan vuosikirja 1980.* Helsinki: Suomen elokuvasäätiö.

Silius, R. (Ed.). (1984). *Studio 14: Elokuvan vuosikirja 1984.* Helsinki: Suomen elokuvasäätiö.

Smith, A. (2000). Images of the nation. In V. Vitali & P. Willemen (Eds.), *Theorising national cinema* (pp. 45–59). London: BFI Publishing.

Soila, T. (1994). Five songs of the scarlet flower. *Screen, 35*(3), 265–274.

Soila, T., Söderbergh Widding, A., & Iversen, G. (1998). *Nordic national cinemas.* London/New York: Routledge.

Staiger, J. (2002/1985). The Hollywood mode of production to 1930. In D. Bordwell, J. Staiger, & K. Thompson (Eds.), *The classical Hollywood cinema: Film style and mode of production to 1960* (pp. 87–153). London: Routledge.

Sundström, H. (1998). Försvunna finska filmer återfunna i Amerika. Hufvudstadsbladet, 5/5/1998.

Thompson, K. (1985). *Exporting entertainment. America in the world film market 1907–1934.* London: BFI Publishing.

Thompson, K. (1988). *Breaking the glass armor. Neoformalist film analysis.* Princeton: Princeton University Press.

Thompson, K. (1999). The rise and fall of film Europe. In A. Higson & R. Maltby (Eds.), *'Film Europe' and 'Film America'—Cinema, commerce and cultural exchange 1920–1939* (pp. 56–81). Exeter: University of Exeter Press.

Thompson, K. (2001). The concept of cinematic excess. In L. Braudy & M. Cohen (Eds.), *Film theory and criticism: Introductory readings* (pp. 513–524). New York: Oxford University Press.

Thompson, K. (2002/1985). The formulation of the classical narrative. In D. Bordwell, J. Staiger, & K. Thompson (Eds.), *The classical Hollywood cinema: Film style and mode of production to 1960* (pp. 174–193). London: Routledge.

Thompson, K. (2004). The cinematic exploration of cinematic expressivity. In L. Grieveson & P. Krämer (Eds.), *The silent cinema reader* (pp. 254–269). London/New York: Routledge.

Thompson, K. (2005). *Herr Lubitsch Goes to Hollywood: German and American Film after World War 1*. Amsterdam: Amsterdam University Press.

Thompson, K., & Bordwell, D. (2010). *Film history: An introduction*. Boston: MacGraw-Hill.

Toiviainen, S. (1975). *Uusi Suomalainen Elokuva*. Helsinki: SKS.

Toiviainen, S. (1999). *Tuska ja hurmio. Mikko Niskanen ja hänen elokuvansa*. Helsinki: Suomalaisen Kirjallisuuden Seura.

Topelius, Z. (1942/1875). *Maamme kirja. Lukukirja Suomen alimmille oppilaitoksille*. Porvoo: WSOY.

Truffaut, F. (1954). A certain tendency of French cinema. *Cahiers du Cinema*, 31/1/1954. Available online: https://soma.sbcc.edu/users/davega/FILMST_113/Filmst113_ExFilm_Movements/FrenchNewWave/A_certain_tendency_tr%23540A3.pdf. Accessed 31 May 2015.

Töyri, E. (1978). *Me mainiot löträäjät… Suomalaisen elokuvan raamikehitysvuodet 1920–1940*. Helsinki: Suomen elokuvasäätiö.

Töyri, E. (1983). *Vanhat kameramiehet: Suomalaisen elokuvan kameramiehiä 1930–1950*. Helsinki: Suomen elokuvasäätiö.

Uusitalo, K. (1972). *Eläviksi syntyneet kuvat—Suomalaisen elokuvan mykät vuodet 1898–1930*. Helsinki: Otava.

Uusitalo, K. (1975). *Lavean tien sankarit. Suomalainen elokuva 1931–1939* (Suomen elokuva-arkiston julkaisusarja). Helsinki: Suomen elokuva-arkisto ja Otava.

Uusitalo, K. (1977). *Ruutia, riitoja, rakkautta…: Suomalaisen elokuvan sotavuodet 1940–1948* (Suomen elokuvasäätiön julkaisusarja n:o 3). Hyvinkää: Suomen elokuvasäätiö.

Uusitalo, K. (1978). *Hei, rillumarei!: Suomalaisen elokuvan mimmiteollisuusvuodet 1949–1955* (Suomen elokuvasäätiön julkaisusarja n:o 5). Helsinki: Suomen elokuvasäätiö.

Uusitalo, K. (1981). *Suomen Hollywood on kuollut: Kotimaisen elokuvan ahdinkovuodet 1956–1963* (Suomen elokuvasäätön julkaisusarja n:o 12). Helsinki: Suomen elokuvasäätiö.

Uusitalo, K. (1984a). *Umpikuja?: Suomalaisen elokuvan vaikeat vuodet 1964–1969* (Suomen elokuvasäätiön julkaisusarja n:o 15). Hyvinkää: Suomen elokuvasäätiö.

Uusitalo, K. (1984b). *Umpikuja? Suomalaisen elokuvan vaikeat vuodet 1964–1969*. Helsinki: Suomen elokuvasäätiö.

Uusitalo, K. (1994). *Kuvaus–kamera–käy. Lähikuvassa suomifilmit ja Suomi-Filmi Oy*. Helsinki: Kirjastopalvelu.

Uusitalo, K. (1998a). Elokuvamies Jörn Donner. In U. Kari et al. (Eds.), *Suomen kansallisfilmografia* (Vol. 7, pp. 363–371). Helsinki: Edita & Suomen elokuva-arkisto.

Uusitalo, K. (1998b). Suomalaisen värielokuvan synty. In U. Kari et al. (Eds.), *Suomen Kansallisfilmografia 7. Vuosien 1962–1970 suomalaiset kokoillan elokuvat* (pp. 205–209). Helsinki: Edita.

Uusitalo, K. (2006). *Tarkastelua: Aarne Tarkas ja hänen elokuvansa*. Helsinki: Like.

Valkola, J. (2012). *Landscapes of the mind: Emotion and style in Aki Kaurismäki's films*. Saarbrücken: Lap Lambert Academic Publishing.

Vasey, R. (1997). *The world according to Hollywood, 1918–1939*. Madison: The University of Wisconsin Press.

Vincendeau, G. (1992). Noir is also a French word: The French antecedents of film noir. In I. Cameron (Ed.), *The movie book of film noir* (pp. 49–58). London: Studio Vista.

Vincendeau, G. (1999). Hollywood Babel: The coming of sound and the multiple-language version. In A. Higson & R. Maltby (Eds.), *'Film Europe' and 'Film America': Cinema, commerce and cultural exchange 1920–1939* (pp. 207–224). Exeter: University of Exeter Press.

Vincendeau, G., & Graham, P. (Eds.) (2012). *The French new wave*. London: BFI, 2009.

von Bagh, P., & Riikonen, M. (1991). SF-elämää. *Filmihullu, 24*(6).

Wagnleitner, R. (1994). American cultural diplomacy, the cinema, and the Cold War in central Europe. In D. W. Ellwood & R. Kroes (Eds.), *Hollywood in Europe—Experiences of a cultural hegemony* (pp. 196–210). Amsterdam: VU University Press.

Wahl, C. (2010). Babel's business: On Ufa's multiple language film versions, 1929–1933. In C. Rogowski (Ed.), *The many faces of Weimar cinema: Rediscovering Germany's filmic legacy* (pp. 235–267). Rochester: Camden House.

Wallengren, A.-K. (2013). *Välkommen hem Mr. Swanson: Svenska emigranter och svenskhet på film*. Lund: Nordic Academic Press.

Wiegand, C. (2012). *French new wave*. London: Pocket Essentials.

Williams, A. (1992). Historical and theoretical issues in the coming of recorded sound to the cinema. In R. Altman (Ed.), *Sound theory sound practice* (pp. 126–137). London/New York: Routledge.

INDEX

© The Editor(s) (if applicable) and The Author(s) 2016
H. Bacon (ed.), *Finnish Cinema: A Transnational Enterprise*, Palgrave European Film and Media Studies,
DOI 10.1057/978-1-137-57651-4